JIM CROW SOCIOLOGY

JIM CROW SOCIOLOGY

THE BLACK AND SOUTHERN ROOTS
OF AMERICAN SOCIOLOGY

EARL WRIGHT II

University of
CINCINNATI | PRESS

About the University of Cincinnati Press

The University of Cincinnati Press is committed to publishing rigorous, peer-reviewed, leading scholarship accessibly to stimulate dialog among the academy, public intellectuals and lay practitioners. The Press endeavors to erase disciplinary boundaries in order to cast fresh light on common problems in our global community. Building on the university's long-standing tradition of social responsibility to the citizens of Cincinnati, state of Ohio, and the world, the Press publishes books on topics that expose and resolve disparities at every level of society and have local, national and global impact.

University of Cincinnati Press, Cincinnati 45221
Copyright © 2020

Published in 2020
Wright, Earl, II, author.
Jim Crow sociology : the Black and Southern roots of American
    sociology / Earl Wright II.
Cincinnati : University of Cincinnati Press, 2020. | Includes
    bibliographical references and index.
LCCN 2019045925 (print) | LCCN 2019045926 (ebook) | ISBN
    9781947602571 (hardback) | ISBN 9781947602588 (pdf) | ISBN 9781947602595
    (epub)
LCSH: Sociology--United States--History. | African American
    sociologists--History. | African Americans--Social conditions. | African
    Americans--Study and teaching--History.
LCC HM477.U6 W753 2020 (print) | LCC HM477.U6 (ebook) |
    DDC 301.0973--dc23
LC record available at https://lccn.loc.gov/2019045925
LC ebook record available at https://lccn.loc.gov/2019045926

ISBN 978-1-947602-57-1 (hardback)
ISBN 978-1-947602-58-8 (e-book, PDF)
ISBN 978-1-947602-59-5 (e-book, EPUB)

On the Cover: © Dr. Ernest C. Withers, Sr. courtesy of the Withers Family Trust
Designed and produced for UC Press by Jennifer Flint
Typeset in Gentium Book Basic

Printed in the United States of America
First Printing

This book is dedicated to ...

My mother, Sandra K. Wright,
who is and will always be the wind beneath my wings.

My wife, Leslie L. Wright,
who has supported me like no one else and I am eternally thankful for all she
has done.

My children, Chasity P. Fleming, Earl "Tre" Wright III, & Alexandria "AJ"
Wright,
for being my inspiration and motivation to keep pushing forward even when
challenges seem insurmountable.

Last, but certainly not least,
to the many unknown and forgotten men and women who contributed to the
Atlanta Sociological Laboratory. It has been my life's goal to bring as many of
your names to the attention of the American public. When your names have
not been available, I have attempted to bring your research accomplishments
to the attention of the world. In these efforts I hope I have been successful and
have represented your memories well.

With love and respect,
Earl Wright II

CONTENTS

PREFACE

The Journey Toward My Life's Work

The journey toward writing this book has been arduous and more than twenty years in the making. It started in the fall of 1995 when I was a first-year master's degree-seeking student at the University of Memphis. While conducting a literature review search for my urban sociology thesis I came across a large number of books and articles lauding the canonical exploits of the Chicago School of Sociology—the moniker bestowed on members of the Department of Sociology and affiliated social scientists at the University of Chicago between, roughly, 1915 and 1930. In numerous seminars my classmates and I were the recipients of lectures centering the accomplishments of the Chicago School within the origin and development of the discipline in the United States. In my neophyte sociological mind's eye, the relevance and significance of the Chicago School was drilled into my classmates and I in a nearly militaristic fashion. The obvious implication of (over)saturating students with the accomplishments of this school was the understanding that no serious sociologist could become credentialed or deemed competent if they could not recite, on command, discipline dogma championing the contributions of the Chicago School, including but not limited to it supposedly being home to the first American school of sociology, architects of urban sociological inquiry and founders of the ethnographic tradition.

During this period, I struggled to overcome the uneasiness I felt while reading publications by and about members of the school and listening to lectures on University of Chicago sociology. I was at a complete loss on the cause of this discomfort that, by this point, had lasted nearly one year. I suddenly gained clarity during a theory class as my professor delivered a nearly flawless and detailed account of Foucault's theoretical genius. As if a bolt of lightning hit me, while daydreaming during the Foucault lecture, my mind flashed back to a moment in my youth.

Similar to others raised in poverty-level, fatherless, and single-parent homes, my childhood was filled with periods of disruption. The types of disruptions included domestic violence, a kidnapping attempt, and parental inattention. During such times I went to live with my grandparents. I welcomed these periods of disruption because, aside from the challenges of home life, I was guaranteed two things: food and physical security. I also enjoyed living with my grandparents because of the exposure I had to things foreign to my life at home with my mother.

One of my grandmother's most cherished possessions was a bookshelf that contained what appeared in my mind's eye as a child more than a thousand books. Of the many books on the shelves two jumped out to me at the age of six years. The first was *Roots* by Alex Haley. This book, later a television miniseries, was the tale of a young African who was kidnapped and brought to America for enslavement. The 688-page book covered the kidnapped African's familial experiences in this nation from slavery to post-emancipation. Immediately the idea of learning about the challenges experienced by this family captivated me. However, since my family had gathered to communally watch the miniseries when it debuted in 1977, I did not feel compelled to read the entire book. To this day I have yet to read beyond page ten.

The second book, conversely, was compelling enough for me to read beyond ten pages. I became interested in reading the book because it was written by a man with a strange and funny name, was published in the 1890s, and had a provocative title. *The Philadelphia Negro* by William Edward Burghardt Du Bois so captured my imagination that I feverishly flipped through its pages on many days and nights. I did not know how to pronounce many of the words, nor did I understand them. That did not prevent me from reading as much of the book as I could. Admittedly, my first attempts at reading the book centered largely on examinations of the meticulously drawn graphs, maps, and pictures. As I aged closer to

ten, I learned how to pronounce most of the words and began to understand some of the major arguments. On many weekend afternoons at my
grandparents' home the only thing I had to keep me company and allow
my imagination to grow was Du Bois's book. While I did not recognize its
significance at the time, I understood that this book, at least to me, was
special. Little did I know *The Philadelphia Negro* would later become widely
regarded as the first scientific urban sociological research endeavor conducted in the United States.

As I entered adolescence, home life with my mother stabilized and I
became a distant acquaintance of Du Bois's book and my grandmother's
bookshelf. Time passed and both faded from my memory. Nearly twenty
years after my introduction to Du Bois's classic work, it was in a graduate
course on classical sociological theory that my consciousness was
awakened and I clearly understood the root of my uneasiness with the
information I was being taught about the exploits of the Chicago School
of Sociology. Succinctly, if sociologists at the University of Chicago were
credited with being *the first* to engage in various forms of urban sociological research starting in the late 1910s, why were Du Bois's works, starting
with *The Philadelphia Negro* in the late 1890s and along similar urban sociological research lines, not similarly recognized? Why were they largely
ignored? These questions, and my awareness of Du Bois's book, explained
my unease with what I was learning about the Chicago School and spurred
a line of sociological inquiry that remains, to this day, my life's work.

My Life's Work

After coming to this understanding, I bought a copy of *The Philadelphia
Negro* and closely examined Du Bois's early sociological works. I learned
he was once on faculty at Atlanta University (now called Clark Atlanta
University) while actively participating in civil rights initiatives including, but not limited to, cofounding the National Association for the
Advancement of Colored People (NAACP). I was previously unfamiliar
with his tenure at Atlanta University and wanted to know as much as

possible about his scholarly activities during that period. I quickly learned
he served as director of the school's annual research study and editor of
the resultant yearly publication. I later discovered that the monographs
published under the title *Atlanta University Study of the Negro Problems* were
the first objective (vis-à-vis the scientific racism products of the era) and
scientific investigations into the social, economic, and physical condition
of Black Americans.

At the time, however, what fascinated me most was discovering
that Du Bois's laboratory at Atlanta University comprised the first institutionalized program of collective sociological research in the nation.
Prior to this discovery, which had not been published in any form at
that point, my singular focus had been on Du Bois's urban sociological
work in Philadelphia. After reading the first three volumes of the *Atlanta
University Study of the Negro Problems (1896–1898)*, two completed prior to
Du Bois's arrival at Atlanta, I immediately understood that I was in possession of an untapped wealth of data on a significant school of sociological
thought. What I understood instantly was that the collective efforts contained in the Atlanta University studies were more groundbreaking than
his Philadelphia effort and the urban-focused investigations of his White
peers at schools including Chicago. At this point I knew Du Bois's research
activities at Atlanta University would be my primary research interest and
life's work.

Within three months I read all twenty volumes of the Atlanta
University publications. I was amazed at the myriad topics covered by the
research team, how data were collected and the structure of the conference where the findings were presented annually. What also fascinated
me was the fact that during its early years the meetings were segregated
by gender and both presented their findings to, seemingly, segregated
audiences. When I juxtaposed what I was discovering within the pages
of the Atlanta University publications with what I was being taught as a
master's degree student, I could not wrap my mind around the fact that I
was being presented with disciplinary *facts* that were demonstrably false.
At this moment I pondered whether or not, with one semester remaining

before completing the master's degree, to change the subject of my thesis from the development of social bonds among African American males at an urban barbershop to an analysis of the Du Bois-led Atlanta University studies. Needless to say, I completed the barbershop thesis and departed Memphis for the University of Nebraska in the fall of 1997 knowing the topic of my dissertation from day one.

During my doctoral training in Nebraska I conducted a thorough literature review of the Atlanta University studies to ascertain if anyone had already published on this topic. To my surprise there existed only one publication, which was singularly focused on the scholarly efforts of the school. In an article published in 1957, Elliott Rudwick offered the first scholarly critique of Du Bois's Atlanta Sociological Laboratory. Rudwick reviewed several volumes of the Atlanta University publications, but not the entire twenty-volume set. From that source he concluded the methods of data collection employed by Du Bois were unsophisticated. As I discuss in Chapter 2, Rudwick's argument is easily debunked when data on the school's groundbreaking data collection techniques and methodological procedures are provided. Moreover, Rudwick proposed that Du Bois's works at Atlanta University were inconsequential because of the renowned scholar's supposed emphasis on self-promotion at the expense of engaging in objective and high-quality sociological research. Beyond the critiques offered above, Rudwick continued his harsh review of the Atlanta University studies and offered a backhanded compliment when he suggested that the one significant outcome of Du Bois's sociological efforts was that he *uplifted* the souls of *Black* folk during a period when positive depictions of the race were needed—despite his having conducted poor and unsound inquiries. Rudwick (1957:475) asserted:

> The Atlanta Studies may not have improved the condition of the race very much, but they probably did improve its morale. At a time when political and social restrictions upon the American Negroes were increasing, the Atlanta monographs must have provided many members of the race with a sense of group integration and ego satisfaction.[1]

It was amazing to discover that Rudwick's article was the only scholarly critique of Du Bois's Atlanta sociological program in the literature as the dawn of the twenty-first century drew closer. Knowing such a large void existed in the literature compelled me to delve even deeper into Du Bois's Atlanta University activities. Moreover, I was excited to inform and reimagine the American sociological world through a lens that, finally, viewed its origin and development from a Black perspective.

Between 1997 and 2000 I absorbed as much information as possible on the Atlanta Sociological Laboratory (the name I coined)—the moniker bestowed on scholars engaged in sociological activity at Atlanta University between 1895 and 1924. During this period, I presented research papers on my findings at sociology meetings including American Sociological Association, Association of Black Sociologists, Eastern Sociological Society, Mid-South Sociological Association, and Southern Sociological Society. After nearly five years of engaged research on the Du Bois-led Atlanta Sociological Laboratory the findings were captured in my 2000 dissertation, "Atlanta University and American Sociology: An Earnest Desire for the Truth Despite Its Possible Unpleasantness." Over the past twenty years I've authored more than twelve peer-reviewed journal publications and one book on this topic, wherein I've argued that the Atlanta Sociological Laboratory, among other achievements, established the first American school of sociology, the first program of urban sociological inquiry, and the first program of sociology of the South studies. It was also the first to institutionalize method triangulation, use of insider researchers, acknowledgment of the limitations of one's research, and a methods section in research papers. After uncovering the achievements of this predominately Black school my attention was drawn to other historically Black colleges and universities (HBCUs). The question I wanted to answer was, "Is Atlanta University an anomaly or did other historically Black colleges and universities (HBCUs) have departments of sociology that made noteworthy contributions to the discipline during its formative years in this nation?" The answer to this question became very clear after I examined the literature and conducted research on departments of sociology at other HBCUs. It was an emphatic Yes!

The Big Four

"Which HBCUs qualify as noteworthy contributors to the discipline of sociology during its formative years in this nation?" is a question that initially dumbfounded me. One way to answer this question is to focus on institutions where individual superstar Black sociologists worked. This is probably the most practical option because of the availability of archival documents that can be used to ground the argument. Another option is to focus on institutions with a critical mass of faculty who contributed to the yearly studies conducted at and published by the Atlanta Sociological Laboratory. The former option is, ideally, not the preferred pathway toward answering the question because a primary objective of this project is to expand recognition for contributions to the discipline by Black scholars beyond the exploits of individual superstar Black sociologists. Indeed, a major goal of this project is to go beyond the exploits of any one individual and explore the collective accomplishments of early Black scholars at one institution and during one period in time. The latter option is not ideal either, because many contributors to the research products of the Atlanta Sociological Laboratory did not have institutional homes that provided the infrastructure necessary for the discipline to have a substantive impact on their campus nor a record of their sociological activities. Therefore, if they did engage in substantive sociological inquiries, there exists today little or no historical record of their works.

After much thought, I remembered a resource that could be a starting point in my quest to identify the leading departments of sociology at HBCUs at the dawn of the twentieth century. In the early 1900s the Atlanta Sociological Laboratory published the nation's first serious examinations of Black Americans and education. Over a ten-year period two studies were conducted on Black Americans and secondary school and Black Americans and college, respectively. In these studies, the nation's leading HBCUs were identified and, in at least one study, the amount of coursework devoted to instruction in sociology vis-à-vis the total curriculum was presented. These data were used to identify schools offering the most coursework in sociology and to determine which, if any, institutional homes of individual superstar sociologists were sufficiently engaged in sociological inquiry. Additionally, in my effort to identify departments of sociology at HBCUs that were engaged in substantive scholarly activities, I pored over the Atlanta University studies looking for institutions that were consistent collaborators with the yearly efforts of the Atlanta Sociological Laboratory. Ultimately, I identified the *Big Four* schools of Black sociology through the extensive examination of the two Atlanta University studies and detailed examination of the collective work of nameless men and women who contributed to the achievements commonly awarded singularly to individual superstar sociologists.

The 1900 Atlanta University study was arguably the first scientific and objective examination of college education and Blacks in America. The methods of data collection for this study included a survey of 12 university presidents, 1,312 Black college graduates, and admissions data from an unknown number of HBCUs. Du Bois used these data to construct a ranking of the top HBCUs. The highest-ranked school was Howard University, since its curriculum was "nearly equal to the smaller New England Colleges [sic]".[2] Second-tier HBCUs, identified as being between one to two years behind New England schools, included (in Du Bois's listed order) Fisk University, Atlanta University, Wilberforce College, Leland College, and Paul Quinn College. The reader is reminded here that most HBCUs were established roughly thirty years post-slavery and experienced huge financial and staffing disadvantages when compared to peer historically White colleges and universities (HWCUs). Moreover, because of the literal lack of public education facilities for Blacks, many newly established HBCUs simultaneously provided instruction to elementary, middle school, high school, and college level students. Despite these and other challenges, Du Bois concluded that a small number of HBCUs offered post-secondary curriculum instruction equal to that of their White peers.

More important than the 1900 study is the 1910 investigation. The methods of data collection for the 1910 study included a survey of more than 800 Black American college graduates, letters from numerous university administrators, and the examination of numerous HBCU catalogs. The 1910 study extended the 1900 effort, as it included an account of the type and amount of instruction offered for the major disciplines at each institution. Specifically, Du Bois's 1910 study listed the exact percent of curriculum time dedicated to each field of study. The disciplines included in the analysis were ancient languages, modern languages, natural sciences, mathematics, English, sociology & history, philosophy, and a category labeled "miscellaneous." Because sociology was a growing field and not well established at many institutions, it was not provided a separate level of analysis. Thus, it is unknown if the time allotted to the area *sociology & history* was dominated by one discipline or divided evenly. Although there is no clear way to ascertain the amount of class time dedicated to instruction in sociology vs. history, we can take guidance from a sociologist of that era, L. L. Bernard, who suggested that HBCUs focused more attention on sociology than their HWCU contemporaries.

In a 1917 study on course offerings at Southern-based institutions, Bernard noted there were more course offerings in political science and economics than other disciplines, including sociology. In fact, he proposed that "sociology was considered only a little more than one-half as important as economics and only one-fourth as desirable educationally as history."[3] Of the four disciplines examined—economics, history, political science, and sociology—the latter would place last in assessments of importance if it were not for the influence of HBCUs. So great an influence was the inclusion of HBCUs in his study that Bernard concluded:

> If these colleges should be eliminated, sociology would rank lowest of the four subjects here indicated in number of courses listed for white male and coeducational institutions, and listings in economics would about double those for sociology, while listings in history would approximate nearly five times as great.[4]

As it related specifically to the amount of instruction time devoted to sociology versus history, Bernard noted:

> Negro colleges "before 1916" give least differential emphasis to history. In fact, the institutions for [N]egroes give, relative to other institutions, little attention either to political science or to history. This is not difficult to understand when the political status and the condition of the [N]egro are taken into consideration.[4]

Bernard's conclusion was a clear indication that during Jim Crow sociologists at HBCUs viewed the discipline as a tool to combat racial inequality and were intentional in the design of institutional curriculums that emphasized its instruction over others even when the name of the department included separate disciplines. The logical conclusion drawn here was that the embrace of sociology at HBCUs was disproportional to that at HWCUs and when paired with other disciplines at HBCUs, instruction in sociology was more likely than not to garner a greater percentage of coursework time.

Relatedly, in the 1900 Atlanta University study Du Bois concluded that Atlanta University required its students to study sociology and history at a rate higher than any HBCU. Nearly 20 percent of Atlanta University's undergraduate curriculum was dedicated to the instruction of sociology and history (19.1 percent). The next highest amounts were Claflin University (16.2 percent), Straight University (13.9 percent), and New Orleans University, Walden University, and Bennett College each graded equally (13.8 percent). After taking into consideration the 1900 and 1910 studies as well as the collective contributions at institutions led by leading Black sociologists pre-1954, a clear understanding of the most influential and important departments of sociology at HBCUs between 1895 and 1970 emerged.

Atlanta University, under the leadership of W. E. B. Du Bois, was the founding member of the Big Four. Not only did Atlanta University offer the most coursework in sociology & history, it was the home of the first American school of sociology where the collective efforts of its research team led to numerous contributions to the discipline in areas including, but not limited to, criminal justice, race, religion, and research methods.

Fisk University, the second of the Big Four, was the first HBCU to offer classes in sociology, starting in 1893, and established a department in 1900. Unlike Atlanta, Fisk enjoyed two periods of influential sociological development. While Charles S. Johnson sits on the Mount Rushmore of superstar Black sociologists, the efforts of an often-overlooked scholar, George Edmund Haynes, laid the foundation upon which the applied sociological efforts of the institution would become known.

While the majority of departments at HBCUs centered their research nearly exclusively on urban issues, the third member of the Big Four focused on racism and discrimination experienced by rural Blacks: the Tuskegee Institute. This school was not listed in Du Bois's ranking of elite HBCUs because its primary curricular focus was technical and vocational education, not liberal arts. However, Tuskegee, under the guidance of Monroe Nathan Work, became the leading disseminator of accurate, scientific, and timely data on Blacks in America after the dissolution of the Atlanta Sociological Laboratory. More important was the fact that, although the school's curriculum did not include sociology in its early years, under the leadership of Booker T. Washington, Tuskegee established the first program of applied rural sociology five years prior to the establishment of the Atlanta Sociological Laboratory, the first American school of sociology and practitioner of urban sociology.

The final Big Four sociology program was Howard University. Similar to Fisk, Howard benefitted from two periods of leadership that extended through nearly the entirety of the Jim Crow era. The first era was guided by Kelly Miller, who was notable for his national relevance as a peacemaker during periods of Black sociological infighting. The subsequent era was led by E. Franklin Frazier, who spearheaded the development of a program that would establish the foundation for what remains to this day the only HBCU with a doctoral program in sociology.

Taken altogether, these institutions comprised the finest exemplars of sociological excellence at HBCUs between 1895 and 1970. Their collective marginalization to date has been shameful. This effort fills a massive void because there currently exists in the literature no book-length treatment on the origin, development, and significance of departments of sociology at HBCUs. Moreover, this book is an important addition to the literature because the historical marginalization of these Black institutions and scholars means accolades for their significant accomplishments have been falsely bestowed upon others. This book corrects the record. Additionally, instead of focusing singularly on individual superstar sociologists, this book contributes to the literature by covering the significance of and contributions made by little-known men and women at HBCUs during the discipline's formative years in this nation. Herein the reader learns of the activities of early Black sociologists from the American South whose efforts were at best minimized and at worst erased. Collectively, this book represents the first of what I hope to be many efforts to reclaim and reframe the legacy of departments of sociology at HBCUs and their contributions to the discipline of sociology.

Were it not for my grandparent's bookshelf I am certain I never would have conceived of this project. It may have been many years before this task would be undertaken by another interested scholar. It is for this and many other reasons that I am grateful to my gone but not forgotten grandparents, Edward and Freddie Mae Davis, for having placed on their shelf a book that forever changed my life: *The Philadelphia Negro* written by William Edward Burghardt Du Bois.

INTRODUCTION

This book is entitled *Jim Crow Sociology* but could have easily been named *Black Sociology*. *Jim Crow Sociology* prevailed because this title refers to a specific period in this nation's shameful history when *separate but equal* segregation between the races in public accommodations was supported by law. Just as important, the title *Jim Crow Sociology* prevailed because of the de jure and de facto policy's impact on institutions. Consequences of the forced separation of Americans by race in public accommodations included, but were not limited to, where and how Blacks and Whites in educational settings engaged the learning process. Keep in mind that this apartheid segregation policy did not take place in a vacuum; it did not affect only limited segments of American society. To the contrary, it affected every aspect of life in this nation. Jim Crow segregation directly impacted the discipline of sociology during its formative years in the United States. Ultimately, *Jim Crow Sociology* is an apt title for this book because it signifies the era in American history that mandated the physical separation of Blacks from Whites in society, in general, and unwittingly created the conditions for a demarcation of the understanding and application of sociology at educational institutions by race.

As previously stated, the title of this book could just as easily be *Black Sociology*. This title, continuing the line of reasoning above, reflects one specific consequence of Jim Crow-era segregation policies. Specifically, the literal physical separation of the races in educational and professional settings created conditions whereby differences in the understanding and application of sociology by early Black and White sociologists emerged. This difference, I argue, resulted in the development of Black sociology.

Just as the two titles of the book are interchangeable, so too is the definitional use of the concept as discussed in the next section. However, Black sociology is the preferred term when used for definitional and conceptual purposes because it is less cumbersome and, more important, it doesn't confine the mind of the reader to a specific and past period of time beyond which it may be difficult for the reader to depart. Ultimately, while the moniker *Jim Crow Sociology* is catchy, the expansiveness of the latter takes precedence in this instance. Below, a definition of and principles for Black sociology are presented, followed by the plan for the book.

Black Sociology

Several years ago Thomas C. Calhoun and I (2006)[1] constructed a definition of Black sociology that departed from the existing literature, which largely did not recognize the role W. E. B. Du Bois played in the creation of this area.[2] Of the collective offering definitions and understandings of Black sociology, only Wilbur Watson acknowledged Du Bois when he wrote, "It was W. E. B. Du Bois who provided the foundation for Black sociology, both in terms of subject and methodology."[3] While he credited Du Bois for being the foundation upon which Black sociology was established, he did not examine his works at Atlanta University to fully tease out his exact contributions. This void was filled with my 2006 article and is discussed in full below. Here Black sociology is defined as the objective and scientific engagement in research investigations into the conditions of Blacks for the express purpose of obtaining data to understand, explain, and ameliorate problems impacting that community, in such a way that the ideal result is the creation of social or public policy to address the specific matter investigated. In its original articulation we assumed Black sociology shared similar theoretical assumptions and methodological research techniques with mainstream White sociology. We were mistaken. I was mistaken. This new iteration of Black sociology that I construct here departs from these notions.

First, my new conception of Black sociology is guided by the idea that the methodological sophistication of the studies conducted by early White sociologists was of lower quality than that practiced by early Black sociologists like W. E. B. Du Bois. A full account of the methodology of Black sociologists can be found in Chapter 2. What is important to note here is Du Bois's awareness of the unsophisticated and low-quality methodological practices employed by some of his White peers and the resulting inaccurate conclusions reached in studies focusing on Blacks. For example, in *The Souls of Black Folk* Du Bois cautions academics on the dangers of engaging in "car window sociology." Car window sociology, according to Du Bois, is one's engagement in subjective sociological inquiry void of objectivity, science, and sound methods of data collection. The lack of these critical components of research often led to inaccurate, even laughable, conclusions reached by leading sociologists at the turn of the twentieth century.[4] Accordingly, Du Bois argued that the car window sociologist is "the [scholar] who seeks to understand and know the South by devoting the few leisure hours of a holiday trip to unravelling the snarl of centuries."[5] His primary argument was that in order to arrive at solid findings upon which theories can be drawn it was imperative that one engage in objective and methodologically sophisticated investigations. Given that most, if not all, research conducted by Whites during the late nineteenth and early twentieth centuries was influenced by scientifically racist theories of the era, Du Bois cautioned academics to have a healthy suspicion of the findings of most, if not all, White sociologists when the topic was Blacks in America. On this issue, Du Bois argued:

> We continually assume the material we have at hand to be typical; we reverently receive a column of figures without asking who collected them, how they were arranged, how far are they valid and what chances of error they contain; we receive the testimony of men without asking whether they were trained or ignorant, careful or careless, truthful or given to exaggeration, and above all, whether they are giving facts or opinions.[6]

Du Bois recognized that even the most-well meaning White social scientist could fall prey to faulty theories and ideas concerning Black life given the racial folkways and mores of the era. Understanding the harmful implications of subjective and unscientific studies on Blacks that formed the basis for many scientific racism theories, Du Bois questioned and challenged the academy to only validate studies on Blacks that were grounded in scientific truths via rigorous methodology. All other scientific efforts should be ignored. Speaking to this notion Du Bois wrote:

> Americans are born in many cases with deep, fierce convictions on the Negro question, and in other cases imbibe them from their environment. When such men come to write on the subject, without technical training, without breadth of view, and in some cases without a deep sense of the sanctity of scientific truth, their testimony, however interesting as opinion, must of necessity be worthless as science.[7]

Du Bois directly challenged his White peers to reject their natural instinct to be subjective and not *value-free* in their scientific inquiries into the lives of Blacks. He essentially asked them to reject car window sociology in favor of scientific sociology.[8]

It bears mentioning here that Du Bois's methodological sophistication was, in part, driven by his understanding that a substantial segment, if not the entirety, of the White scientific community would not accept his research, nor that of any Black scholar, as valid because of their belief that his primary, if not exclusive, goal was to produce findings promoting positive aspects of Black life and not simply the pursuit of objective scientific facts.[9] Consequently, in his quest to counter biased and unscientific research conducted on American Blacks, Du Bois and his sociological team spearheaded groundbreaking research methods and practices. Thus, the idea that Black sociology shared methodological consistency with that of early Whites who, in notable cases, engaged in the sociological malpractice otherwise known as scientific racism is rejected.[10]

The original articulation also suggested there were no differences between the theoretical assumptions of White sociology and Black sociology. The idea that no distinction existed between the theoretical assumptions of Black sociology and the scientific racism theories embraced by early White sociologists was flawed. What was not addressed in the original articulation was the fact that a good number of White sociologists (if not all) embraced, and in many cases promoted, existing and new theories of Black inferiority and pathology that were often based on unscientific car window sociological studies or investigations conducted with low-quality methods of research. This important point was not included in the original articulation and enabled one to infer that early Black sociologists accepted and possibly promoted scientific racism theories of the era such as, for example, *drapetomania*—the supposed *mental condition* that compelled enslaved persons to consider or attempt to escape slavery despite the benign and beneficial features and conditions of the peculiar institution. While early Black sociologists like Du Bois occasionally attributed deficiencies in the Black community to matters of personal responsibility instead of institutional structure(s), none supported, my research indicates, scientific research and theories that promoted the notion that Blacks were biologically and intellectually inferior to Whites and that their condition was pathological. Now that a definition for Black sociology is established and a correction made concerning the methodological and theoretical (dis)similarities with White sociology, what follows is an overview of the five principles of Black sociology.

Principles of Black Sociology

The first principle of Black sociology mandates that research endeavors be led, primarily but not exclusively, by persons of African descent. This principle comes from Atlanta University president Horace Bumstead, who argued at the inaugural 1896 Atlanta University Study of the Negro Problems conference, "the problems of Negro city life must be settled *largely* [emphasis mine] by Negroes themselves."[11] Arguably, the biggest misconception of Black sociology is the idea that one must be Black to engage with this work. What is true is that anyone with a commitment to the definition and principles of this area is welcome to contribute to the

Black sociology literature. To expound further on this matter, just because one is of African descent does not automatically mean one's efforts are or should be construed as engagement in Black sociology. Further, just because one is of African descent doing research focusing on Black folk does not automatically mean those efforts should be construed as engagement in Black sociology. Conversely, just because one is not of African descent does not mean one is automatically disqualified from participation in this research endeavor.

While he does not directly articulate this point, one surmises from President Bumstead's position that he is promoting agency for the race and understands that Blacks in America have a specific standpoint and set of experiences they bring into the social science enterprise. Among other things, this knowledge enables them to raise questions uniquely reflective of their lived experiences. Assuredly, many, if not most, of the research questions raised by Black social scientists only a few decades removed from chattel slavery differed from many, if not most, questions raised by Whites who uncritically accepted popular scientific racism theories of the day. Thus, per Bumstead, it is without question that Blacks should be the principal, not exclusive, investigators of their social, economic, and physical condition because they are more likely than not to challenge the reigning beliefs of Black inferiority and the methods by which those conclusions are reached.

The second principle of Black sociology is that the research center the experiences of Blacks. Prior to the Atlanta University studies, Blacks in America were rarely the subjects of objective, scientific, and *non-deficit-centered* studies. President Bumstead articulated this principle at the inaugural 1896 conference:

> Very little attention, too, has been given to the specific problems arising out of the changed conditions under which this large proportion of the Negro population is now sharing the city life of their white brethren. The Negro has been thought of chiefly as a tiller of the soil, as in fact he is; and much has been done, and very properly, for the improvement of his plantation life. But the problems connected with his life in the cities and larger towns need even more careful study and thorough treatment.[12]

Atlanta University's centering of urban Blacks as research subjects in the middle 1890s is significant because it was a counterbalance to the subjective and unscientific existing literature and contemporary research of the era. Despite the prevalence of scientific racism theories, one can find solace in the fact that there was a paucity of social science investigations into the condition of Blacks in America. The lack of a critical mass of investigations is partly explained by the fact that many White social scientists did not view Blacks as subjects worthy of scientific investigation.

When faced with, arguably, the greatest social experiment in the world's history, the infusion of a formerly enslaved populace numbering millions into a society that largely considered their existence *the White man's burden*, the scientific community, with the exception of those engaged in scientific racism, opted not to fully engage the subject. Du Bois lamented:

> We have been unable as yet to convince any considerable number of the American people of the burning necessity of work of this sort and its deep scientific significance. . . . The mass of thinking people, however, fail to recognize the true significance of an attempt to study systematically the greatest social problem that has ever faced a great modem nation.[13]

To Du Bois and the growing number of Black sociologists and social scientists, the idea that most scientists were not interested in studying this topic was hard to process. Du Bois believed, "Such an attitude is allowable to the ignorant—it is expected among horses and among the uncultivated masses of men, but it is not expected of the scientific leaders of a great nation."[14] He theorized that the lack of substantive investigations into the social, economic, and physical conditions of Black Americans by Whites was because White sociologists did not deem them worthy of scientific inquiry. Stated more explicitly, if American Blacks were viewed by Whites as full members of the family of humanity, whose existence was deemed to produce positive benefits to the nation, they would have been judged worthy of the time and energy required to be the focus of *true* objective scientific research investigations. Instead, as Du Bois argued:

> If the Negroes are not ordinary human beings, if their development is
> simply the retrogression of an inferior people, and the only possible
> future for the Negro, a future of inferiority, decline and death, then it
> is manifest that a study of such a group, while still of interest and scien-
> tific value is of less pressing and immediate necessity than the study of
> a group which is distinctly recognized as belonging to the great human
> family, whose advancement is possible, and whose future depends on its
> own efforts and the fairness and reasonableness of the dominant and
> surrounding group.[15]

A final factor to consider concerning the lack of interest by Whites
in studying Blacks is objectivity. Du Bois's writings are, again, important
here as he explains why the existing literature on research about Blacks by
Whites is limited. Speaking to this idea, Du Bois said:

> It is of course perfectly clear as to why scientific men have long fought
> shy of [the study of Black Americans]. The presence of the Negro in
> America has long been the subject of bitter and repeated controversy—of
> war and hate, of strife and turmoil. It has been said that so dangerous a
> field, where feelings were deep-seated and turbulent, was not the place
> for scientific calm of clear headed investigation.[16]

While the discipline has today progressed to a space whereby it is assumed
that research, on some level, can be value-free, Du Bois's explanation for
the lack of sociological studies on Blacks by Whites is certainly plausible. Summarily, the second principle of Black sociology, mandating that
Blacks be the subject of research investigations, emanated from the lack
of interest on the topic by early White sociologists, their lack of objectivity
on the topic, and the desire for Black sociologists to infuse objective investigations into the literature.

The third principle of Jim Crow sociology promotes the idea that
research should, ideally, be interdisciplinary. This principle was derived
through an examination of twenty volumes of the *Atlanta University Study
of the Negro Problems* (1896–1917) wherein it was uncovered that the school
investigated a range of topics including business, criminal justice, economics, education, and health. In the school's attempt to understand the
social conditions impacting Black Americans at the turn of the twentieth

century it was necessary that the research endeavors be interdisciplinary and not constricted to one myopic disciplinary home.

The fourth principle of Black sociology requires the findings, whenever possible, to be generalizable. This principle was derived, again, from President Bumstead, who admonished attendees at the 1896 meeting to

> not forget that the general subject of this and succeeding conferences—the study of Negro city life—and the particular subject of this year—the morality of Negroes in cities—constitute a human problem far more than a Negro problem. We shall use the words "Negro" and "colored," not to emphasize distinctions of race but as terms of convenience. We are simply to study human life under certain conditions—conditions which, if repeated with any other race, would have practically the same result.[17]

Even before Du Bois's tenure, the Atlanta University studies were designed to explore social conditions that, while using Blacks as the primary subject group, could be generalizable to other race groups. For example, the 1897 Atlanta University study, the last conducted prior to Du Bois's arrival, examined the living conditions of Blacks in cities. A major conclusion drawn in that investigation was that the high rate of consumption, now called tuberculosis, was caused by poor ventilation in multistory apartment buildings. This finding came from a sample that only included Blacks. Despite consisting of a homogenous racial population, the findings of the study were undoubtedly applicable to non-Black Americans as well—that is, unless one were to believe that only Black Americans lived in multistory apartment buildings during this era or that diseases impacted Blacks and Whites differently. Sadly, on the latter point, one is reminded that during this era the medical community promoted studies indicating there existed biological differences between Blacks and Whites and that health outcomes for persons of different races afflicted with similar diseases produced different outcomes. One product of this reasoning was the inhumane, unscientific, and morally bankrupt research project called the Tuskegee Study of Untreated Syphilis in the Negro Male. Under the sponsorship of the United States government from 1931 to 1971, this study resulted in the deaths of

scores of Black men decades after it was known that the disease impacted
Blacks and Whites similarly. Despite its focus on a seemingly homogenous
population, a number of findings of the Atlanta Sociological Laboratory
were, in fact, generalizable. Unfortunately, because of the racialized veil
through which the scientific studies were interpreted by their White peers
and because the subject pool consisted nearly exclusively of Blacks, the
prevailing White racial logic of 1897 unfortunately and incorrectly deemed
this and similar Atlanta University studies ungeneralizable.

The final principle of Black sociology mandates that the findings,
whenever possible, have social policy implications. Early Black sociologists did not engage in abstract sociological theorizing for the purpose
of enhancing the discipline's status among its positivistic and scientific
peers. Instead, they conducted social science research investigations on
the social, economic, and physical conditions experienced by Blacks in the
hopes of using the discipline as a tool to positively impact the group's life
outcome and life chances. Early Black sociologists understood that social
reform and policy development were important components of their work.
Just as important, they were acutely aware that reform efforts should not
be the immediate objective of their research. They believed scientists
should strive for the acquisition of objective scientific truths in answer to
questions impacting their community. The ideal outcome of such a philosophy was that others could use their research products for social policy
purposes. As best as possible, they believed scientists should be detached
from the promotion of their research for policy implementation. However,
in the event that one's impactful research was not used proactively on
an important topic such as, for example, lynching, then the researcher
should be ready to engage in direct social reform. Du Bois, well aware
of the heightened distrust of Whites toward research with social reform
aims, especially that conducted by Black Americans, did not support the
latter position during his time as an institutionally affiliated scholar.

Although Du Bois did not support direct social policy/reform efforts
while an academic, he championed the use of research for those aims by
interested parties. He distanced himself from direct reform efforts as a

scientist to assure, as best he could, that his research was not unneces-
sarily invalidated and marginalized within the academy because it was
believed to be subjective or conducted in a manner designed to unethically
produce results favorable to Black Americans. Toward this end Du Bois
proclaimed, "any attempt to give [science] a double aim, to make social
reform the immediate instead of the mediate object of a search for truth,
will inevitably tend to defeat both objects."[18] Du Bois simply wanted to
study social problems and discover scientific truths that, if utilized by
the proper stakeholder(s), could be used to impact social policy or social
reform efforts. However, it was his preference that others, not scientists,
engage in direct social reform / policy development with the findings of
their investigations. To this idea Du Bois said:

> [I] put no special emphasis on specific reform effort, but increasing and
> widening emphasis on the collection of a basic body of fact concerning
> the social condition of American Negroes, endeavoring to reduce that
> condition to exact measurement whenever or wherever occasion per-
> mitted. As time passed, it happened that many uplift efforts were in fact
> based on our studies.[19]

The definition of and principles for Black sociology are taken from
the words of Atlanta University president Horace Bumstead and gleaned
from the scholarship of W. E. B. Du Bois. Black sociology was established
at Atlanta University but its philosophy, vicariously and not explicitly,
extended to other early departments of sociology at HBCUs between 1895
and 1970. While there was no codified messaging of the idea that an alter-
nate branch of sociological practice existed, most, if not all, of the principles of Black sociology are found in the scholarly activities conducted at
Fisk University, Tuskegee Institute, and Howard University. What follows
is an outline of the remainder of the book wherein an examination of the
Black sociological practices at the Big Four between 1895 and 1970 is made.

Jim Crow Sociology: The Black and Southern Roots of American Sociology is an
examination of the scholarly and disciplinary impact of four departments
of sociology at HBCUs during Jim Crow. Before I outline the specific

components of this book, let me be clear in articulating what the objective of this project is and is not. The primary objective of this book is to uncover the seminal contributions of sociologists at educational institutions that, by my definition, practiced Black sociology. The primary objective of this book *is not* to provide comprehensive coverage of all the contributions of all early Black sociologists, nor to highlight the major contributions of already well-known early Black male sociologists. I purposely do not center the efforts of early *superstar* Black male sociologists because bodies of literature, albeit not as extensive as one would desire, currently exist on them. By not centering early Black male sociologists, the contributions of lesser-known and unknown early Black sociologists, including those who are female and LGBTQ, are privileged. This book's focus provides an opening to expand the canon of early contributors to the discipline: people whose sociological works have been hidden in the shadows of superstar sociologists such as W. E. B. Du Bois, E. Franklin Frazier, and Charles S. Johnson. While these men and some of their significant contributions to the discipline at their respective institutions are addressed here, it is important that the reader takes away from this project the contributions made by others within their networks, without whom their accomplishments may not have been possible nor their institutions relevant.

This book opens with an overview of the early educational opportunities available for Blacks in America immediately after the end of slavery. This is an important starting point because most of the schools established for the education of Blacks included classrooms filled with children eager to learn what the world had to offer and adults desirous of an opportunity to finally, and legally, learn to read, write, and do arithmetic as freepersons. Almost all of the HBCUs established to educate the freedmen and freedwomen included the name *university* or *college* but were little more than the equivalent of contemporary junior and high schools at the time of their establishment. The titles "university" and "college" were more aspirational than accurate accounts of the quality of education offered during the early years. Beginning with the extremely limited educational opportunities available during slavery and the opening of schools during

Reconstruction, a snapshot of the challenges and obstacles to educating the freedmen and freedwomen is presented. Infused into this narrative is the irony that as America grappled with its transition from a slaveholding to non-slaveholding society, a scientific tool of human uplift was developing simultaneously at some of the nation's elite institutions of postsecondary learning. As sociology emerged at HWCUs like Yale College and the University of Chicago, its White practitioners were more preoccupied with validating its existence through positivism and abstract theorizing than using it as a tool for the advancement of social justice, challenging inequality, and debunking scientific racism theories.

More troubling than the embrace of scientific racism was the engagement of sociologists at HWCUs in research that was either wholly unscientific or employed low-quality methods of research—especially when Blacks were the subjects of investigation. The *science* of this era was nearly universally guided by racist theories depicting American Blacks, even when adults, as in a perpetual state of childhood, impervious to diseases impacting Whites and biologically and intellectually inferior to Whites. The pushback against this body of sociology began with the establishment of the sociological laboratory at Atlanta University. Important to understanding Atlanta University and other HBCUs' embrace of sociology was its promise as a tool for social uplift that directly aligned with the mission of most institutions established for the education of Blacks during this period. It is quite clear that one objective of early HBCUs was the development of sociology programs that would use the discipline as a tool to challenge and/or ameliorate social inequality: a posture opposite to that assumed by HWCUs. In Chapter 1, the foundation for the relevance of research through the lens of Black sociology is established with an examination of the *sociology of the South* efforts of early White sociologists. The early and intensive embrace of the discipline by southerners was rooted nearly exclusively in their desire to wield the new *science* as a tool in the justification of continued racial inequality in this nation. Accounts of this particular chapter of the discipline's emergence in America are almost always hidden. However, this inquiry firmly establishes the growth of this body of research grounded in scientific racism as an impetus for the creation of Black sociology.

Chapter 2, "The Atlanta Sociological Laboratory," includes an examination of the origin, development, and major contributions of the sociology program at Atlanta University to the discipline. Significant moments in the program's history include the introduction of sociology to the institution by Howard Hincks and its ascension to sociological prominence under the leadership of W. E. B. Du Bois. The accomplishments made under Du Bois's leadership include, but were not limited to, being the first American school to institutionalize the use of insider researchers, method triangulation, a section acknowledging the limitations of one's research, and a section articulating the method(s) of research in one's publication.

The major point of departure for this book from other conversations on the Atlanta Sociological Laboratory is the examination of the contributions of lesser-known members of the school. One critique made concerning historical examinations of the origin and development of sociology in the United States is the failure to include the scholarly efforts of early African American women sociologists. Accordingly, emphasis is placed on the pre-Du Bois years of the Atlanta University studies, when women such as Lucy Laney and Georgia Swift King presented research papers based on their studies. Additionally, the conference participation of women including Jane Addams and Mary Church Terrell is examined. An additional critique of historical examinations of the origin and development of sociology in the United Sates is the failure to include the contributions of LGBTQ sociologists. This book fills this void by examining Augustus Granville Dill's contributions to the Atlanta University research effort and the impact that his life as a queer Black man in the early twentieth century had on his career.

Atlanta University's impact on the scientific community via its research on Blacks, starting in 1895, was immense. However, Du Bois's departure from the school and academia in 1913 began the decline of its sociological influence and prominence. Although the annual conference continued until 1924, its annual studies, if conducted at all, were much less scientifically significant. More important, Atlanta University's de-commitment to groundbreaking sociological research created a void in the pursuit of research not based on scientific racism on Blacks in America. This void was eventually filled, but by an unlikely person at a most unlikely location.

In Chapter 3, "Tuskegee and Rural Sociology," the unlikely sociological impact of Booker T. Washington on the discipline is examined. While the efforts at Atlanta University centered largely on the challenges facing urban Black Americans, relatively little sociological attention during this period was focused on the conditions experienced by their rural brethren. Booker T. Washington recognized this void and in 1892 initiated the Tuskegee Negro Conference, later renamed Tuskegee Farmer's Conference. The primary purpose of the Tuskegee Negro Conference was to teach Black farmers how to improve their life chances and life outcomes by becoming proficient in agriculture through the combination of scientific knowledge and real-world applications. The unintended result of this effort was the establishment of an area of applied sociological inquiry that did not previously exist. It is argued in this chapter that under the direction of Washington, Tuskegee became the first school in the nation to engage in applied rural sociology. Although the scientific rigor of the applied rural sociology program initiated at Tuskegee was underwhelming when compared to that taking place at Atlanta, that an HBCU was the first to engage this work was a significant, yet unknown and groundbreaking achievement. The efforts at Tuskegee were scientifically significant because they were, at a minimum, on par with *sociology of the South*-influenced research of the era. This accomplishment is even more significant because Tuskegee didn't officially embrace the formal instruction of sociology until after the turn of the century. After the school infused social science courses into the curriculum it hired one of the leading scholars of the era and, unknowingly, situated itself as the transitory agent between the herculean efforts at Atlanta University and the forthcoming Golden Age of Black Sociology.

Tuskegee, under the guidance of Monroe Nathan Work, succeeded Atlanta as the primary conduit of data on the social, economic, and physical condition of Blacks in America. This task was not accomplished through yearly scientific investigations, conferences, and publications, as had been done at Atlanta University. Instead, Work created and edited *The Negro Year Book*, an annual publication that included the most accurate and up-to-date information on the social, economic, and physical condition of Blacks in America during the era. Foremost among the issues addressed in *The Negro Year Book*, and one especially relevant to rural Blacks, was lynching. In this chapter Tuskegee's publication of lynching data and, circuitously, anti-lynching legislation efforts are highlighted. Also included in this discussion are the exploits of an influential researcher, independent scholar, and from my perspective a citizen sociologist, Ida B. Wells-Barnett. Wells-Barnett also gathered lynching data on Blacks in an effort to influence public policy toward the elimination of the abhorrent spectacle through the introduction of severe penalties for its practitioners. No examination of (anti)lynching can be considered complete without a review of her important, and sociological, contributions. The efforts of Work and Wells-Barnett are highlighted to note early, albeit unsuccessful, efforts to elicit public policy legislation directed at curtailing lynching. Ultimately, this chapter includes significant information because it uncovers the hidden sociological importance of Washington's technical and vocational school and opens discussions on its fitness to be recognized as one of the discipline's foundational units.

Both Fisk University and Howard University have storied sociological legacies. Unfortunately, most sociologists recognize these institutions because of the exploits of their respective superstar sociologists and not the foundational figures upon which both departments were established. This chapter focuses on the foundations established by George Edmund Haynes at Fisk and Kelly Miller at Howard that led to the accomplishments later made by Charles S. Johnson and E. Franklin Frazier, respectively. In Chapter 4, "Fisk and Howard: Laying the Foundation," the reader learns that Atlanta University was not the only HBCU engaged in high-quality sociological research during the latter years of the Atlanta Sociological Laboratory's duration and prior to Monroe Nathan Works's continued efforts at Tuskegee. Fisk, under the leadership of George Edmund Haynes, established one of the earliest programs of applied sociology in the United States. With an emphasis on translating sociological theory into practical application, Haynes's applied sociology program was a forerunner to contemporary efforts to bridge theory and praxis. In this chapter I note that the apex of Haynes's applied sociology program was its response to and assistance in the rebuilding of East Nashville after a fire in 1916 that destroyed the homes of more than 600 Black and White families. Although Hayne's tenure at Fisk was short, school administrators understood the utility of the discipline and were committed to its expansion after his departure.

The focus on departments of sociology at HBCUs has centered, to this point, on Deep South states. At least one *Up South* institution was central to the development of Black sociology. Chapter 4 includes an examination of the origin and development of sociology at Howard University, in Washington, D.C. Under the leadership of Kelly Miller, the school established one of the earliest departments of sociology in the nation. While Miller did not produce a voluminous body of sociological scholarship, as he was a trained mathematician, he is a noteworthy figure because of his role in the community of Black sociologists and intelligentsia. His most noteworthy role, perhaps, is that which he played in deftly mediating the ideological disagreement between W. E. B. Du Bois and Booker T. Washington. Though he largely aligned with Washington, Miller attempted to bring the two giants of the Black community to a mutual understanding of one another with the political acuity of a seasoned statesman. This chapter explores his nearly universally recognized status as a marginal man, one who did not neatly fit within the Black nor White worlds, and its possible impact on the development of sociology at Howard. Also discussed is how the school's disciplinary impact was possibly neutered by its complicated financial relationship with the federal government. More specifically, I argue that Miller's pragmatic worldview combined with the realities of the financial relationship between Howard and the federal government may have contributed to the lack of critical race scholarship published by members of the unit during Miller's term of leadership. Regardless of his personal positions, it was his moderate philosophical perspective and temperament that provided the foundation upon which the school was able to amass, arguably, America's finest collection of social science minds toward the end of the Jim Crow era. Conclusively, it is because of the efforts of Haynes at Fisk and Miller at Howard, in addition to their contemporaries at other institutions, that foundations for the growth of sociology were established. It was upon their shoulders that the Golden Age of Black sociology emerged.

Chapter 5 is titled "The Golden Age of Black Sociology" because this era represents the apex of sociological practice, instruction, and leadership at HBCUs. This period begins circa 1930 with the arrival of Charles S. Johnson at Fisk and E. Franklin Frazier at Howard. The talent displayed by an array of brilliant Black American sociologists during this era is undeniable. During this period a fair number of Black sociologists gained recognition beyond their segregated academic spaces as the White sociological community began to accept these long-marginalized academics into their formerly homogenous professional sociology organizations and spaces.

Moving beyond George Edmund Haynes, the chapter highlights Charles S. Johnson's efforts on researching and improving relations between the races. The point of departure for this book from existing examinations of Johnson's impact on the discipline is the emphasis on the research unit he spearheaded. Johnson's tenure as director of Fisk's Race Relations Institute is central to understanding how he and his colleagues, in the tradition established by Haynes, used sociology as a tool to challenge racial folkways and mores impeding the complete attainment of civil rights for Black Americans. Less a treatise on Johnson, as indicated earlier, this chapter centers the school's engagement in applied sociological research to improve the condition of Blacks in general, and southern Blacks specifically.

Similar to Johnson, E. Franklin Frazier built upon the foundation laid by his predecessor at Howard, Kelly Miller. In addition to conducting groundbreaking research and becoming the first Black president of the American Sociological Society (now called American Sociological Association), Frazier was the central figure in the greatest collection of intellectual talent at an HBCU during Jim Crow. Collectively, Frazier, Abram Harris, and Ralph Bunche represented the Howard School of Thought. More importantly, this chapter outlines the institutional support for the department that enabled it to erect facilities suitable for the development of a doctoral program in sociology and the school's complicated relationship with the federal government, which provided substantive fiscal support for these efforts.

The Golden Age of Black Sociology cannot be written without including the era's founding voice. After a twenty-year absence W. E. B. Du Bois returned to Atlanta University in 1933. Upon returning to academia, his unofficial title as leader of the Black sociological and intellectual community had been usurped by moderate and politically savvy newcomers who, while similarly desirous of confronting and ameliorating racism and inequality, employed different tactics. Included in this chapter are Du Bois's efforts to navigate this new reality vis-à-vis Frazier's Howard collective and his efforts to revive the research program at Atlanta University that had ended shortly after his departure in 1913. Although he produced studies at Atlanta University between 1941 to 1943, it was clear that Du Bois no longer wielded enough influence in the discipline to carry out his plan for a massive social science research initiative spearheaded by land-grant HBCUs. Du Bois's presence at Atlanta University, despite his minimized research influence, contributed to the strong production of sociological research and training at HBCUs during the Golden Age.

The Golden Age of Black Sociology not only included Du Bois's return to Atlanta, but Charles S. Johnson's ascension from faculty member to becoming the first Black president of Fisk and E. Franklin Frazier's ascension to becoming the first Black president of the American Sociological Association. The stable of rising Black sociologists, while not large, was indeed talented; it quickly increased in ways unimagined by the first Black American to take the doctorate with a specialty in sociology, James R. L. Diggs (Illinois Wesleyan, 1906), the first Black American to take the doctorate from a department of sociology, R. R. Wright (Pennsylvania, 1911), or the first Black woman to take the doctorate, Anna Johnson Julian

(Pennsylvania, 1937). Unfortunately, this era was short-lived. The Golden Age of Black Sociology began its decline after the historic 1954 Supreme Court decision outlawing segregation in public education, *Brown v. Topeka Board of Education*. By 1962, when the deaths of Johnson, Frazier, and Du Bois had occurred, the Golden Age of Black Sociology was over, and a period of darkness began.

Chapter 6, "Whither Black Sociology," begins with an examination of the impact of desegregation on the employment choices of Black sociologists and the resultant implications for departments of sociology at HBCUs. Prior to the 1970's Black sociologists were nearly exclusively employed at HBCUs. As discussed in the preceding chapters, these institutions were the primary producers of objective and scientific research on Blacks up to this point. The demise of Black sociology, as an institutional concept, began in 1954 with the *Brown v. Topeka Board of Education* decision that was intended to erase the stain of educational inequality from the American fabric. In this chapter I posit that an unintended consequence of the *Brown* decision was that the eventual desegregation of White American educational institutions created opportunities for Black sociologists to depart HBCUs and seek employment at HWCUs. Like the majority of their White colleagues, HWCUs required Black sociologists to engage in effective teaching and high-quality research. Unlike their White colleagues, HWCUs also expected their newly embraced colleagues to spend a disproportionate amount of time serving as mentors to the increasing numbers of Black students on campus. Increasingly, high-performing and exceptional Black sociologists were no longer accepting invitations to join departments of sociology at Atlanta, Fisk, Tuskegee, and Howard after completing doctoral work. Instead, the new generation of Black sociologists was taking their talents to better-funded and better-resourced institutions like Chicago, Columbia, Stanford, and other HWCUs. Thus, one theme in this chapter is the unintended and harmful impact of the *Brown v. Board of Education* decision on the production of Black sociology at HBCUs.

A second theme in this chapter is that desegregation led to the death of Black sociology. Combined with the departure of talented Black faculty was the de-emphasis on innovative sociological research at formerly high-performing HBCUs. The most far-reaching impact, however, is the idea that combined with the departure of talented Black faculty was the de-emphasis on innovative sociological research at formerly high-performing HBCUs. The slowed production of quality sociological research at HBCUs led to the demise of Black sociology as an institutionalized practice. Thus, the era of Black sociology is ended. Ultimately, I propose in this chapter that despite the negative and unintended impact of civil rights victories on Black sociology as an institutional entity at HBCUs, the parallel world of social science inquiry as an institutionalized academic endeavor did not disappear. This chapter concludes with the proposition that Black sociology reemerged in the late 1960's serendipitously as Black Studies. I conclude this book with the argument that Black sociology is the foundation upon which Black Studies was established and that the tenets of Black sociology continue to exist organizationally, primarily via the Association of Black Sociologists.

Significance

Jim Crow Sociology: The Black and Southern Roots of American Sociology is the first book-length examination of the significant contributions to the discipline of Black sociologists at multiple departments of sociology at HBCUs. Moreover, it includes several groundbreaking claims. For one, it is demonstrated that Booker T. Washington's Tuskegee Institute comprised the nation's first applied rural sociology program while debunking the long-held notion that the Wizard of Tuskegee was vehemently opposed to social science research. Also, data indicate that Fisk University, under the leadership of both George Edmund Haynes and Charles S. Johnson, comprised an early forerunner of what is known today as community-based participatory research. Additionally, this book expands the literature on our understanding of the contributions of people associated with the first American school of sociology not named W. E. B. Du Bois and who were women, namely Lucy Laney, Georgia Swift King, Jane Addams, and Mary Church Terrell, in addition to Ida B. Wells-Barnett, who is recognized for her anti-slavery works. Last, this book is noteworthy for its examination of an early Black queer sociologist, Augustus Granville Dill, who participated in the efforts of the first American school of sociology as an undergraduate and later replaced Du Bois as the chairperson of the department of sociology after his departure.

Ultimately, this book forces sociologists to grapple with our problematic history concerning which individuals and institutions are and should be included among the canonical figures and works students should be expected to know. Beyond deemphasizing the herculean efforts of individual superstar Black sociologists, *Jim Crow Sociology* contextualizes the collective contributions of multiple units of sociologists at HBCUs that embraced the discipline as a tool to improve their condition in this nation while, simultaneously, making groundbreaking contributions. This narrative describes how each school utilized its specific strength(s) to address the pressing problems of the day, individual and institutional racism, using the scientific method. Accordingly, the sociology practiced at Atlanta differed from that practiced at Tuskegee. This fact does not prioritize the contribution of one over the other, nor are comparisons between the two intended to lessen the importance of either to the discipline. Howard's sociology differed from that practiced at Fisk and both made substantive contributions to the discipline, but more importantly to American society. One was through the production of community-grounded and impactful research and the other through the development of a program of doctoral study where Blacks would be trained to fight proactively against scientific racism and in defense of those unfairly characterized as suffering pathological deficiencies via the leading research studies of the day. Regardless of the type of sociology practiced, what is certain is that for more than one hundred years, American sociologists and students of sociology have been deprived of learning the significant accomplishments of these men and women. This void, as discussed in full later, has hindered the development of the discipline for nearly a century.

It is my expectation that this book, written for use in undergraduate and graduate courses as well for scholars with little knowledge of the subject matter, will stimulate sociologists to consider how the canon of sociological excellence is created, reified, and, where necessary, reimagined. The long-overlooked contributions of Blacks to the discipline articulated in this book should motivate us to more fully engage in works exploring the contributions of non-Whites, non-males, and non-heterosexuals, especially during the discipline's foundational years. Imagine how different sociology would look now if the works of early Black sociologists had been critiqued and implemented and their findings promoted, and published, as regularly and enthusiastically as the early White sociologists we know all too well. What would we have learned? We would have learned that the founding practitioners of sociology were Black, southern, and worked at HBCUs. We would have learned that W. E. B. Du Bois established the first American school of sociology at Atlanta University. We would have learned that Booker T. Washington established the first applied rural sociology program at Tuskegee Institute. We would have learned that Fisk University, under George Edmund Haynes and Charles S. Johnson, was prominent in the maturation of applied sociology and race relations research, which could be considered a forerunner to what we now call community-based participatory research. And we would have learned that Howard University was the intellectual touchstone of Black sociology, with a collection of faculty, university-wide, that were as accomplished as any assemblage in the nation. Had the discipline of sociology not allowed its race-tinged glasses to prevent it from fully viewing the sociological activities conducted at HBCUs during the discipline's formative years in this nation, then, at a minimum, the scholarly exploits of the schools identified herein would already be infused into the sociological canon and the fruits of their research efforts given life to and for interested parties. To not take this moment to promote their enshrinement into that hallowed collective today with as much vigor as the HWCUs currently canonized is an affront to everything that is good and right in this world. The nation and this discipline owe them nothing less than full and complete entry into the canons and curriculums of sociology programs across this nation.

CHAPTER 1

The Black and Southern Roots
of American Sociology

The instruction of sociology in the United States dates back to the 1872–1873 academic year, when William Graham Sumner "gave up one of the three terms of his course on Political and Social Science to a discussion of Spencer's [*Study of*] *Sociology.*"[1] The discipline's emergence at the religiously affiliated Yale University gave rise to some consternation: "Theologically it is probably the most objectionable book Spencer has written, making no secret of its contempt for believers in the Christian religion, who are told that they must lay aside their faith if they wish to study sociology."[2] Due to religious resistance, sociology disappeared from the college's curriculum from 1880 to 1885. Sumner's role in establishing sociology as a legitimate area of academic study in the United States, despite its brief banishment from Yale, was key in the discipline's early acceptance and development. While not diminishing his important role in spearheading the academic instruction of the discipline in America, a moderated view of his significance to the discipline may be appropriately characterized by noting that "Professor Sumner's priority in the sociological field may be referred to as incidental to the more general fact of awakening academic interest in social science."[3] Therefore, although Sumner's instruction of the discipline was an important milestone, more central to the discipline's development was its institutionalization at postsecondary institutions across the nation.

The accepted narrative on the development of sociology in America leads one to believe the discipline's roots are grounded singularly within the soil of elite White institutions in America's Midwest and Northeast regions. This narrative is incorrect. The early instruction and overall acceptance of the discipline in academia was nearly geographically homogenous and not dominated exclusively by elite institutions. A more accurate narrative on the institutional acceptance of the discipline is that in the years immediately following Sumner's course at Yale a diverse array of largely southern institutions embraced and expanded the instruction of sociology. Although the sociology community acknowledges Sumner's course at Yale as a defining disciplinary moment, a little-known fact is that the second institution in this nation to list a course in sociology was the University of Arkansas in 1881.

Instruction in the discipline in the South at this time extended beyond Arkansas and into areas that once comprised the Confederate States of America during the Civil War. Beyond Yale and Arkansas, the first schools to infuse sociology into their curriculums were largely southern-based institutions including, but not limited to, Trinity College of North Carolina (now called Duke University), Atlanta University (now called Clark Atlanta University), the Woman's College of Maryland, and West Virginia University.[4] That a discipline rooted in objectivity and the scientific understanding of human behaviors and interactions was warmly embraced in states where slavery and segregation were commonplace only a generation prior was understandable given the specific objectives of its use. I address this point later in this chapter when an explanation is offered for the divergence between the way sociology was practiced at Black versus White southern institutions. What is noteworthy at this juncture is that the early southern embrace of and influence on the discipline was prominent and, unfortunately, has been and continues to be largely ignored.

As sociology became more popular and expanded to campuses across the nation there soon came a demand for instructors trained in and specifically assigned to teach courses in the discipline. The listing of the word *sociology* in the title of a professor teaching classes in the discipline did not occur until thirteen years after the first sociology course was taught in this country. "The first university [faculty position] to be created with

sociology designated by title as part of the professor's teaching responsibility was probably that established at the University of Indiana in
1885," for Arthur B. Woodford.[5] The school listed Woodford as an assistant
professor of economics and sociology and his assigned responsibilities
included teaching a course entitled *Sociology* in 1885.[6] Between 1885 and
1889 Woodford taught this course at Indiana University and used the textbooks "Spencer's *Study of Sociology*, Wilson's *Anthropology* and Letourneau's
Sociology Based upon Ethnography during the first and second terms on three
days a week."[7] Despite the discipline having its first named instructor at
Indiana University in 1885, no institution at this time had established an
academic department that included the word *sociology*.

It is accepted as common knowledge in most polite American sociological circles that the University of Chicago established the nation's first
department of sociology. Whether or not one deems this assertion true
depends on how one operationalizes the word *department*. The distinction
of establishing the first department of sociology is accurate when applied
to Chicago if it is explicitly understood that one is referring to a unit having
only the word *sociology* as its *singular* department title. However, if the
distinction of establishing the first department of sociology includes the
simple inclusion of the word sociology as *part* of an academic unit's title,
then the answer is quite clear. The University of Chicago did not establish
the first department of sociology in the United States. This distinction
belongs to the University of Kansas and is a fact acknowledged by Chicago
sociology's founding department head, Albion Small.

In 1889 the University of Kansas established the Department of
History and Sociology, making it the first department of sociology in
the nation. Kansas's path toward this founding was a curious one, which
included overt and covert political interventions and concessions. More
specifically, the direct involvement of political officials and the intensity
of pressure placed upon school administrators was critical in the institution's circuitous route toward establishing the department. The endeavor
began with the institution's nationwide search for a person to lead the
newly proposed social science department. This task began in a low-key

manner and led to the doorstep of an early and prominent sociologist. The institution's search "for a man to take charge of a new department to be formed in the University of Kansas" led them to Frank Blackmar of Johns Hopkins in Baltimore, Maryland.[8] Blackmar, once a classmate of Albion Small at Johns Hopkins, differed from the founder of the unit in Chicago in that he "took [his] major in history of institutions" while Small majored in sociology.[9] Despite not majoring in sociology, Blackmar was selected to chair the new department. Moreover, he was charged with naming the new unit.

Blackmar's initial recommendation for the department name, History and Politics, was rejected because "the regents were very much excited, telling me it would not do to give a department that name, because 'the people of Kansas would not tolerate a Department of *Politics* [sic] in the University, as they had enough politics in the state already.'"[10] Seemingly undaunted at the rejection of his first recommendation, he offered the Department of History and Political Science as an alternative. Again he was rebuffed. The inclusion of a word similar or relating to *politics* or *political* was a deal-breaker for politicians whose support was critical for school administrators, who were thought to have ulterior progressive motivations in establishing the unit. Again, political opposition and the unease of the school and its supporters with a unit that, in their opinion, may have led to taxpayer-funded engagement in matters of government and politics on a college campus was untenable. This posture led to the establishment of the first named sociology department in the nation.

In making the decision to title the unit Department of History and Sociology, Blackmar noted, "So far as my knowledge goes, this was the first time that the word 'sociology' was used in connection with the name of a university department in the United States."[11] This distinction was also noted and bolstered by the founder of the Department of Sociology at the University of Chicago, Albion Small, who wrote, "Professor Blackmar seems to be correct on this point. No evidence of priority in this respect over the University of Kansas is known [to me]."[12] Despite Chicago not being the location of the nation's first formalized department, sociologists historically and naively believe the discipline began in earnest upon the establishment of sociology at the University of Chicago three years after the Kansas effort.

When the University of Chicago opened in 1892 one of its primary charges was to become one of the finest research-intensive institutions in the United States. Reflecting on the school's founding, assisted amounted to more than $25 million in today's dollars, the University of Chicago Committee on Development proclaimed:

> "Here is to be found intellectual freedom." [The University of Chicago] established as its official motto, and has kept it: "Let knowledge grow, that life may be enriched." By setting up lofty ideals of scholarship, by recognizing research as one of its primary aims, and by encouraging freedom of investigation as a prime condition of success in research, [the University of Chicago] began on a plane to which many other institutions have been slowly ascending.[13]

The institution's commitment to the emerging discipline was evidenced by the fact that shortly after Chicago's founding it established one of the nation's first departments of sociology. Reflecting on the school's establishment and commitment to its departmental founder, the Committee on Development proclaimed:

> In Sociology, the name of a man like Professor Albion W. Small, Head of that Department of the University, stands for pioneer work in organizing a subject that belongs to the present generation and has made for a broader view of human society.[14]

While the Chicago School of mythical sociological renown did not emerge until the arrival of Robert Park, Ernest W. Burgess, and other members of the second-generation cohort circa 1914, Small created a formidable team of first-generation Chicago School scholars: William I. Thomas, Charles R. Henderson, George E. Vincent, and Charles Zeublin among them. Although Small acknowledged Kansas's distinction in establishing the first department of sociology in the nation, he was adamant that the sociological research program he spearheaded in Chicago was the primary reason the discipline developed as fully in this nation as it did.

"After 1892 sociology came out into the open as an accredited university subject," says Small, "but I very strongly [sic] doubt if this consummation would have been reached at that time—I am not sure that it would have occurred at all—if the University of Chicago had not been founded."[15] Allowing for a possible exception, Small stated, "In some respects Leland Stanford Junior University [Stanford University], founded the same year, was a similar dynamic factor, but it was so remote geographically that it did not produce the same visible effects."[16] Small was adamant that the development of sociology in America would not have occurred as fast, or possibly at all, without the substantial financial largess and commitment to excellence in research at schools like Chicago, Stanford, Princeton, and Johns Hopkins. In addition to these schools' financial backing and commitment to social science research, Small argued, competition among the presidents of these elite institutions contributed to the discipline's ascension in the early twentieth century.

Small lauded University of Chicago President Harper's commitment to "opening the way for the subject of sociology in curricula which might not for years have made room for that division of social science."[17] The implication here was that many institutions did not share Chicago's zeal for social science or sociological expansion. Add to this argument the fact that many institutions did not have access to the financial largess of a John D. Rockefeller to shepherd their ambitions into fruition, and we find that institutions not hampered by financial limitations and insufficient social science interests were establishing, supposedly, the most impactful sociological units in the nation. Curiously, the majority of these *influential* institutions were, largely, located in the Midwest and Northeast. A reasonable question to ask is, "did schools outside these regions make substantive contributions to the discipline during its formative years in this nation?" The answer to this question is a resounding yes.

The development of sociology at institutions in the Midwest, Northeast and, to some degree, west of the Mississippi River is well known.

Less known are the sociological origins and exploits of southern-based institutions. Even less known are the sociological activities conducted at HBCUs. Before one can fully understand the development of sociology at HBCUs and HWCUs in the South, one must understand the social and racial milieu within which they emerged. Because the path to understanding the contributions of Blacks to the discipline uniquely and directly connects to this nation's original sin, slavery, and includes the criminalization of education, a brief overview of the education of Blacks pre-emancipation and the establishment of HBCUs is offered.

The Audacity of Learning

Key to the development of Black sociology was the segregation of Blacks and Whites in education. This division forced the discipline to develop without intimate equal-status professional interactions between Blacks and Whites that could have led to innovative methodological, theoretical, and substantive scientific collaborations and advances. When the teaching of sociology began in 1872–1873 American Blacks were only seven years removed from their status as the legal property of other human beings. Though no longer bound by chains, the second-class status of Black Americans was affirmed over many decades and in a variety of legal manners, which included decisions rendered by the Supreme Court of the United States of America. For example, the Supreme Court affirmed the second-class status of free Blacks in America when it ruled in Dred Scott v. Sanford (1857) they were not eligible for American citizenship. This decision certainly tortured the souls of scores of Blacks whose desire to continue living in a nation rife with the constant threat of death was predicated on the possibility they could one day gain citizenship and, in theory, achieve a quality of life equal to if not greater than their White peers. What is lost in the general understanding of the outcome of the *Dred Scott* decision is that the Supreme Court concluded that Blacks in America could secure citizenship status in specific states, but that they were ineligible for federal or national citizenship. Because of their non-federalized citizenship status, the Supreme Court reasoned that Blacks in America were disqualified from filing lawsuits in federal court to obtain their freedom and to becoming full-fledged citizens. A little more than ten years later the legislative branch of the government accomplished a feat the judicial branch was unwilling to perform.

After the 14th Amendment to the United States Constitution awarded citizenship to Blacks in America in 1868, judicial challenges to their efforts to participate in American society as full, equal, and complete citizens not bound by race were immediately initiated. A collection of such efforts, known as the Slaughter-House Cases (1873), effectively empowered states to continue or establish segregation policies, including those related to education, to severely limit the movement and social and economic opportunities available to Blacks in America. That this decision was rendered nearly simultaneously with the introduction of sociology in America virtually guaranteed, at least for the foreseeable future, the preservation of educational settings where there would be no, or very limited, integrated spaces where debates among professional and student peers concerning academic matters could take place if the participants were of different races. While the aforementioned cases and their circuitous impacts are historically significant in their own right, perhaps the most infamous and impactful civil rights case of this era was *Plessy v. Ferguson*.

Although the Slaughter-House Cases provided legal cover for the separation of the races in this nation, Black Americans continued to petition the courts to reverse those collective decisions. Their efforts to overturn segregationist laws were unsuccessful. Unfortunately and unintentionally, the persistence of Blacks in America to gain equal status citizenship and human rights under the law led to the formal introduction of segregation, commonly known as Jim Crow, in education. In *Plessy v. Ferguson* (1896) the Supreme Court upheld previous legal decisions that supported segregation on the basis of race. This decision bolstered earlier rulings by promoting the notion that segregation by race, with respect to public accommodations, was permissible if the facilities were *separate and equal*. The separate but equal mandate applied to all aspects of formal American institutional life, including education. This decision solidified the divide between Blacks and Whites and further delayed potential collaborative efforts that could have molded the emerging discipline of sociology into unknown forms. It was within this cultural milieu and bank of court decisions that Blacks in America, now barely twenty-five years removed from legalized enslavement, pursued educational opportunities previously denied under the malignant institution of slavery—but were now only free to do so within the restrained legal confines of Jim Crow segregation.

The Costs of Learning

The fight by Blacks in America to obtain formal and informal education dates back to slavery. During enslavement it is reasonable to suggest that minus the penalties for such actions, most Blacks desired and many attempted to obtain at best a formal education or at worst simple book learning. Because slave owners feared the potential consequences of an educated slave labor force, education was prohibited and whipping and/ or death were promoted as penalties for such ambitions. Many enslaved men and women risked and lost their lives to become educated despite the desire of slave owners to maintain a largely uneducated labor force, except in certain cases. So strong was the desire of enslaved Blacks to become educated that states began passing legislation to prevent them from becoming literate. For example, in the 1770s the penalty for teaching enslaved Blacks to read and write in South Carolina was a $100 fine.[18] The desire to prevent Black literacy and education was so strong in some states that legislation was enacted to penalize Whites for assisting the enslaved to become educated. In Georgia the teaching of Blacks to read and/or write by another Black person was punishable:

> By fine and whipping, or fine or whipping, at the discretion of the court; and if a white person so offended, he, she or they shall be punished with a fine not exceeding $500 and imprisonment in the common jail at the discretion of the court.[19]

The fear of enslaved Blacks becoming educated in nontraditional ways, such as in small groups located in public spaces, led to the passage of additional punitive anti-education legislation. Some states went so far as to implement laws to prevent the free assembly of Blacks because they were concerned with the possible consequences of having an educated and literate non-White and enslaved population within their midst. Many Whites feared public gatherings of Blacks would become covert attempts at becoming proficient at 'readin, 'riting, and 'rithmetic. Once educated and literate, Blacks, they feared, would become discontent with their lowly status and attempt to strive for rights equal to those of Whites who, in the throes of the scientific-racism era, believed themselves to be of a higher human rank. This fear was exemplified in the laws of at least two states.

In 1819 Virginia forbade "all meetings or assemblages of slaves or free Negroes or mullatoes [sic], mixing and associating with such slaves . . . at any school or schools for teaching them reading and writing, either in the day or night."[20] In 1847, less than twenty years prior to the end of legalized slavery, Missouri "passed an act saying that, 'No person shall keep or teach any school for the instruction of Negroes and mulattoes in reading or writing in this state'."[21] The conscious and legal denial of educational opportunities to Blacks in America was nearly crippling to a group newly released from bondage and forced into a situation where they, as Frederick Douglass argued, *were free to die.* That roughly 80% of Blacks were illiterate when the 15th Amendment to the United States Constitution, giving Black men the right to vote, passed in 1870 was an indicator of the need for and establishment of centers of learning to prepare the freedmen and freedwomen for, theoretically, the wide array of opportunities available to the unbonded.[22]

Secondary schooling in the pre–Civil War Southern United States was essentially nonexistent for Blacks and paltry, at best, for most Whites. With the exception of Kentucky and North Carolina, there existed no statewide supported school system in the South for Whites. While educational opportunities for Blacks in the South were limited for the reasons discussed earlier, "From about 1835 on it became general for the Northern states to support wholly a separate system of Negro schools. They were usually poorer than the whites, worse taught and worse equipped, and wretchedly housed."[23] It was not until 1870 that an earnest push for the establishment of schools for the education of Blacks in America was initiated nationally.

Although Blacks in America were able to legally establish schools after the abolition of slavery, they continued to experience obstacles in their educational pursuits. Since America's formerly enslaved populace did not receive formal schooling prior to emancipation, there was little to no differentiation, relatively speaking, between the level of *book-learning* one could accomplish relative to the age of, contemporarily speaking, typical students. Therefore, during the years immediately following slavery the schooling of Black students was largely conducted in rooms where instructors simultaneously taught multiple grade levels in the same classroom among ages that varied widely. These early schools were called common or normal schools and often were components of the education system delivered by local and newly established HBCUs. "Common school" was the name assigned to institutions dedicated to teaching the core principles of reading, writing, and arithmetic. Normal schools were dedicated to training Blacks to become teachers in order to fill the demand for such professionals. After completion of common or normal school, a college education could normally begin.

Although it was illegal to educate Blacks during enslavement, and despite their mis-education during the Reconstruction and Jim Crow eras, there are some examples of Black academic excellence and achievement during this period. For example, the first Black person to graduate from an American college was John Brown Russworm, who earned a degree from Bowdoin College (ME) in 1826.[24] Despite the challenges of the era, competition for the distinction of becoming the first Black person to graduate from an American college was close. Russworm garnered this distinction because his graduation preceded another candidate by only two weeks. Edward Jones, who took his degree from Amherst College (MA), was the second Black college graduate in America.[25] It is noteworthy that the two institutions to provide opportunities for the first Black college graduates in America were located in the North when the overwhelming majority of Blacks lived in the South. For southern Blacks, the establishment of HBCUs post-slavery signaled the first legitimate opportunity for them to obtain both secondary and post-secondary educations while remaining in or near their hometowns.

The Rise of HBCUs

When Blacks in America were emancipated from slavery in 1865 there were practically no institutions dedicated to educating the millions of freedmen and freedwomen. When specifically considering post-secondary institutions, the educational opportunities available to Blacks were even fewer. The obvious and pressing need in the years immediately following emancipation, other than food, clothing, and shelter, was the establishment of post-secondary institutions for their education. Because of the lack of basic K–12 facilities in most densely populated Black areas, many *colleges* and *universities* established by and for Blacks simultaneously provided instruction for all grades and to different levels of students. Although early HBCUs labeled themselves with titles including the word "university," in many cases little to no instruction was offered at the post-secondary level during the school's early years. According to Frank Bowles and Frank DeCosta:

> Literally hundreds of [Black institutions] were founded with "normal," "college," and "university" in their titles. Of course, they were largely elementary and secondary schools, but their titles were selected with the aim of indicating the eventual purpose they were to serve.[26]

As discussed earlier, in the South the majority of states did not provide support for a public system of education even for Whites. This made the task of educating millions of Americans, Black and White, a daunting task. Similar to early HBCUs, HWCUs were called upon to provide instruction for secondary education on their campuses. Thus, the inclusion of secondary

instruction at colleges and universities was not limited to newly established Black schools but took place at HWCUs as well. For example:

> As late as 1895, all of the white colleges in Alabama, [with the exception
> of the University of Alabama], reported preparatory enrollments. . . .
> Even in Massachusetts, Boston College and Tufts College reported pre-
> paratory enrollments.[27]

As Bowles and DeCosta noted, early Black schools labeled themselves with
names that foretold what they aspired to become. This notion was not new
and was also common at now-elite HWCUs. According to Augustus F. Beard:

> Oxford when it began more than a thousand years ago was not Oxford
> of today. Yale University, which lately celebrated its two hundredth
> birthday, began when half a dozen ministers of the gospel brought
> together a few books and said, We give these to the founding of a college.
> The name is in the interests and purpose, in the faith of what is to be,
> and in the hope of final achievement. Let us wait two hundred years
> and then ask whether or not this [Black institution] was rightly named
> University.[28]

Dwight Holmes informed us, "It must constantly be borne in the mind in
any consideration of the Negro college that at the beginning of the Civil
War the Negro, generally considered, began his academic education at
zero."[29] For this reason, it was important that a vast number and diversity
of colleges and universities for Blacks were established post-emancipation.
By establishing schools for their own education Black Americans could
supply teachers for their institutions and build upon or create new stocks
of knowledge.

The origin, number, and diversity of HBCUs was outlined by W. E. B.
Du Bois, who authored arguably the first objective and scholarly investigation into the education of Black Americans in 1900. He concluded that the
origin and development of HBCUs could be categorized into five distinct
groups. The first group, *Ante-Bellum* schools, "were established before the
[Civil W]ar and represent[ed] the abolition movement."[30] These schools
included Lincoln University (PA), established in 1854 and the oldest HBCU

in the nation, and Wilberforce University (OH), established in 1855. The second group, *Freedman's Bureau Schools*, "were established directly after the [Civil W]ar . . . by Missionary and Freedman's Aid Societies under the protection and for the most part under the direct patronage of the Freedman's Bureau."[31] Schools established under these auspices included Fisk University (1866), Atlanta Baptist College (1867), now known as Morehouse College, Atlanta University (1867), Howard University (1867), and Rust University (1868). The third group, *Church Schools*, "were established mainly by Church Societies after the closing up of the Freedman's Bureau"[32] and included Knoxville College (1879), Benedict College (1870), Clark University (1870), Wiley University (1873), and Philander Smith College (1876). The *Schools of Negro Church Bodies*, the fourth group, were established after "the first forward rush of the freedmen [to pursue an education] after emancipation [that] culminated in the eighties and led to a movement to found schools among the Negro churches."[33] These schools included Livingstone College (1880), Allen University (1881), Arkansas Baptist College (1884), Morris Brown College (1885), and Paul Quinn College (1885). The final group of schools listed by Du Bois were *State Colleges*. "The establishment of these colleges was due almost entirely to the United States' statutes of 1862 and 1890 donating public land to the several states for endowing agricultural colleges."[34] These schools included Branch Normal College (1875), now known as the University of Arkansas at Pine Bluff, Virginia Normal and Collegiate Institute (1882), now known as Virginia State University, Georgia State Industrial College for Colored Youth (1890), now known as Savannah State University, and Delaware State College (1891).

Simultaneous with the establishment of HBCUs was the emergence of sociology into a legitimate academic field. Current sociology students are taught that the discipline's expansion is *largely* due to the efforts of White sociologists at HWCUs in the midwest and northeast regions. A more accurate understanding of the discipline's history acknowledges that the American South is where the discipline was first embraced and employed as a scientific tool to understand the life chances, life outcomes, and experiences of its peoples. Although, as discussed later, Black and White sociologists utilized their tools differently, it is a fact that sociology was institutionalized in curriculums at southern institutions before those in other regions.

Sociologist L. L. Bernard wrote extensively on the development and history of the discipline in the early twentieth century. One of his primary research topics was the South's role in expanding the popularity of sociology and how Black and White sociologists employed the discipline differently. Concerning the growth of the discipline and the fact that institutions in the South included sociology in their curriculum earlier than other regions, Bernard concluded, "I think it is quite clear that sociology is, historically considered, more largely than not a product of our American South."[35] While Black and White institutions in the South embraced the discipline during its formative years, their reasons for doing so differed sharply.

The discipline's early embrace by southern sociologists and HWCUs was largely rooted in their attempts, as discussed in the next section, to rationalize and promote racial segregation, racist policies and scientific racism. HBCUs, conversely, focused on using the discipline as a tool to improve the life chances and life outcomes of Black Americans within the post-slavery world that witnessed the birth of the most notorious American domestic terrorist group to ever exist, the Ku Klux Klan. These facts led Bernard to conclude:

> But as the known facts now stand, it is apparent that sociology was first accepted by the smaller institutions of the South and by the Negro colleges. The reason for Negro interest is, I think, sufficiently evident in the fact that a minority group was trying honestly to understand the social situation in which it found itself.[36]

The social situation Black Americans found themselves in included, but was not limited to, state sanctioned segregation, domestic terrorism, unequal protection under the law, lynching, and a convict lease system that served as a shadow conduit for slavery many years after its legal death. Therefore, Black Americans, more than their White peers, viewed sociology through an emancipatory lens that had the potential to provide practical possibilities of eradicating the harmful injustices facing them. The lens through which Black American sociologists viewed the discipline is what I call "Black sociology." This brand of sociology emerged in the segregated American South during the Reconstruction and Jim Crow eras and was used as a tool to challenge biased and unscientific investigations into the condition of Blacks in America. In so doing, this particular strand of sociology rejected racially subjective paradigms promoting the intellectual and biological inferiority of Blacks and superiority of Whites; much of which was produced and promoted by southern scholars. Conversely, Whites used their sociology (of the South) as a tool to rationalize, weaponize, and promote scientific racism and racial inequality.

Sociology of the South

The traditional narrative on the origin and development of sociology in the United States tends to align closely with that presented in the introductory section of this chapter, whereby the efforts of White sociologists at midwestern and northeastern HWCUs are championed. What has historically been ignored, and continues to be, are the contributions of southerners, Black and White, to the development of the discipline. More specifically, what has been largely ignored or minimized is the role racism played in the South becoming the first region to fully embrace the emerging discipline. The early embrace of sociology by southern Whites, as indicated previously, differed from that of Blacks, who viewed the emerging discipline as a tool and weapon in the fight for their rights as human beings. White sociologists in the South, on the other hand, viewed their *sociology (of the South)* as the basis for a scientific appeal to the nation on the benefits and utility of (re)establishing and maintaining the racial social order that existed during the years of Black enslavement. The topical area *sociology of the South* defined this period of *scholarship* and, unlike its later iteration authored by Howard W. Odum, centered squarely on scientific racism.

Heretofore, discussions of the topical area "sociology of the South" have centered largely, if not exclusively, on Howard W. Odum's emphasis on regionalism and the unique aspects of southern culture he explored beginning in the 1920s. As an aside it must be noted that, despite historical arguments to the contrary, W. E. B. Du Bois, and not Odum, was the first to initiate a "sociology of the South" program of research.[37] Nevertheless, the focus on Odum's sociology of the South ignores the fact that the racist inclinations of many early White sociologists helped expand the discipline, at least in the South, on the foundations of racial superiority and segregation under the umbrella term and guise of "sociology of the South." This brief and important period of American sociological history is largely missing from traditional accounts of the development of the discipline. Despite its exclusion from traditional narratives describing the discipline's origin and development, the South's early and racially motivated embrace of the discipline is central to understanding the factors leading to the creation of Black sociology. An understanding of why the discipline was first embraced by institutions in the South provides a larger understanding of the subsequent differences between the sociology practiced at HBCUs and HWCUs. The utility of the discipline as a tool by Black sociologists to improve their social, economic, and physical condition has already been presented. What follows is an examination of how sociology as practiced by Whites in the American South was weaponized to promote scientific racism theories of Black American inferiority and subordination.

Fitzhugh and Hughes

Attacks against slavery and its primary practitioners, southern Whites, were mounting before the formal cessation of the peculiar institution as both average citizens and the intelligentsia were applying pressure on the nation's leaders to end this crime against humanity. In defense of southern sensibilities, ideas, and ways of life there arose a social philosophy of the *Old South* that became known as *sociology of the South*. The primary goal of this iteration of sociology of the South was the defense of White southerners who wanted to maintain the existing racial order of subordination and the idea of separate and (un)equal as espoused in the *Plessy v. Ferguson* case. Sociology of the South during this period was described as a "social philosophy that . . . was a curious mixture of logical reasoning and illogical guesses, profound arguments and stupid utterances, and subtle distinctions and blatant paradoxes."[38] While this area of *sociological inquiry* was, obviously, scientifically limited, "this body of social thought became the 'blue print' for shaping the pattern of defense for Southern institutional life and for attacking the theory and practice of free society, and sociology became one of these agencies."[39] Laid bare here is the reality that the regional embrace and development of this brand of sociological inquiry was grounded, largely if not exclusively, on subjectively validating the subordination of one human group by another. This effort was led by two southern lawyers and authors of books that were used in universities across this nation until the turn of the twentieth century—*Sociology for the South* (1854) by George Fitzhugh and *Treatise on Sociology* (1854) by Henry Hughes.

Fitzhugh's book, according to Edgar T. Thompson, asserted indirect support for southern mores and folkways and his was "a sociology battling in behalf of a regional interest and a sectional sentiment."[40] I contend, however, that Fitzhugh's publication was a direct—and supposedly *scholarly*—defense of the legalized enslavement of one group of human beings by another. Fitzhugh argued that if slavery had been the primary practice of the nations of the world there would not have been a need for the establishment of the discipline of sociology. Seemingly, his argument was based on the idea that chaotic social events such as the French Revolution, which spurred the development of sociology, would not have occurred in the context of the legalized enslavement of one group of people by another. This assertion was quite breathtaking and Fitzhugh amplified this point in the preface, where he wrote that:

> our book is intended to prove that we are indebted to domestic slavery for our happy exemption from the social afflictions that [necessitated the establishment of sociology]. . . . The fact that, before the institution

> of Free Society, there was no such term [as sociology], and that it is not
> in use in slave countries, now, shows pretty clearly that Slave Society,
> ancient and modern, has ever been in so happy a condition, so exempt
> from ailments, that no doctors have arisen to treat it of its complaints, or
> to propose remedies for their cure.[41]

Hughes made equally impassioned and direct "sociology of the South"
arguments in defense of slavery. Again, evidence of the author's position
is found in the preface. Hughes wrote:

> Some think that the Societary [sic] Organization of the American South,
> is morally evil, and civilly inexpedient. Others, who understand the
> working principles of what is called Slavery [sic], do not think so. They
> think that it is both morally and civilly good. This [book] is their opinion
> of its great and well known essentials. These they think, ought to be
> unchanged and perpetual. This Treatise essays amongst other things,
> to expound the philosophy of the Perpetualists; or in other words, to
> express some of the views of the Southern people on the subject of
> Slavery [sic].[42]

Collectively, and most germane to the point raised herein, these books
were required readings at post-secondary institutions across the nation,
and were embraced as legitimate sociological analyses on the development,
or lack thereof, of American society thru the lenses of White southern
lawyers whose goals were to promote *rational, objective,* and *scientific*
propositions on the usefulness of slavery-era relationships between the
races while offering theoretical arguments on why the peculiar institution
should be continued. What is important to note, and what is emphasized
here, is that these books were not ignored, marginalized, or hidden from
the mainstream societal consciousness. Instead, I repeat again, both were
adopted as university texts between 1854 and 1893.[43]

Scientific Racism

Is it fair to suggest that during Jim Crow sociologists outside the American
South were less dedicated to promoting theories and perspectives on the

biological and physical inferiority of Blacks in America and asserting what their status in the natural order of American society should be? No, it is not. Americans of all stripes and from all geographic regions embraced the scientific and cultural racism postures of the era. The list of participants included non-southern sociologists, contributors to the discipline's flagship journal *American Journal of Sociology* (*AJS*), and early presidents of the American Sociological Association. Below are a few representative examples of the scientific racism promoted by each grouping.

Francis Galton, a eugenicist, published a paper in *AJS* wherein he questioned the intellectual development of Black Americans. Galton believed the principles and implementation of eugenics could improve the stock of most races, but pondered "while most barbarous races disappear, some, like the Negro, do not."[44] In Galton's estimation Black Americans were scientifically proven to not be able to develop as a race past the stage of barbarism, with the exception of their childlike behaviors demonstrated during enslavement. Galton's conclusion, published in the leading sociology journal of the era, was reached without the presentation of any method(s) of data collection. Additionally, he did not indicate the body of information from where his conclusion was derived. One is left to conclude that his study was informed, at best, by what W. E. B. Du Bois called *car window sociology* or, at worst, from mere unscientific theoretical musings from the perspective of one who quite possibly never viewed Black Americans as full members of the human family.

G. E. Howard offered an equally offensive *scientific* and *scholarly* assessment. Howard's study focused on the impact of alcohol consumption on different race groups. His assessment was expansive and included Native Americans. According to Howard:

> The intoxicated Indian is bestial, almost fiendish, in his depravity. No depth of immorality, we are told, is too low for him. The lust of killing is aroused by the "fire water." . . . The case of the Negro is unique. He is not a habitual drunkard. As a rule the Negro of the South does not use liquor in his home. He indulges in orgies of intoxication on Saturdays, on Christmas, or other holidays. Then his evil passions are released and he

> is prone to commit acts of violence; but in a less degree than the white
> man is his efficiency or earning capacity impaired by these excesses.[45]

Again, this theoretical argument was presented without supporting data or articulation of the method(s), if any, of data collection.

Overt racism, unbothered with the absence of objective scientific data, espoused by early White sociologists was a constant staple of articles published in *AJS* pre-World War I. According to Elliott Rudwick:

> It is true that the *Journal* did carry articles by a man like W. I. Thomas, who criticized racist theories, but other items displayed the racial biases of their authors. The September 1903 issue included an article by H. E. Berlin entitled "The Civil War as Seen through Southern Glasses," in which the author described slavery as "the most humane and the most practical method ever devised for 'bearing the white man's burden.'" The publication of such views in the *American Journal of Sociology* reflected theories about race held in the profession at the time.[46]

Rudwick continued:

> Books by known racists were reviewed and often warmly praised. In 1906, Thomas Nelson Page's *The Negro: The Southerner's Problem* was glowingly lauded by Charles Ellwood, who had been Small's graduate student (*American Journal of Sociology* 11[1905–6:698–99]; Barnes 1948, pp. 853–55). In another review, Ellwood gratuitously commented, "it is only through the full recognition that the average Negro is still a savage child of nature that the North and South can be brought to unite in work to uplift the race."[47]

Early Black sociologist E. Franklin Frazier noted the attitudes of his White peers on the general condition of Black Americans and how their research was intentionally designed to subjectively prove their preexisting beliefs on the inferiority of those considered to be *the White man's burden.*

> As Frazier has described the situation, the "general point of view" of the first sociologists to study the black man was that "the Negro is an inferior race because of either biological or social hereditary or both." . . . These conclusions were generally supported by the marshaling of a vast amount

of statistical data on the pathological aspects of Negro life. In short, "The sociological theories which were implicit in the writings on the Negro problem were merely rationalizations of the existing racial situation."[48]

Green and Driver supported Franklin's critique of early sociologists, in general, and leaders of the American Sociological Association, specifically, when they wrote:

Examination of the writings of [the "Big Five"] presidents of [the American Sociological Association] from 1905, when the Association was founded, to 1914, reveals that this general ideology [was] present, varying from one president to another in its degree of subtlety.[49]

Green and Driver probed deeper and, using the work of R. Charles Key, concluded that the racism of many early White sociologists was to be expected given their racial socialization during that era.

Key's analysis of the writings of Sumner, Giddings, Small, Ward, and Ross leads him to conclude [that] . . . the racism of the pioneer sociologists and the incidents of racism found in their works seems to range from unashamed bigotry to tacit acceptance. Their racism can be understood in the same manner by which their theories and prophecies can be understood; with reference to the socio-culture in which they took meaning and shape; their opportunity structures, "styles of life," and worldviews.[50]

While attempts to rationalize the racism of early White sociologists can be appreciated, what is missing from Green and Driver's critique is the impact the racially charged scholarship and the resultant implications on notions of Black American intellectual acuity had on the development of the discipline. Stated more clearly, what is missing is an understanding that the preconceived notions of Black American inferiority contributed to the lack of equal-status partnerships among early Black and White sociologists who, according to Du Bois, failed to seriously grapple with one of the most unique social problems the world had ever faced; the assimilation of millions of formerly enslaved persons into the very society that had held them in bondage. Despite the lack of collaborative partnerships, Blacks at HBCUs scientifically and objectively pursued the social problems articulated by Du Bois as thoroughly and systematically as anyone in the nation.

What is argued to this point is that the White American sociological enterprise from the late 1800s to the mid 1900s collectively created and sustained a body of racist *scientific* literature that largely supported existing beliefs of Whites regarding the supposed intellectual and physical inferiority of Blacks in America. Prior to the passage of the 13th Amendment of the United States Constitution there was little, if any, scientific pushback against these notions. The counterbalance to the mountain of data scientifically validating the subordinate status of Black Americans was the discipline of sociology as employed by Black sociologists at HBCUs in the American South. It was within the Jim Crow segregation environment that HBCUs emerged to educate the millions of formerly enslaved Africans who had been legally prevented from securing an education in most of the states of this nation during enslavement and subjected to poorly funded miseducations after gaining their freedom. It was in the Jim Crow segregation environment that Black sociologists began to employ sociology as a tool to study the social, economic, and physical condition of Blacks in the United States such that the data could be used to improve or ameliorate the problems discovered via, among other ways, public policy. Because of their utilization of sociology as an emancipatory device as opposed to a theoretical formula to better understand the principles of society, what developed through the works of early Black sociologists was a parallel world of investigation and analysis called "Black sociology" that was best exemplified by the efforts of social scientists at Atlanta University, Tuskegee Institute, Fisk University, and Howard University.

CHAPTER 2

Atlanta Sociological Laboratory

The First American School of Sociology

Atlanta University was established in 1867 by the American Missionary Association. Guided by a cadre of 1863 Yale graduates, the university's administration set out to create the best post-secondary educational institution available to Blacks in America. As important as its emphasis on a strong curriculum was the school's commitment to assuring that its graduates obtain holistic and scientifically grounded understandings of the late nineteenth-century world in which they lived. This objective was championed by the university's White faculty and administrators, as they expected their students to, in addition to excelling academically, be change agents within a society that largely viewed them as unintelligent, inferior, and in some cases, subhuman. Additionally, Atlanta University faculty and administrators expected their students to exercise agency in their lives and not passively stand aside as the social, economic, and physical conditions of their people were deteriorating. School officials understood clearly that the fight to obtain civil rights for Blacks should be led, primarily, by Blacks. The school's White administrators and faculty knew and embraced the idea that their role was to provide the academic training necessary to assist their students in the fight for equality. Yes, the school's White administrators and faculty played a supportive role by providing physical space, academic training, and mentoring. But Black Americans, themselves, were best suited to articulate and lead the fight for the improvement of their future. In order to properly train its students for the challenges of life in late nineteenth-century America, Atlanta

University's curriculum emphasized instruction in the emerging discipline of sociology, which, as presented in the introduction, by the early twentieth century comprised roughly 20 percent of the school's entire academic curriculum.

Sociology was infused into the curriculum at Atlanta University because school officials wanted to provide students with a tool of scientific research they could use in their attempts to challenge the racial hierarchy of an American society where they were treated like second-class citizens. In short, Atlanta University faculty and administrators were consciously attempting to change the world, circuitously, through their graduates. Russell W. Irvine noted:

> The faculty at Atlanta University were principally interested in training leaders for work among blacks in the south. Knowledge of how the world is organized, what principles drove it, what motivated people within it, and how human relationships are ordered was essential to the work of leading a newly freed population. Graduates of Atlanta University were conceived of as agents of change and directors of the affairs of the black community. *It was imperative, if for no other reason, that they knew how the world they were charged to lead worked.* [my emphasis][1]

The emerging discipline of sociology could not have arrived in this nation at a more opportune moment. Just when the formerly enslaved populace was in need of allies and additional tools to fight for their human rights during Reconstruction, Atlanta University made a commitment to the instruction of sociology and scientific research at a level that outdistanced most post-secondary institutions in the nation.

John Howard Hincks, Professor of Social Science and History, introduced sociology to Atlanta University during his tenure, which lasted from 1889 to 1894. His tenure was brief because of his unexpected and untimely death. While Hincks, a White male, introduced sociology to the institution, it is unclear which, if any, sociology textbooks were used during his tenure. What is known is that he used non-sociology textbooks, including James Fairchild's *Moral Philosophy*, Francois P. Guizot's *History of Civilization in Europe*, and Frank Wayland's *Political Economy*. The difficulty in identifying whether or not sociology textbooks were used by Hincks stems from the university's unease with requiring its students to read books that may have been perceived by the city's White residents, and financial support-ers of the then-taxpayer funded institution, as promoting notions of racial equality, at best, and of complete liberation from the region and nation's accepted racial hierarchy, at worst. Despite the institution's commitment to encouraging the agency of its students, faculty, and administrators, all were well aware of the volatile and dangerous racial climate of Atlanta, Georgia in the late nineteenth century. Atlanta University officials under-stood the potential backlash, both physically and financially, that could arise if White residents discovered that its hometown institution was teaching Black students about the liberating possibilities of a science that could disprove supposedly *scientific* theories of racial superiority while simultaneously increasing the self-esteem and self-value of the freedmen and freedwomen. This is why the instruction of sociology during this early period was conducted in a clandestine manner and with textbooks that received little scrutiny from city residents who supported the public insti-tution through their tax dollars.

The books selected by Hincks, despite not being purely sociological, were carefully examined by school officials to assure they did not promote notions of racial inferiority or include faulty conclusions about Blacks based on groundless *scientific* racism foundations. That school officials proactively selected books that did not demean, belittle, or promote lies about Blacks reflected the seriousness with which they were committed to building holistic intellectuals to challenge American inequality. Toward this end Irvine reported, "Perceptively and wisely the leadership of Atlanta University understood that the force of ideas can wreak havoc as surely as weapons of personal injury. For that reason per se, they chose to teach around [sociology]."[2] During Hincks's tenure the cloaked instruction of sociology at Atlanta was the norm. However, shortly after his premature death the school fully and publicly embraced the discipline in complete view of the world.

By 1898 the Department of History and Sociology was established and openly promoted at Atlanta University. If there was any lingering concern about the negative consequences of teaching sociology at the public institution they were clearly dispelled in the unit's mission statement that year.

> It is intended to develop this department not only for the sake of mental discipline, but also in order to familiarize our students with the history of nations and with the great economic and social problems of the world. It is hoped that thus they may be able to apply broad and careful knowledge to the solving of the many intricate questions affecting their own people. The department aims therefore at training in good intelligent leadership; at a thorough comprehension of the chief problems of wealth, work and wages; and at a fair knowledge of the objects and methods of social reform.[3]

Free to assign readings without the fear of political oversight and retaliation, records indicate that textbooks used by sociology students during this period included *Civil Government* by Fiske, *The State* by Wilson, *Economics* by Hadley, and *Statistics and Sociology* by Mayo-Smith. While the public embrace of sociology was significant, more important to the trajectory of the discipline was the school's full-throated support of a research program that led to the establishment of the first American school of sociology, the Atlanta Sociological Laboratory.

From George G. Bradford to W. E. B. Du Bois

By 1895 Atlanta University could boast that its graduates included college presidents, business leaders, politicians, and persons of influence in their respective communities.[4] These alumni and other Black Americans witnessed rapid societal transitions and some were beginning to understand the need for scientific investigation into how the shifts from slavery to freedom and rural to city life were impacting the new Americans. Many graduates contacted administrators and faculty at their alma mater to push for scientific studies on the social, economic, and physical conditions impacting Blacks they were witnessing in their respective communities.

Despite their training in sociology at Atlanta, many graduates did not deem themselves qualified to spearhead scientific investigations into the societal transitions identified. While they could most certainly serve as citizen researchers and collect data in supplementary roles, graduates were confident their alma mater could procure the services of someone qualified to lead the research initiative they proposed. Given its formal and informal mission to develop cadres of social activists, no other American institution, Black or White, was better situated to lead such an effort than Atlanta University.

Requests from Atlanta University graduates for its alma mater to marshal scientific investigations into the social, economic, and physical conditions of Blacks in America did not fall upon deaf ears. In 1895, and at the behest of alumni, school trustee George G. Bradford and President Horace Bumstead presented to the board of trustees a proposal to establish an annual program of sociological inquiry into the social, economic, and physical condition of Blacks in America. Bradford and Bumstead proposed that data be collected during the summer and fall of each year and that the findings be presented the following spring. The proposal was immediately approved and, with Bradford as the founding director, data collection began soon afterwards. Bradford served as director of the research program for the 1896 and 1897 studies and was removed from this position because school officials wanted to enhance the scientific rigor of the studies. More specifically, they wanted to hire a director with a specialty in sociological research and academic training in the field. Although Bradford provided capable leadership during his brief stint, the school desired a director with actual research experience, not someone whose acknowledged qualification for initial selection as director was his cursory interest in the study of Black Americans. The search for a new director was brief and led to the hiring of the most talented sociologist in the nation.

W. E. B. Du Bois assumed leadership of the Atlanta University Study of the Negro Problem at Atlanta University in January 1897. Upon assuming leadership he changed the research program in a number of ways. One of his first acts as director was to place an *s* after the word "Problem" in the official title of the annual investigations. By shifting to the plural, Du Bois pivoted from the original director's goal of simultaneously investigating multiple social issues impacting Blacks in America. Also, the shift to the plural avoided the silent implication that Blacks themselves constituted the "Problem," and made clear that the study was of problems that Blacks suffered under because of racism. Du Bois's directive was that the research unit focus on one specific topic per year, not a hodgepodge of subjects, as practiced in the first two studies. This allowed the investigations to be more focused and thorough. Additionally, since only one topic was addressed per year (e.g., education, health, etc.) he proposed that after a ten-year period had elapsed, the research unit would return to the same topic to note changes that may or may not have occurred over the past decade.

Du Bois also (re)focused the annual conference toward the presentation of scientific papers and lectures. In order to accomplish this, he removed from the yearly conference or minimized the presentation of nonscholarly and nonscientific speeches by political officials, and eliminated sessions where attendees simply *discussed* problems of the day sans scholarly guidance and proposals for change.

The final substantive change Du Bois made was to provide clarity on the scientific integrity of the studies, given the school's overt and covert missions. Du Bois decided it was prudent to change the research unit's focus from direct social reform to objective, but covert, scholarly inquiry. In so doing, the research findings of the school would, theoretically, be less susceptible to subjective critique and/or dismissal by White sociologists, who were already predisposed to summarily dismiss as flawed and subjective scholarship by Black sociologists that was favorable to Black Americans. To this notion, Du Bois noted:

> This program at Atlanta, I sought to swing as on a pivot to one of scientific investigation into social conditions, primarily for scientific ends. I put no special effort on special reform effort, but increasing and widening emphasis on the collection of a basic body of fact concerning the social

condition of American Negroes, endeavoring to reduce that condition to exact measurement whenever or wherever occasion permitted.[5]

To be clear, the position posited here does not suggest that Du Bois was not an active agitator for societal reform regarding the social, economic, and physical condition of Blacks in America. It is suggested, however, that within the realm of science Du Bois believed social reform should be the mediate, and not immediate, objective of the researcher. His position on this topic was grounded in the racial realities of early twentieth-century America.

In 1898 Du Bois wrote an essay on the importance and necessity of objectivity in research. In the piece he argued that sociology's acceptance into the family of science as an equal was largely dependent on the quality of research produced by its practitioners. In what could be described as his answer to Max Weber's notion of value neutrality, Du Bois wrote:

> Students must be careful to insist that science as such—be it physics, chemistry, psychology, or sociology—has but one simple aim: discovery of truth. Its results lie open for the use of all men—merchants, physicians, men of letters, and philanthropists, but the aim of science itself is simple truth. Any attempt to give it a double aim, to make social reform the immediate instead of the mediate object of a search for truth, will inevitably tend to defeat both projects.[6]

Clearly, Du Bois did not diminish the importance of agitation and resistance in the fight for social justice. What he did suggest, in no uncertain terms, was that the scientist, as he or she engaged in their craft, must be fully aware of their responsibility to be objective and honest brokers in matters of science. This idea was especially important during Jim Crow, when it was widely accepted that Blacks and Whites were members of separate strains of humanity. Any suggestion otherwise, especially one espoused by Black scientists, received extreme pushback from Whites. Du Bois, speaking to how difficult it was for Black scientists to have their works embraced by the American public at the turn of the twentieth century, said:

> There will first be some difficulty in bringing the Southern people, both
> black and white, to conceive of an earnest, careful study of the Negro
> problem which has not back of it some scheme of race amalgamation,
> political jobbery, or deportation to Africa.[7]

It is quite ironic that Du Bois proactively fended off critiques of his
research as racially subjective during an era that produced a cottage
industry of scientific racism scholarship from the pens of White social
scientists. This foresight is evidence of how his scientific sociology was far
more developed than that of his White peers.[8] The ultimate objective for
Du Bois, then, was not subjective or altered realities of the Black American
experience but the production of objective science that could be used by
interested parties to improve the social, economic, and physical condition
of Blacks in America. Du Bois noted:

> Only by such rigid adherence to the true object of the scholar, can states-
> men and philanthropists of all shades of belief be put into possession of
> a reliable body of truth which may guide their efforts to the best and
> largest success.[9]

Upon his arrival at Atlanta University Du Bois drastically altered the
direction and scientific rigor of the annual investigation and conference.
It was upon this foundation that a reliable body of data on the condition of
Blacks in America developed, which eventually led to the establishment of
the first American school of sociology, the Atlanta Sociological Laboratory.

The Atlanta University study of the Negro Problems

Between 1895 and 1914 Atlanta University conducted yearly studies
on the social, economic, and physical condition of Blacks in America.
The topics of investigation included, but were not limited to, business,
crime, deviance, family, health, religion, secondary education, and
post-secondary education. It is important to note that the research accomplishments of the Atlanta Sociological Laboratory were not the result of
the singular herculean performance of W. E. B. Du Bois. Numerous, mostly

unnamed and unknown, men and women participated in the Du Bois-led Atlanta Sociological Laboratory; some of whom are discussed in this chapter. It is known that data for most of the annual studies were collected by Black and White sociologists, Atlanta University students and alumni, and students and alumni from other various HBCUs. Additionally, research papers in many volumes of the Atlanta University publications were written by leading scholars in their field of study. Participants at the annual conference included academics as well as local residents and government officials. Through the efforts of these disparate groups of persons, and under the leadership of Du Bois, this school made significant yet little-known contributions to the discipline. While a few of the school's accomplishments are discussed below, a more thorough analysis of the annual investigations can be found in my book *The First American School of Sociology: W. E. B. Du Bois and the Atlanta Sociological Laboratory*: the first book-length examination of the origin, development, and contributions of an HBCU department of sociology.

The Atlanta Sociological Laboratory was the first social science unit to recognize the need for insider researchers for data collection.[10] The idea that the researcher and subject should share some common trait was not an issue that White sociologists were concerned about during this period. Members of the pre-Du Bois Atlanta Sociological Laboratory, on the other hand, understood clearly the difficulties that could arise when White researchers attempted to gather data from Blacks, especially in rural areas, during Jim Crow. One must be mindful that when data collection for the Atlanta University studies began slavery had only been ruled unconstitutional for a scant thirty years. Moreover, during this era the domestic terrorism of Blacks in America by Whites via organizations like the Ku Klux Klan resulted in the deaths of thousands of innocents. It stands to reason that Blacks in rural and southern America would be extremely cautious, if not outright deceptive, when approached by even well-meaning White researchers attempting to obtain data, for example, on their family income, wealth, household structure, and leisure activities. Understanding this situation, the Atlanta Sociological Laboratory utilized insider researchers to obtain data that could not be elicited by White researchers.

In addition to the collection of data possibly not attainable by White researchers, utilization of insider researchers was important because it potentially offset acts of car window sociology and preexisting beliefs concerning Black inferiority that White interviewers, by the very nature of their racial socialization in late nineteenth-century America, may have held. This matter, along with information on the benefits of employing insider researchers, was addressed in the Atlanta University publication immediately preceding Du Bois's arrival. Atlanta University officials argued:

> All the data gathered by this body of trained colored leaders, are believed to be, perhaps, more than usually accurate because of the investigators' knowledge of the character, habits, and prejudices of the people, and because of the fact that they were not hindered by the suspicions which confront the white investigator, and which seriously affect the accuracy of the answers to his questions.[11]

A second contribution of the Atlanta Sociological Laboratory to the discipline was its institutionalization of triangulation, or mixed methods.[12] It is generally accepted that triangulation, the use of two or more methods to investigate a research question, was established in the late twentieth century. This assumption is false. Upon his arrival, Du Bois was intentional in his efforts to upgrade the scientific rigor of the studies because he believed the two investigations conducted prior to his arrival lacked scientific depth. Indeed, the studies conducted under Bradford were largely collections of census and public records data on Blacks in America. The majority of studies conducted under Du Bois's leadership, however, emphasized method triangulation through the collection of original data using techniques including, but not limited to, blanks (known today as questionnaires), interviews, and community studies.

The Atlanta Sociological Laboratory's third contribution to the discipline was that it was the first unit to institutionalize the inclusion of a *limitations of research* section in its reports.[13] Prior to the Atlanta

Sociological Laboratory, the practice of acknowledging the limitations of one's research was not widely practiced, let alone institutionalized, by any sociologist or academic unit. The decision to include a section articulating the limitations of the research was an extension of Du Bois's decision to alter the research unit's emphasis from direct to indirect social reform. He wanted to preempt, as much as possible, arguments by White sociologists that the work conducted by the largely Black research team at Atlanta was, by definition, subjective and nonscientific. By clearly articulating the limitations of the investigations, he believed concerns over the scientific rigor of his studies could be allayed. An example was found in the 1908 Atlanta University study on the Black family, where Du Bois acknowledged that the findings

> do not, however, represent properly the proportion of different types among the masses of Negroes. Most of the families studied belong to the upper half of the Black population. Finally, to repeat, this study is but a sketch with no pretense toward attempting to exhaust a fruitful subject. The main cause of its limitation is lack of material.[14]

The Atlanta Sociological Laboratory's fourth accomplishment was its institutionalization of a methods section within its research reports. Prior to the Atlanta Sociological Laboratory, no sociologist or sociological unit consistently included within their research publications information on where or how their data were collected. Daniels and Wright found that the overwhelming majority of articles in the *American Journal of Sociology* between 1897 and 1917 did not include statements or sections on how or where data were collected. Amazingly, the first *American Journal of Sociology* article to include a section titled *Methods* was penned by W. I. Thomas in 1912. Conversely, beginning with its first publication in 1896 the Atlanta Sociological Laboratory included a section on data collection often called "The Scope of Inquiry (and Methods)."[15] In these sections the school provided exact information on how data are collected.

Collectively, the contributions of the Atlanta Sociological Laboratory to American sociology in research methods included institutionalization of insider researchers, triangulation, limitations section, and methods section. These accomplishments were immense. However, the school's most significant accomplishment was its establishment of the first American school of sociology.

The First American School of Sociology

When the question, "Who established the first American school of sociology?" is raised, the answer given by most sociologists is, the Chicago School of Sociology. Chicago's misplaced acknowledgment is largely based on its establishment of the first singularly named department of sociology in the nation and its scholarly contributions to the discipline in the period after the arrival of Robert Park and Ernest Burgess. From the discipline's emergence in this nation until the year 2000, the idea that Chicago was home to the first American school of sociology went unchallenged and was promoted by sociologists at institutions well beyond the Windy City campus. Despite the discipline's wholesale embrace of this notion, the first American school of sociology was not established at the University of Chicago. Before discussing the school rightly deserving of this honor, the key to understanding who established the first American school of sociology is ascertaining what is meant by the term "school."

What is a sociological school? Although there exist varying definitions for the term, generally speaking, a school of sociology is understood as a cadre of scholars who are primarily located at one institution or unit who collectively engage in the scientific study of social problems via the tools of sociology. The idea that schools exist in academia is, seemingly, anathema since the common conception of academics is that we engage in individual research projects and do not participate in large-scale research efforts involving multilayered collaborative relationships. So, the idea that a school can emerge in an environment where individuality is the norm, not the exception, means those eligible for consideration for comprising a school in academia are limited.

Prior to the 1980s the understanding of what comprised a school of sociology was limited by the broad definition articulated above. However, in 1984 Martin Bulmer offered a narrower understanding of what was required to be considered a school, specifically a school of sociology. Bulmer identified nine criteria that a unit must exhibit in order to qualify for school status. Bulmer applied his nine criteria to the Park and Burgess led unit and concluded that the University of Chicago housed the first American school of sociology. Bulmer's effort was a tremendous contribution to the literature, but not because of the conclusion he reached. His article was important because it represented the first attempt to articulate specific criteria for what constituted such a school. Effectively, Bulmer created a model that could be used to ascertain whether or not other departments of sociology were eligible for school status. Through the use of Bulmer's model, I determined that the Atlanta Sociological Laboratory also comprised a school of sociology. Not only did the Atlanta Sociological Laboratory comprise a school, it predated the Chicago School by nearly twenty years, thus becoming the first American school of sociology.[16] Below, Bulmer's nine criteria for a school are applied to the Atlanta Sociological Laboratory to dispel the notion that Chicago was the first such school.

The first criterion of a school is that it be organized around a central figure. One misnomer concerning the Atlanta Sociological Laboratory was that Du Bois singlehandedly founded the Atlanta University Study of the Negro Problems. This is incorrect. George G. Bradford and Atlanta University president Bumstead co-founded the research program and Bradford served as director of the first two investigations. However, it is clear that upon Du Bois's arrival in 1897 he became the central figure around whom the school was organized until his departure in 1913.

The second criterion of a school is that it should exist in a university setting and have direct contact with a student population. Du Bois's research program satisfies this requirement since it was housed in the Department of Sociology & History at Atlanta University where faculty interacted with students through course instruction. As discussed in the

Preface, the undergraduate curriculum in sociology at Atlanta University comprised a higher percentage of general education coursework than any other HBCU and many HWCUs. In addition to undergraduate instruction, the school offered graduate work in sociology. In the 1901 Atlanta University publication, Du Bois noted, "special research courses are offered to graduate students."[17] A year later Du Bois provided additional information on the expectations of the school's undergraduate and graduate students in sociology when he wrote:

> Instruction is given by means of a special class room library with reference books and the leading text books, the arranging of charts and tabular work, the presentation at regular intervals of special reports and theses, and field work in and about the city of Atlanta for the observation of economic and social conditions.[18]

In addition to coursework, upperclassmen were allowed to assist with fieldwork for the annual Atlanta University Study of the Negro Problems. Occasionally, the work conducted by students was included in the annual publication. For example, in Du Bois's groundbreaking 1908 study of religion, noted by Phil Zuckerman as the first purely sociological study of religion conducted in the United States, students from Atlanta University and other HBCUs participated in data collection and their written report was included in the annual publication.[19] Specifically, data were collected from 32 Black families by 16 students from the graduating classes of 1909 and 1910. Also, the 1913 study on the social uplift efforts of Blacks included data collected by Atlanta University students and their written report was included in the annual publication.

The third criterion for a school is that there be interaction between it and the community within which it is located. A primary means of interaction between the Atlanta Sociological Laboratory and community was through research. While it was already noted that graduates of Atlanta University participated in the annual investigations as data collectors, what is less known is that other members of the community participated also. The school used, as citizen researchers, persons with good reputations and high community status, graduates of other HBCUs living in the area, and members of the community who may have never attended college but were able to carry out the tasks assigned.

In addition to interactions with members of the community that involved their direct participation in the investigations, some members of the Atlanta Sociological Laboratory participated in community organizations like the local First Sociological Club of Atlanta. Du Bois, on at least one occasion, delivered a controversial talk to the organization where he directly reprimanded the organization for having accomplished little along the lines of scientific sociology and challenged them to engage more fully with the liberating potentials of the discipline. One can only imagine that his critique was received lukewarmly and his participation in club matters brief. Nevertheless, this is an example of community engagement.

The fourth criterion requires the school's leader to have a dominating personality. Evidence of Du Bois's dominating personality, as discussed earlier, included his refocusing the annual investigation to one topic per year, not a hodgepodge of issues; placing the studies on a cycle where the same topic was revisited every ten years; minimizing the amount of non-scientific presentations and speeches at the yearly conference; and implementing scientific rigor that led to the advances in research methods articulated previously.

The fifth criterion of a school indicates that its leader must possess an intellectual vision and have a missionary drive. Du Bois's intellectual vision and missionary drive for the Atlanta University Study of the Negro Problems included an ambitious plan to engage in a one-hundred-year program of sociological research on the Black American experience. During each ten-year period investigations would cover one specific topic such as business, crime, education, or health. Ten years after the original study the same topic would be revisited to note any changes. The goal of the longitudinal study was to gather the richest and most scientific data ever collected on one race of people such that theories on the social, physical, and economic development of the race could be developed. Du Bois was driven to accomplish this goal because of his belief that the Black American experience could be used as a template for subsequent race groups as they sojourned through the American racial and class minefield. Du Bois believed the opportunity to study a group starting, essentially, at their release from bondage to their acquisition of civil rights was a tremendous scientific opportunity. Unfortunately, Du Bois's one-hundred-year plan did not come to fruition because of disinterest from White sociologists, lack of resources for Black sociologists, and his two untimely departures from Atlanta University. Instead of lasting one hundred years, the Atlanta Sociological Laboratory only managed to produce two decades' worth of data on the Black experience in America.

Reflecting on his original vision for the conference more than fifty years after his first departure from Atlanta University, Du Bois conceded that he should have been more narrowly focused. He acknowledged he should have placed more emphasis on the impact of capitalism and global economic forces on Blacks in America as they transitioned from slavery to freedom and rural to city life. To this idea Du Bois said both the studies and conference were:

> weak [on the] economic side. [The conference] did not stress enough the philosophy of Marx and Engels and was of course far too soon for Lenin. The program ought to have been—and as I think would have been if I had kept on this work—the Economic Development of the American Negro Slave: on this central thread all the other subjects would have been strung. But this I had no chance to essay.[20]

The sixth criterion for a school is that there be intellectual exchanges between colleagues and graduate students (e.g., seminars) and that the school must have an outlet for the publication of its scholarship. Intellectual exchanges between colleagues were evidenced by the school's annual investigation and conference. Examples of intellectual exchanges were discussed above and included the school's outline of a program of research for graduate students. Additionally, that Atlanta University undergraduate and graduate students participated in data collection for a number of studies, as indicated earlier, was further evidence of intellectual exchanges. Last, this school fulfils the publication requirement because the *Atlanta University Study of the Negro Problems* was published by Atlanta University throughout its duration, 1896–1917.

The seventh criterion for a school is that it has an adequate infrastructure. This means the school should have demonstrated advances in research methods, have institutional links, and maintain strong philanthropic support. The Atlanta Sociological Laboratory's significant accomplishments in research methods were discussed in full earlier. However, the reader is reminded here that the school's advances included institutionalization of insider researcher, triangulation, and the institutionalization of sections in research reports indicating the limitations of one's methodology and its data collection method(s). Proof of the school's institutional links were found in the pages of the Atlanta University studies where the participation of faculty, students, and graduates from a myriad of schools—including, but not limited to, Berea College, Fisk University, Howard University, Lincoln University, Meharry Medical College, Spelman College, and numerous other HBCUs—were noted.

Unquestionably the philanthropic support for Atlanta University paled in comparison to that procured by well-resourced and funded schools like the University of Chicago and Stanford University. The gap between the financial gifts for Atlanta and that of its better-financed institutional peers was monstrous even during the best of periods of yearly fiscal growth for the Black and southern institution. The gap increased even further when Georgia withdrew its taxpayer-based funding from the school because Atlanta University, against a directive from state politicians, dared to openly allow admission to its campus for Black and White students. Despite what most reasonable persons may consider to be obvious financial realities, I argue that Atlanta University meets the requirement of having strong philanthropic support. This claim rests not on the actual dollars amassed by the school. Instead, this position is grounded in the fact that for twenty years the school was able to produce the most scientific and rigorous program of research the nation had ever witnessed. This school produced the first American school of sociology and was the home of scientific sociology.[21] That Black sociologists at an HBCU located in the American South during a period of racialized domestic terrorism when Black men and women were murdered for the simplest of crimes were able to advance the discipline for two decades in ways unmatched by their White contemporaries is sufficient evidence to support this criterion. Despite the fear of directly teaching the discipline; the possibility of physical harm to faculty, administrators, and students because of its mission; losing state funding and many philanthropic gifts to the school because of the conclusions reached in many of the Atlanta University studies—despite all this, the research program lasted two decades. Is there any evidence in the literature to indicate that another school of sociology faced such extreme conditions and managed to impact the discipline in ways that are still being uncovered to this day? Unless and until such an example is found, I argue that the Atlanta Sociological Laboratory demonstrated strong philanthropic support; that is, it garnered the monies needed to perform the work it did, despite immense obstacles.

The eighth criterion of a school is that it could not last beyond the generation of its central figure. Prior to Du Bois's arrival two studies were published, and under his tenure he led the preparation of sixteen volumes of the *Atlanta University Study of the Negro Problems*. After his departure in 1913 the school only managed to publish two additional volumes. One consisted of original research on the general condition of Blacks in America and the other was a collection of papers on the race question. Although annual conferences continued until 1924, the Atlanta Sociological Laboratory essentially ended upon Du Bois's departure in 1913.

The ninth criterion of a school is that it must be open to ideas and influences beyond its home discipline or engage in interdisciplinary work. The Atlanta University studies were established on the foundation of interdisciplinary scholarship. The school explored areas that today are compartmentalized into separate and distinct disciplinary silos, including business, crime and deviance, education, health, and religion. The foundation of the Atlanta Sociological Laboratory, if nothing else, was girded by interdisciplinarity. Let us look at two examples of the school's interdisciplinary work.

In 1903 Du Bois spearheaded a study on religion. Although Black sociologists have long recognized this effort as a massive contribution to the discipline, this investigation has been largely ignored by main-stream (White) sociologists for over one hundred years; that is, until Phil Zuckerman made an argument for the canonization of Du Bois's study. While he recognized the important works of Emile Durkheim, Charlotte Perkins Gilman, and Max Weber, Zuckerman believed that Du Bois

> should be regarded as the first American sociologist of religion ... [because] he employed standard sociological research methods to a degree unparalleled by the canonized classical sociologists of religion ... [and because his research] stressed the ways in which religious institu-tions can be recognized as social, communal centers which provide this worldly rewards and comforts.[22]

In addition to serving as an example of the interdisciplinary work of Du Bois's Atlanta Sociological Laboratory, this study is deserving of canon-ical status. Another example of groundbreaking interdisciplinary work of the Du Bois-led Atlanta Sociological Laboratory is the 1906 study, *Health and Physique of the Negro American.*

A major conclusion reached in this study was the debunking of the *scientific* theory undergirding the argument that Black Americans were physically inferior to Whites. Using 1,000 Hampton University students as subjects, Du Bois concluded there was no evidence to support the medical science supported position that there were inherent physical differences between the races. This was, arguably, the earliest and most successful debunking of the scientifically racist medical literature, but it was largely ignored by the medical and sociology communities. This point was high-lighted by Dr. Montague W. Cobb of the Howard University School of Medicine who stated:

> [This inquiry was the first] significant scientific approach to the health problems and biological study of the Negro. ... "But," said Cobb, neither the Negro medical profession nor the Negro educational world was ready for it. Its potential usefulness was not realized by Negroes. Whites were hostile to such a study. ... This study, Du Bois's single excursion into the

health field, was, said Cobb, "an extraordinary forward pass heaved the length of the football field, but there were no receivers."[23]

Using the most detailed model of a "school" in the literature, we know the Atlanta Sociological Laboratory comprised the first American school of sociology and did so nearly twenty years prior to Park and Burgess's appearance in Chicago. The accomplishments made at Atlanta University during the post-Reconstruction and Jim Crow eras are impressive when one considers the challenges faced by early Black sociologists. While the accomplishments and advances made by Du Bois and the Atlanta Sociological Laboratory were impressive, one must be mindful that the achievements made at the school were not singularly due to the efforts of W. E. B. Du Bois. Countless numbers of professional sociologists, undergraduate and graduate students, and citizen researchers participated in the effort that resulted in the establishment of the first American school of sociology. Two particular groups of contributors to the school who are almost always overlooked are Black women and queer men. In the next section we explore the contributions to the Atlanta Sociological Laboratory of several women and a little-known Black queer sociologist.

Beyond W. E. B. Du Bois

Women of the Atlanta Sociological Laboratory

Women were important contributors to the Atlanta Sociological Laboratory's research investigations, publications, and conferences during its early years. Although the traditional thought is that Du Bois singularly constituted this school, countless Black and some White women contributed to its now seminal status in the discipline, either through participation at the conference or through written works to the yearly publication. Below are a few examples.

In its early years, conference attendees included prominent figures such as Mary Church Terrell, who was a civil rights activist who fought for racial and gender equality. Born into an affluent family in Memphis,

Tennessee the year Lincoln signed the Emancipation Proclamation, Terrell did not rely on her class privilege, inasmuch as a Black American woman could stake such a claim in Jim Crow America, to live a life above the color and gender lines. Instead, she fought to improve the social, economic, and physical condition of her people. She is known to have attended at least one Atlanta University conference.

At the May 1903 conference Terrell, in her capacity as the president of the National Federation of Colored Women's Clubs, delivered a lecture during the gendered Women's Meeting session of the conference. More significant than the message she delivered before conference attendees is that she, along with Du Bois and Kelly Miller of Howard University, were signatories to the resolutions of that year's study. The resolutions were a staple of the conference since its inaugural 1896 meeting; Terrell was the first woman to be a signatory to these resolutions in the short 8-year tenure of the program of sociological research. Resolutions were prescriptions for addressing the problems uncovered in each year's investigation. In many respects, and as I have argued previously, many resolutions offered by the school should be considered theoretical contributions. That is:

> If one defines a theory as a set of interrelated statements that attempt to explain, predict, or understand social events, and that can be replicated and generalizable, then the resolutions offered in the conclusion of the Atlanta University Conference Publications, after being tested by interested social scientists, qualify as systematic theoretical constructions.[24]

Another participant at the annual conference was early sociologist and founder of the Chicago-based Hull House Settlement Home, Jane Addams. Addams's May 1908 lecture at the Mother's Meeting offered a comparative analysis of the difficulties cultural groups experienced when attempting to adapt their family to life in America. In her example, Addams contrasted the experiences of European immigrants, the focus of her sociological inquiry, and Black Americans. She noted the difficulty European immigrants had adjusting to and embracing life in America while grappling to maintain their *old folk ways*. Black Americans, on the other hand, did not share that experience, according to Addams. Instead, she suggested the institution of slavery had broken the bonds of family tradition that Africans brought with them from their home continent. According to Addams, "The habits which you might have had from your ancestors were all broken into . . ., they were all scattered, and especially the habits connected with family life."[25] She suggested that the benefit of the broken family traditions of Africans was their willingness, unlike European immigrants, to use their increasing levels of education to properly assimilate into American society. The downside, however, was their inability to successfully resist the harmful aspects of the impact of American society on the Black family. Jane Addams was not the only White woman or member of Hull House to participate at the Atlanta University conference. Other notable participants included Florence Kelley and Mary White Ovington. While attendance at the conference signified interest in the subject addressed for that year, a greater measure of the role of women in the Atlanta Sociological Laboratory was their inclusion in the annual publication.

The publications released prior to Du Bois's arrival included substantive sections written by Black women. After Du Bois's arrival, and consistent with the fact that his domineering personality led to numerous changes in how the studies were conducted, publications constructed, and conference formatted, the number of contributions to the annual publication from persons not named Du Bois decreased. While articles written by Black women were not completely eliminated, it is obvious that in the years preceding Du Bois's arrival women's publications reached their high-water mark. Foremost among the women contributing to the annual publication prior to Du Bois's arrival, and continuing their presence within the Atlanta Sociological Laboratory via their participation at the annual conference throughout its existence, were Georgia Swift King and Lucy Laney.

Georgia Swift King, an 1874 graduate of Atlanta University, was an intermittent participant in the Atlanta Sociological Laboratory from 1896 to 1904. Her essays were published in the 1896 and 1897 publications and she appeared in an additional two conference programs, with the last being in 1904. King's essay in the 1896 publication, "Intemperance as a Cause for Immorality," was one part an overview of the existing literature on the dangers of alcoholism for Black Americans, and also a plea for diversion programs for youthful Blacks who, because of their lack of parentage, became offenders, were sent to prison, and were housed alongside adults. Knowing the shadow worlds of slavery, now known as sharecropping and the convict lease system, awaited new laborers who, once ensnared, were overtaken by death at an early age, King pleaded:

> Let Georgia lessen the death-rate among the Negro population by establishing at once a reformatory for juvenile offenders. . . . I beg your aid in the attempt to secure the pledge of the representatives of the approaching legislature to enact a law providing a State reformatory.[26]

King's second and final publication, "Address at Mother's Meeting," centered on the plight of Black women who experienced high levels of racial and gendered inequality that led, to name a few consequences, to decreased birth rates, high numbers of infant deaths, and high levels of infanticide. Her solution to these problems, and more, was to proactively engage and inform Black women on these topics and provide them with the best practices to reduce those rates, because of their disproportionate impact on Black women. Ideally, King wanted women within the immediate Atlanta area to attend the annual conference and participate in a session set aside for mothers titled "Mother's Meeting." According to King:

> Observation and experience lead me to conclude me that a most excellent medium for effectual instruction of the masses is, "Mother's Meetings," where all questions of human interest are pertinent and may be freely discussed; where all classes of women may become better informed; where even the illiterate, by regular attendance, may gain such essential knowledge of . . . vital subjects.[27]

Although the desired location for this informational session was the annual gathering at Atlanta University, King understood that the best way to make substantive change on these topics was to take the information directly to the targeted populations. Possibly, this is why her essay ended with the message, "When difficulty is experienced in getting the mothers to these meetings I have met with some success by taking the meetings to the mothers, that is, to their immediate neighborhood."[28] In effect, King's proposal was a call to engage in community outreach. While King participated in a number of Atlanta University studies and conferences, her appearances were outnumbered only by Lucy Laney.

Lucy Laney, an 1873 graduate of Atlanta University, is, arguably, best known for her contributions to the education of Black children, which include her establishing the first school for Blacks in Augusta, Georgia, in 1883. Less well known was her participation in the Atlanta Sociological Laboratory prior to, during, and after the directorship of W. E. B. Du Bois. Prior to Du Bois's arrival Laney wrote reports on the condition of the Black community and her works appear in the first two volumes of the Atlanta University publications. During and after Du Bois's tenure, Laney's reports were read at the conference but not included in the final publication (as was the case with the overwhelming majority of contributors to the Atlanta University studies). Her two brief published reports prior to Du Bois's arrival are summarized here.

In her 1896 report, "General Conditions of Mortality," Laney outlined differences between families based on class and ethnicity. Using Augusta as the site of data collection, Laney proposed that Blacks in America were more susceptible to disease than Whites because they lacked sufficient knowledge concerning hygiene and because of their proximity to hazardous environmental sites. She chastised Blacks for not embracing medical science supporting the idea that a relationship existed between hygiene and sickness, a notion that a good number of African religion-based Blacks did not hold. However, she did note that Black neighborhoods, as they continue to be today, were more likely to be located in areas where the risk of sickness was enhanced due to the presence of hazardous waste sites. She concluded her essay by arguing that the more educated members of the race, the talented tenth, should take more active roles in leading the less-informed members of the race away from *old world* traditions that caused them to not engage in the best health practices of the day. This foretelling of Du Bois's theory of the talented tenth was her opportunity to promote the utility of formal education for Blacks in America as one, if not the exclusive, key to securing social, economic, and physical advancement for the race.

In her 1897 essay, "An Address Before the Women's Meeting," Laney argued that the development of a strong Black family was the foundation for successes in other areas of life. A strong family unit, according to her argument, grounded itself in one's religion of choice, and would lead family members to make informed decisions on employment and, most important, to guide their children to becoming successful contributors to society. Noting that the duty of mother was supreme over any title one could carry, she cautioned mothers to not allow their girls to be socialized in ways that harmed them. Moreover, she was careful to note that boys and girls, as much as possible, should be held to similar standards of performance and expectations. Speaking to this idea, Laney said:

> Too often that mother who is careful of her daughter's environment, the formation of her girl's character, is negligent as to her sons.... Our boys need the careful loving hand of a mother; perhaps not more so than girls—but certainly not less.[29]

This speech before the women attendees, in the tradition of Black feminism, was representative of the types of conversations that permeated the yearly conference, and most certainly in the women's meetings. Laney participated in more Atlanta University conferences than any other woman. It is unfortunate that only two of her essays were included in the Atlanta University publications. Despite this limitation, it is clear from the readings of Georgia Swift King and Lucy Laney that women were central to the establishment and development of the Atlanta Sociological Laboratory prior to Du Bois's arrival. Although very little written documentation of their contributions to the school remain, the efforts of the women of the Atlanta Sociological Laboratory should not be unnoticed.

Augustus Granville Dill

Augustus Granville Dill was born in 1881 in Portsmouth, Ohio, and in 1906 graduated from Atlanta University. When he entered the school in 1902, Du Bois's sociological laboratory was nearing its apex of sociological greatness. As a student interested in sociology, Dill took classes in the discipline under the guidance of Du Bois, who would be his mentor the remainder of his life. Because of his interest in the discipline it is almost certain that he participated in some aspect of the annual investigation and conference. While this is a reasonable assumption to make given that the research requirements for sociology students required their participation in the studies, there is little evidence of Dill's actual contribution(s). The closest one can come to noting his participation is his listing in the preface of the groundbreaking 1903 publication, *The Negro Church*, as someone who performed a bulk of the proofreading, in what would have been Dill's sophomore year. Students from Atlanta University and Virginia Union were also recognized for their participation in what is now called the first sociological study of religion conducted in the United States, *The Negro Church*.[30] Unfortunately, Dill's specific contributions to the research effort as an undergraduate are murky. Better known is his tenure as chairperson of the Department of Sociology and director of the Atlanta University Study of the Negro Problems.

When Du Bois resigned from the school's faculty in 1913 because of the deleterious impact his presence was having on fundraising efforts, Dill was selected to succeed him. It is possible that Dill was the ideal candidate because he was Du Bois's mentee and the two had a relationship that enabled the jettisoned scholar to maintain a modicum of control over the sociology operations at Atlanta University. Regardless of the rationale for his selection, Dill was given charge of the first American school of sociology. Sadly, neither archival data nor the existing literature feature inquiries centering on his tenure as director or record as a sociologist. Instead, Dill is mentioned tangentially as Du Bois's mentee, who was best known for losing his job at the National Association for the Advancement of Colored People (NAACP) that his mentor had secured for him, because of an arrest in a gay sex sting operation in New York City in 1928. Dill was an early Black queer scholar whose academic and (public) sociological activities are noteworthy. He should not be reduced to tabloid headlines or to the footnotes of accounts of Du Bois's tenure at the NAACP. Instead, Dill should be provided a platform appropriate for insightful analyses of his academic and public sociology. Only the former is addressed here.

Although Du Bois left the faculty at Atlanta University in 1913 he continued to serve as co-director of the annual investigation for a number of years thereafter with Dill. Together, Dill and Du Bois co-edited four monographs: *The College Bred Negro American* (1910), *The Common School and the Negro American* (1911), *The Negro American Artisan* (1912), and *Morals and Manners Among Negro Americans* (1913). Similar to accounts of his undergraduate career, Dill's specific contributions to the publications he co-edited are not clear. The only publication that specifically references Dill's contribution is the 1912 monograph, *The Negro Artisan*. This effort is important because, of the twenty volumes released by the Atlanta Sociological Laboratory, it is the most methodologically sound.[31] Dill and Du Bois employed mixed methods data collection via questionnaires from 1,300 subjects that were cross-compared with data among employees as well as between employers. Questionnaires were collected from ninety-seven trade unions, two hundred from local trade organizations representing more than thirty states, thirty-two reports from citizen researchers representing more than thirty states, Canada, Costa Rica, and Puerto Rico, and a few responses from the presidents of vocational schools from across the nation. Added to this were the collaborative efforts of a Tennessee newspaper, *Chattanooga Tradesman*, that conducted a similar but smaller-scale study nearly ten years earlier. Unfortunately, there is no detailed account of the distribution of responsibilities as it relates to data collection or analysis on the part of Dill or Du Bois. While we do not know how Dill's participation impacted the essential facts amassed, we do know he presented the data collection strategy to the attendees of that year's conference. The 1912 publication lists Dill as being responsible for the session, "Methods of the Present Investigation." That the publication offers detailed descriptions of data collection and a verbal articulation of the methodology at the conference speaks volumes about the sophistication of this school in comparison to the discipline in general, which didn't witness its first methods section in the *American Journal of Sociology* until 1912 while Atlanta's first articulation was 1896.[32] Sadly, very little is known about the life and career of Dill.

W. E. B. Du Bois did not raise the Atlanta Sociological Laboratory to its high sociological status alone. He was assisted through the participation of many men and women. This brief overview of some of the contributors to the school is not meant to be exhaustive. Instead, the reader should view these accounts as an opportunity to more fully consider the contributions of members of the Atlanta Sociological Laboratory not named Du Bois. Du Bois remains the central and most dominating figure associated with the Atlanta Sociological Laboratory, but it would be criminal not to note the contributions of the many other members of the Atlanta Sociological Laboratory. They may not have made as substantial an individual impact on the discipline as Du Bois, but it is certain that without their collective efforts the Atlanta Sociological Laboratory would not have been as impactful as it was.

Summary

The Atlanta Sociological Laboratory not only comprised the first American school of sociology, it was the first school of Black sociology. Because of the perceived threat of an educated cadre of Black Americans with skills in sociological knowledge and inquiry, the *discipline* was initially taught in a clandestine manner at Atlanta University. Fear of negative public reaction to the emerging discipline by Atlanta University officials gave way to the reality that the school's mission was uniquely connected to the promise of Black sociology. Toward this end, a department of sociology was established with the overt objective of developing a curriculum to transmit to its students the requisite skills and training to obtain well-paying jobs in their profession of choice. The covert, and arguably more important, objective of the institution's support for the department was to instill into its graduates the notion that they should use their training to positively impact their respective communities and serve as leaders in the fight for racial equality and civil rights.

In order to accomplish the latter, according to school administrators, by the time a student graduated from Atlanta University they would know how to use the discipline of sociology as a tool to develop solutions for existing social problems. Thus, as discussed previously, a premium was placed on sociological inquiry, as it was viewed as a vehicle to facilitate the liberation of Blacks in America. Atlanta University was the template for other HBCUs to follow, whereby its students completed a rigorous sequence of courses in sociology and were taught to use their sociological imagination to analyze, investigate, and understand the social, economic, and physical conditions impacting Blacks. Although Atlanta University was the first to do so, it wasn't the last. In fact, the location of the second school of Black sociology may be shocking to most trained sociologists.

CHAPTER 3

Tuskegee Institute and Rural Sociology

It is well documented that William G. Sumner taught the first course in sociology during the 1872–1873 academic year at Yale. What is less known is that C. R. Henderson taught the first course on rural sociology at the University of Chicago in 1894. Although rural sociology was not a primary interest of Henderson, he understood the necessity of sociological study of the geographical area that, heretofore, was the primary residence of the majority of Americans pre-industrialization. His support for the burgeoning area is noteworthy as he was "apparently the first person to direct the attention of other sociologists to the importance of the rural studies."[1] Henderson's concern was that interest in rural areas, unlike cities, was minimal and a consequence of this neglect was that the tools of sociology were not being applied to that space in ways that could improve the lives of its residents. Henderson contended in 1901 that "we actually have more and better books on breeding cattle and marketing corn than on forming citizens or organizing culture. Is it not worthwhile to attempt social technology of the rural community?"[2] It is noteworthy that Henderson, a member of the influential department of sociology at the University of Chicago which was nearly exclusively known for its urban research efforts, was a principal figure in the growth of this substantive area. While Henderson's early support of the area was important, many figures beyond the Windy City contributed to the expansion of rural sociology.

In order for any field of specialization to exist there must be persons trained in the area. A key figure in this substantive topical area was

Kenyon L. Butterfield. Butterfield was a prominent figure in rural sociology who took his bachelor's degree from Michigan Agricultural College
(now called Michigan State University) and master's degree from the
University of Michigan. During his academic career he developed an
expansive knowledge of and interest in agricultural matters, particularly
as an undergraduate at a land grant institution. One year after taking the
master's degree Butterfield was offered employment at the University of
Michigan as an instructor of rural sociology. With this appointment, in
1902 Butterfield is believed to be the first person hired in the United States
with the title *instructor of rural sociology*.[3]

The expansion of rural sociology continued through 1913 when the
first textbook in this area was written. *Constructive Rural Sociology* by John
Gillette is recognized as being the first textbook in the field, although
it was not the first textbook to include a discussion on rural sociology.
Gillette's book is recognized because it was the first textbook intended
exclusively for a rural sociology audience, not an interdisciplinary assemblage of audiences including, but not limited to, education and religion.
Probably the most noteworthy contribution of Gillette's effort was its definition of rural sociology. By any standard conception, Gillette's definition
of the substantive topical area was broad and general. Nevertheless, it
was an early attempt to provide structure to the burgeoning field. "Rural
sociology," Gillette wrote, "has as its particular task to take full inven-
tory of the conditions of life in rural communities. It must discover their
tendencies and deficiencies, map out the special problems and indicate
ways of betterment according to the best ideals of life."[4] This definition
hinted at the applied, or practical, ambitions of the practitioners of rural
sociology. While the 1913 definition seemed a bit broad, the 1923 edition
of his textbook included a conception that was more focused concerning
the aims of rural sociology. Gillette defined it as "that branch of sociology which systematically studies rural communities to discover their
conditions and tendencies, and to formulate principles of progress."[5]
This definition of rural sociology clearly suggested that its practitioners
should engage in the application of sociological research, methods, and

knowledge in rural settings, a.k.a. applied sociology. It is also noteworthy that Gillette's definition and understanding of rural sociology is consistent with that expressed by Kenyon L. Butterfield twenty years prior. Nearly thirty years after Henderson's call, the leading textbook on rural sociology explicitly pushed for a sociology of rural communities that, in some ways, mirrored the urban exploits of W. E. B. Du Bois and the men and women of the Atlanta Sociological Laboratory.[6]

The professionalization of rural sociology began in 1912 at a meeting of the American Sociological Society (now called the American Sociological Association). The theme of the meeting, Rural Life, aroused the interest of an expanding group of folks interested in what later became rural sociology. During the meeting one group of men were so interested in infusing rural sociology into the discipline's curriculum that they held a meeting in one participants' hotel room to develop a strategy to accomplish their goal. "From this meeting grew annual informal gatherings [during the annual American Sociological Association conference], which eventually expanded into the rural section of the society and then into the Rural Sociology Society."[7] Rural sociology's most defining moment, however, came in 1937 when several members of the American Sociological Association's Rural Sociology section formed their own professional organization. The Rural Sociological Society (RSS) was formed to provide a platform for supporters and practitioners of rural sociology to promote and advance this area of research. To this day RSS adheres to these founding principles.

Although some suggest the origins of rural sociology go back as far as the 1820s and began in earnest after the publication of United States President Theodore Roosevelt's commissioned 1909 *Report of the Country Life Commission*, the focus here has been on early efforts to institutionalize and formalize the area.[8] Accordingly, emphasis has been placed on the establishment of courses on the topical area starting in 1894 at the University of Chicago and its coming of age in 1937 with the establishment of an independent professional organization. While the narrative provided here is not exhaustive, it does provide a sequential record of how the history of the area of study unfolded. Although this accounting may appear to be a representative historical account, there exists a major shortcoming of the narrative on the origin and development of rural sociology in the United States. The shortcoming of this narrative is the discipline's historical exclusion of the applied rural sociology program initiated at Tuskegee Institute. The following section fills this void and includes an argument for Tuskegee's recognition as the nation's first program of applied rural sociology.

The Wizard of Tuskegee

Many Americans today fail to understand that after the emancipation of Africans from the peculiar institution of slavery in 1865, a race of people numbering around five million were effectively destitute and homeless. No longer covered by the economically driven interests of *beneficial* Whites to provide the bare necessities of life to their property, after passage of the 13th Amendment to the Constitution of the United States Blacks in America were essentially *free to die.* They were free to die because they owned no homes, were impoverished, and were literally exposed to the meteorological elements of the moment. They were free to die because they did not have money for food. They were free to die because they did not have the basic protections of human life that were afforded to each and every *free* White American citizen. Faced with this dire situation the options available for survival to most Blacks in America, especially those in rural areas, were limited. Two distinct paths to economic stability and independence were immediately presented to the freedmen and freed-women. One path emphasized the utilization of the skills learned during enslavement and their application to agrarian life, which could lead to entrepreneurship, fiscal independence, and racial cooperation. The other path emphasized the acquisition of holistic academic training that could serve as a springboard to economic stability and evidence to Whites that Blacks were not biologically or intellectually inferior. These paths pit two giant figures in American life against one another: W. E. B. Du Bois and Booker T. Washington.

The ideological debate between Du Bois and Washington over the most appropriate and feasible type of education Black Americans should pursue post-slavery is well covered in other spaces and not repeated in full here. However, I devote some space to correcting a misunderstanding concerning Du Bois's position on liberal arts vis-à-vis vocational and technical training. I emphasize here that, despite notions to the contrary, Du Bois did not argue that Blacks in America should not engage in vocational or technical training. Conversely, he believed there was space within the Black community and academia for institutions emphasizing both liberal arts and vocational and technical instruction. The point of departure in Du Bois's argument that continues to be lost in many volumes of writings is that he believed there should not be a singular or exclusive emphasis on vocational and technical education. Unlike Du Bois, Washington questioned the very utility of a liberal arts degree within an American society he believed reserved no occupational space for persons so educated. His solution was found in the land that he believed would lead to entrepreneurship. Washington believed Black Americans singular engagement with vocational and technical education would develop the requisite skills to gain immediate employment such that the basic necessities for life would be provided for their families and themselves. Instead of adhering to an either-or position, Du Bois posited a *both/and* model that only privileged liberal arts because of the need for intelligent and holistically educated persons to serve as teachers *in* vocational and technical institutions. Du Bois addressed this notion in his classic article on the talented tenth where he wrote:

> I would not deny ... the paramount necessity of teaching the Negro to work ... or seem to deprecate in the slightest degree the important part industrial schools must play in the accomplishment of these ends, but I do say, and insist upon it, that it is industrialism drunk with its vision of success, to imagine that its own work can be accomplished without providing for the training of broadly cultured men and women to teach its own teachers, and to teach the teachers of the public schools.[9]

Despite historical notions to the contrary, Du Bois did not believe non-liberal arts programs should assume a subordinate status to the liberal arts or that they should not exist at all. Instead, he contends that a pragmatic system of developing a lineage of holistically trained teachers and scholars grounded in the liberal arts must be established before advancing to a more comprehensive focus on vocational education. This position by Du Bois is prophetic when one considers the unexamined sociological activities at Tuskegee and, by happenstance, the school's significance to the discipline of sociology.

Washington can rightly be characterized as a "drunkard industrialist" because of his belief that American Blacks should exclusively commit their labor and educational efforts to the soil on which they toiled for hundreds of years as enslaved human beings. Becoming proficient in vocational and technical education, according to Washington, provided avenues for financial independence, economic uplift, and the potential to improve race relations because Whites would appreciate, in theory, the work ethic of those members of the human family. It is with these principles in mind that Washington established Tuskegee Institute for instruction in vocational and technical education. Beyond merely establishing an institution for its instruction, the Wizard of Tuskegee wanted his school to become the nation's leader in such ambitions for Black Americans.

If the school's production of graduates and their chosen occupations are an indicator of its effectiveness, then Washington's school manifested many successes in its early years. Despite the effectiveness of his school's vocational education program, Black Americans living in the American South in the late 1800s remained a vulnerable population whether they possessed a college education or not. Often the former was sufficient cause to justify attacks by Whites on *uppity Negro* graduates of schools that specialized in liberal arts and technical vocations. By 1881 Washington was well aware of such attacks on Black Americans by their White neighbors. Adding to the challenges experienced by America's second-class citizens was the agricultural depression that severely impacted rural Blacks and the harmful impact of the crop-lien system (or sharecropping) on those attempting to pull themselves up by their bootstraps. Seeking to better understand the condition of rural Blacks, to develop strategies to improve their condition and to improve relations between the races, Washington called for a conference to be held at Tuskegee in 1882 on the condition of rural Blacks in America.

Tuskegee Negro Conference

When Washington announced his plan to host the inaugural Tuskegee Negro Conference, he believed the number of attendees would not exceed one hundred. His expectation was that the small gathering of famers and vocational professionals would be a space where Blacks working in rural occupations and agricultural work could discuss "their present condition, their helps and hindrances, and to see if it were possible to suggest any means by which the rank and file of the people might be able to benefit themselves."[10] When the first meeting was held, to Washington's pleasant surprise, more than four hundred attendees showed up. What Washington initially planned as a modest maiden effort focused on gathering empirical data on the condition of rural life for Blacks in America morphed into a long-term event with far-reaching impact. That the number of attendees at the first conference exceeded his expectations fourfold dumbfounded Washington and strengthened his belief that this program of vocational education for students and the training of members of rural communities were invaluable contributions to American society. More importantly, the outpouring of support for his conference steeled his goals for the annual gathering.

The goals for the Tuskegee Negro Conference as articulated in his 1901 autobiography were:

> First, to find out the actual industrial, moral and educational condition of the masses. Second, to get as much light as possible on what is the most effective way for the young men and women whom the Tuskegee Institute and other institutions are educating, to use their education in helping the masses of the colored people to lift themselves up.[11]

On his first goal, Washington suggested that data be collected on rural communities such that one would be in possession of accurate information from which prescriptions for improving the condition of attendees and members of their respective communities could be developed. His second goal centered on the application of book learning to the practical data garnered at the annual meeting. Clearly, when both goals are considered collectively, Washington was effectively articulating the school's intention to employ the scientific method to investigate the real-life experiences of rural Blacks to then develop strategies to improve their life chances and life outcomes. This was a clear articulation of applied sociology. Taking this idea to a deeper level, let's examine more fully Washington's stated scientific goals.

In a 1904 publication, twelve years after the first Tuskegee conference, E. J. Scott reported that the annual event hosted by Washington was not conceived as the kind of car-window sociological effort practiced by many if not most White sociologists of the era, as unmasked by Du Bois in his seminal book *Souls of Black Folk*. Instead, as Scott reported (1904:9), "the Conferences [were] not devoted to abstractions, but to concrete problems, and what is most important, solutions of these problems."[12] The solution to these problems included the amassing of accurate data that could be used to develop the best practices in rural sociology by Black Americans in the South. Toward this end, at the first Tuskegee conference Washington insisted on the *accuracy of statements* by attendees when presenting their first-hand accounts. Accuracy and specificity of material facts were important for Washington when attendees reported on, for example, discrepancies in income and debt levels between Black and White farmers. Speaking to this matter specifically in 1893, Washington, as reported by a newspaper attendee, contended that a goal of the conference was "to present the real condition of the people, and to find, if possible, a way out of their difficulties."[13] One tacitly finds in this statement the promotion of the gathering of scientific facts to bolster programs to improve the lives of Blacks in the South, or, again, an applied sociology agenda. In other words, herein is found the outlines for engagement in what is today called applied rural sociology.

While the method of data collection employed by attendees of the conference were, as compared by the standards of today, underdeveloped, when compared to the methodological practices of sociologists of the era, particularly those engaged in sociology of the South and other methodologically unsophisticated works identified earlier, Washington's attendees' efforts were exemplary.[14] Again, no argument is made here suggesting that the methodological sophistication of Washington's annual gathering came close to that at Atlanta University by trained social scientists like W. E. B. Du Bois. However, it is argued here that the methodological sophistication of the presentations offered at Tuskegee was comparable to the majority of articles submitted to the *American Journal of Sociology* between 1895 and 1917, wherein roughly only 20 percent (and this is a generous estimate) of all contributions during this period included *any* discussion of how, where, or when data were collected.[15] It must be stated as clearly as possible here that the number of articles reported (20 percent) to have some articulation of research methods in the *American Journal of Sociology* is generous, as the authors of the study emphasized the difficulty they had in simply identifying methods of research and the stretch they made when labeling some pieces as "articulating a research method." If the articles examined were judged by a more fair and strict measure, only 7 percent of the articles published by the nation's leading sociology journal would have qualified as identifying a method of research between 1895 and 1917.

The argument concerning Tuskegee's methodological or scientific sophistication is strengthened not only when compared to early sociology of the South and mainstream disciplinary practitioners, but also against early rural sociologists. In a 1927 article titled "Research in Rural Sociology," Carl C. Taylor laments the dearth of quality scientific inquiries in the area. According to Taylor:

> Research is science in the making. Science used to be simply defined as the classification of knowledge or as the description and explanation of phenomena. Only by use of such an inadequate definition can there be said to be any research in rural sociology. I suppose we rural sociologists do, to some degree, classify knowledge. We do describe rural social

> phenomena and we do attempt to explain them. Even so, there has been
> little, if any, rural social investigation which has risen to the level of
> science.[16]

Taylor made this observation during the third decade of the twentieth
century, when the discipline was making forward progress at becoming
more rigorous and positivistic in its attempt to legitimize itself among its
peers. This admission of the discipline's, or more accurately sub-area's,
methodological shortcomings more than thirty years after the inaugural
conference makes the Wizard of Tuskegee's attempts at such an effort even
more impressive. Thus, when compared against the research products of
trained White sociologists of the era, the farmers attending the conference at Tuskegee compared quite favorably.

A final statement on Washington's attempt to obtain accurate and
scientific data on the rural conditions of Blacks in America was discerned
from his pronouncement at the 1894 conference: that participants should
"tell things just as you see them and understand them. These meetings are
for you. If you don't get benefits from them they are of no use."[17] Taken
collectively, Washington's statements on the necessity of accurate and, as
closely as possible, scientific data run counter to one's historical understanding of his resistance to liberal arts education and the gathering of
scientific data. Unquestionably Washington, while not necessarily a pro-
ponent of liberal arts education, was indeed aware of the importance of
the tools of sociological investigation and analysis in finding solutions to
the problems experienced by rural Black Americans. Thus, attendees, in
accordance with his guidelines that the meetings include the presentation of factual information on the condition of Black American rural life,
provided accounts that were used by others to improve their agricultural
productivity and lives in their respective rural towns.

"One Day's School of Practical Sociology"

After experiencing high attendance at its inaugural effort and facing an
increasing demand for facts and solutions to the pressing rural sociological

issues of the day, the Tuskegee Negro Conference expanded to become a multiple-day event that overtly embraced (while not overtly espousing) the tenets of Black sociology. The second day of meetings, now called the Worker's Conference, "was appropriately styled a 'one day's school of practical sociology'."[18] Although sociology was not a staple of the institution's curriculum there was awareness within the university community of the utility of the discipline as a tool for improving the condition of the race through applied means. Practical sociology, as evidenced at the Tuskegee Negro Conference, included taking personal accounts from multiple sources on a specific topic (i.e., data collection), teasing out the most salient and viable practices (i.e., analysis), then implementing that best practice in one's local community (i.e., application). Essentially, the Worker's Conference was where Black agricultural workers listened to speakers from every southern state, and some from the North; discussed best practices in the profession; and then learned the methods of implementation. Examples are offered below.

Before examples of research presentations at the conference are offered, a statement must be made about the documents used here. Unlike the Atlanta University studies that were led by Du Bois, Tuskegee did not regularly publish the reports and findings of each conference. In fact, there is only a scant record of actual proceedings of the meetings. The most reliable record of events at the Tuskegee Negro Conference, at least during its early years, comes from *The Southern Workman*, which was a monthly periodical produced by Hampton Institute, Washington's alma mater. Given the tremendous national and international stature of Washington and the fact he was a proud graduate of the institution, a reporter was sent to the meeting annually. Further, unlike Du Bois's Atlanta University studies, and the majority of mainstream sociology for that matter, the few existing records of the early meetings did not include many detailed articulations of the methods of data collection. As indicated earlier, the methods of data collection were largely taken from reporter accounts, which noted how they were derived from the *accurate* and *honest* statements of attendees as Washington requested and mandated.

One attendee account is taken from the inaugural meeting. An article in *The Southern Workman* indicated that teachers from more than twenty counties reported on what they believed to be a pressing need in their community. To a person, teachers reported that their community was in dire need of buildings for the instruction of students and additional teachers to meet the increasing demand. Moreover, they lamented the fact that the school year, due to children's responsibilities on the farm, was generally restricted to three months. Another group of speakers noted the difficulties many freedmen and freedwomen experienced making their monthly mortgage payments. Often the cause of their financial distress was excess or overspending, but in many other cases it was reported that farmers did not completely understand the details and responsibilities associated with signing a mortgage. In each of these cases attendees reported the condition of their respective community to the best of their ability and, as discussed later, their concerns were eventually resolved.

Repeatedly, while there is no suggestion that the first-hand accounts of participants were examples of rigorous scientific inquiry, it is worth reminding the reader, again, that the quality of *scientific* inquiry conducted by sociologists of all stripes during this era varied wildly. Speaking to the quality of the (data) presentations, *The Southern Workman* reported:

> [The Tuskegee Negro Conference] not only answered most interestingly, graphically, at first hand, the inquiries proposed as to the actual condition and needs of the masses of the people, and suggested the best direction at least for efforts to help them help themselves, but it also revealed elements of character and strength in the people themselves.[19]

An important part of Tuskegee's applied rural sociology program was the yearly assessment of the skills and information offered at the previous year's meeting. In a normal year, previous years' attendees returned to provide updates on the progress, or lack thereof, made since the last meeting. For example, at the 1893 Tuskegee Negro Conference reports were received from teachers and educators on the implementation of recommendations made at the previous year's meeting. It was concluded, "The reports brought in from different [communities] showed already good effects from last year's Conference and brought out, as that did, the marked difference between communities with and those without a district school and live teacher."[20] Essentially, due to the efforts of teachers and educators via their participation at the Tuskegee Negro Conference, more schools were built and teachers hired in communities where the need was great, and children were allowed to attend classes more regularly than before.

The 1894 meeting included additional evidence that the application of the skills and information learned at the previous year's meeting were being implemented and greatly impacted the communities where participants were engaged. Specifically, reference was made to continued efforts to enhance schooling for Black Americans, and to assessing the impact of the annual conference on attendees. In the conference declarations, where the findings of each conference and recommendations for engagement were presented, it was noted:

> The building of decent school houses and cabins, the purchase of lands, the raising of food crops and stock, has been going on steadily; receiving a new impetus at each meeting of the conference, by the actual demonstration that the reports brought in give, of the possibility of getting out of debt and up in the world.[21]

Speaking directly to the exchange of best practices in education and the sharing of data points, *The Southern Workman* reported:

> Here were [former slaves] mustered out of the army of the Republic thirty years ago, straight into the work of educating the Negro, comparing their observations and experiences with the observations and experiences of those who had recently gone from Hampton or Tuskegee, straight into the little log houses of the plantations.[22]

Again, I ask, is an argument being made here that the sophistication of the data collection and its application are comparable to today's standards or that of the Atlanta Sociological Laboratory? No. Nor should they be compared against one another. However, the quality of methodological rigor performed at Tuskegee starting in 1892 is comparable to that demonstrated in the pages of *AJS* between 1895 and 1917.

In addition to schooling, another topic of importance at the early meetings was home mortgage. Many freedman and freedwomen found themselves trapped in a state of perpetual debt after enslavement for a variety of reasons including their misunderstanding of home mortgages or the lack of good faith dealings with unscrupulous Whites with whom the deals were made. This topic was discussed at the 1894 conference where first-hand data were presented. A formerly enslaved Black American recounted, after an admonishment from Washington to all speakers to only speak of things that were factual, how he was trapped in a mortgage/lien contract during the previous year's conference. Because of the information he learned at that meeting he managed to improve his skills as a businessperson and lift himself from debt caused by the mortgage/lien contract. Conversely, as reported by *The Southern Workman*, some attendees presented accounts revealing lesser levels of success. One farmer recounted the difficulty he had keeping up with his monthly mortgage payments. "He explains his present situation by stating that after 'mancipation he was tu'ned [sic] loose with a great stream of little children, and they were small—very small. He then started wrong with mortgages and has been wrong ever since."[23] The farmer, although discouraged with his present condition, remained hopeful the one day of practical sociology at Tuskegee would render him positive results in the future. There was no further record of this farmer's success, or lack thereof, in achieving his goal of financial security.

The final example of the type of data presentations made at the early meetings also tapped into Washington's latent goal for the annual event, to improve race relations. At the 1896 conference a first-hand account of the improving race relations between Blacks and Whites in at least one community was noted. A "*Southern white gentleman*" from Snow Hill, Alabama, a town southwest of Tuskegee, was invited to offer his thoughts on Washington's annual event. A former slave owner, the man attested to the difficulty some Blacks experienced as landowners. His theory on the struggles of his fellow farmers centered on the idea that some Blacks bought more land than they could work and/or afford. Additionally, he, as did others at this and all previous meetings, lamented the burden Blacks in America experienced when attempting to pay off mortgages. The former slave master's advice to attendees was for them to "get rid of mortgages" since they damaged both races. Presumably, for Blacks the damage was caused by the inability to pay their bills which often led to one entering debtors' prison and becoming a participant in the convict leasing system. For Whites, presumably, the damage was the lack of effective use of fertile farmland and loss of revenues. Speaking to the impact of Washington's yearly gathering and its potential impact on Black Americans in his community he said, "I attended this Conference on last year, and it did me good. Whatever is for your good is for my good."[24]

Washington's commitment to developing a solid applied rural sociology program can be captured in two changes that extended his original idea beyond only holding a yearly conference. It is likely that the success of the meeting's second day of practical sociology, the Worker's Conference, inspired the Wizard of Tuskegee to consider additional ways to positively impact farming communities year-round. What emerged was a course entitled, "Short Course in Agriculture." This course "was designed to provide the farmers in surrounding counties, at the season when most of them were idle, several weeks of study and observation of the school's farm and Experiment Station."[25] Attendees, including spouses and children for whom courses were developed, were not charged a fee and received expert instruction from Tuskegee faculty as well as persons from the United States Department of Agriculture, state of Georgia, and Auburn University. In these classes attendees received intensive and consistent instruction on the best practices in agriculture on topics including, but not limited to, "general farming, livestock, dairying, poultry raising, fruit growing, and truck gardening".[26] This course started in 1908 with 11 enrolled students and by the seventh year more than 1,500 were enrolled. The success of his Short Course in Agriculture led Washington to consider additional ways of reaching farmers, resulting in his second addition to the applied rural sociology program.

Washington was fully committed to the idea that his emphasis on agriculture was in the best interests of Blacks and he wanted to make the opportunities at his institution available to as many people as possible. He also understood that, for any number of reasons, many farmers were unable to attend the yearly conference or free agricultural course, both of which took place at Tuskegee. His solution to this challenge was the establishment of a "Movable School." Between 1906 and the start of World War II Washington's Movable School travelled across the South promoting best practices and the latest advances in agriculture. At its peak the school is estimated to have reached at least 2,000 persons per month.

> The wagon carried different kinds of plows and planters, a cultivator, a cotton chopper, a variety of seeds, samples of fertilizers, a revolving churn, a butter mold, a cream separator, a milk tester, and other appliances useful in making practical demonstrations, and it had the immense advantage of carrying scientific agriculture directly to the farmers in the fields. After making the rounds of the small and large farms of a community, the "Movable School" located at a central point and conducted an open-air demonstration for a gathering of farmers and their families.[27]

There are a number of issues that Washington can be taken to task for and in a number of areas. Unquestionably, his belief in and commitment to the use of the resources Blacks were more familiar with, those emanating from agriculture, led him to not only establish a conference where attendees from all over the South could receive at least one day of practical sociological training, but also mini-semester courses where more intensive training could take place as well as a Movable School that could make the resources offered at Tuskegee available to those unable to attend the yearly conference. In the existing literature there is no evidence of another scientific program of rural sociological education and application existing prior to Washington's efforts at Tuskegee. That Washington not only embraced this work, as others lamented the relationship of Blacks to agriculture and rural areas while fleeing to emerging cities, but was creative in the promotion of science and technology as tools to be used in the best interests of Blacks is commendable, despite his low opinion of liberal arts education and (perceived) acquiescence to the racial folkways of Jim Crow.

The primary conclusion reached after examining the fragmented records of the Tuskegee Negro Conferences and early history of rural sociology is that Tuskegee Institute comprised the first applied rural sociology program in the United States. By this, I mean Tuskegee was the first academic entity to engage in an institutionalized and annual research inquiry into the social, economic, and physical condition of rural folk with the objective of developing solutions to address the problems discovered. It is true that early individual sociologists and social scientists engaged in what can be described as applied rural sociology activities. However, it is also true that no evidence exists of an academically housed institutional and annual program of inquiry into the social, economic, and physical condition of rural folk prior to that initiated at Tuskegee. Instead, it is largely agreed upon that no real and concerted institutional effort to study rural areas emerged until after Theodore Roosevelt commissioned the 1909 *Report of the Country Life Commission*. Taylor is again a guide as he argues that true rural sociological research of any kind did not commence in the United States until the start of the second decade of the century:

> Rural social research in the United States can be said to have begun with Dr. C. J. Galpin's study of The Social Anatomy of an Agricultural Community in Wisconsin in 1911. This was followed by Dr. Warren H. Wilson's rural church surveys from 1913 to 1916. Studies—chiefly surveys—sprang up here and there in a haphazard manner until 1919, when the Division of Rural Life Studies was established in what is now the Bureau of Agricultural Economics in the United States Department of Agriculture.[28]

The question that arises is, why have the activities at Tuskegee been ignored? Again, it is possible that questions regarding scientific rigor may come forward. Collectively, the reports reviewed earlier are examples of the types of presentations made by typical attendees and participants of the early Tuskegee Negro Conferences. While they may be considered scientifically rudimentary by today's standards, the idea that Washington, consistently labeled anti-liberal arts, insisted on the presentation of scientific facts such that those experiences could be packaged into an application of best practices was significant. Moreover, Washington's historically perceived dismissal of liberal arts may have given past scholars pause when considering whether or not, or even how, to describe the annual conference. When one considers the state of social science research at that time in the United States, the activities at Tuskegee are extraordinary. They were conducted during a period when they were the only ones engaged in such an institutionalized and systematic endeavor. Although Washington's statements affirming a commitment to practical sociology are amplified here, at least one scholar suggests that his commitment to scientific research may have been more talk than action.

Paul Jefferson argued that Washington was not overly concerned with his stated scientific aims of the conference. Jefferson based his assertion on a quote that Washington is reported, but not confirmed, to have made. According to Jefferson, the "primary objective [of the Tuskegee conference], as Washington was reported as stating, was 'not so much to gather scientific information as to encourage and inspire the people to better living'."[29] Jefferson posited, "Tuskegee's was a show-me empiricism" where "personal histories tell at Tuskegee the story of progress or discouragement for the year."[30] The crux of Jefferson's argument was that Washington was simply paying lip service to the proposed scientific aims of the conference while being resigned to only noting stories of success or failure, devoid of the impact of the previous year's conference or past attendances of the individual.

The counternarrative to this position is found in the writings of Washington, who argued, "We didn't let [participants] generalize or tell what they thought ought to be or was existing in somebody else's community, we held each person down to a statement of the facts regarding his own individual community."[31] Washington made another statement on the employment of science at his meetings when he wrote:

> After we had got hold of facts, which enabled us to judge of the actual state of affairs existing, we spent the afternoon of the first day in hearing from the lips of these same people in what way, in their opinion, the present condition of things could be improved, and it was most interesting as well as surprising to see how clearly these people saw into their present condition, and how intelligently they discussed their weak points as well as their strong points.[32]

Not only did attendees appear to embrace the admonition to express only facts at the meeting, they applied the information learned at Tuskegee in their own communities. According to Alan Jones, "The stories heard at the conference were carried home by the delegates and became a sort of oral literature that spread gradually over the entire black South."[33] Moreover, upon returning to the next year's meeting it was not uncommon for "a large number of the delegates [to give] encouraging evidence of how, as a result of the previous meeting, homes had been secured, school houses built, school terms extended and the moral life of the people bettered."[34]

The Tuskegee Negro Conference was one of several hosted by HBCUs, aimed at improving the condition of Blacks in America. While Tuskegee emphasized rural issues, Hampton focused on industry and Atlanta on urban issues. Despite Du Bois's and Atlanta's focus on urban issues, he was aware of the scientific studies on rural sociology taking place at Tuskegee. In an essay titled, "Results of Ten Tuskegee Negro Conferences," Du Bois reported that he attended the 1901 conference and conducted a quick study on whether or not Washington's gathering was accomplishing its stated goals. In the introduction he noted the school's intention to lift rural Blacks out of poverty and ignorance when he writes, "Here is a school planted in the midst of the rural black belt which has sought to raise the standard of living, and especially to change the three things that hold the Negro still in serfdom—the crop lien system, the one-room cabin, and the poor and short public school."[35] During his visit he randomly interviewed two hundred attendees on topics including, but not limited to, home structure, home ownership, income, and, most important, impact of the conference on attendees. Du Bois concluded that his "reports showed too, that this work has not been in vain. Not only was this manifest in the tone of the discussions and general atmosphere, but also in the more exact reports of the selected two hundred."[36] It is important to note here that Du Bois provides first-hand knowledge of Washington's admonition that reports of attendees be as exact and accurate as possible. In attesting to this methodological expectation of full member participant observation accounting, the architect of some of the most advanced scientific practices of his era provides a convincing and supportive statement on Tuskegee's fitness for canon status, as argued herein.

Clearly, it is not an exercise of intellectual fairness to judge the scientific practices of an earlier generation with advances made over the course of one hundred years or more and practiced by a later generation. Certainly the scientific rigor Washington articulated would be questioned, if not downright dismissed, by today's scientific standards. However, a more nuanced interpretation of Washington's program is that it should be considered the first example of applied rural sociology. More germane to Washington than establishing what I argue is the first applied rural sociology program, however, was the possibility of improving race relations.

Paul Jefferson's critique of the Tuskegee Negro Conference was not limited to the idea that Washington was unconcerned with the actual scientific aims of the conference. He also argued that Washington's circuitous goal was not a conference that centered the presentation of scientific research for the benefit of rural Black Americans, but a platform whereby he could assuage the concerns of southern Whites worried about the potentially rebellious activities of persons recently released from bondage. Contrasting the Negro conferences held during this era at Atlanta, Hampton and Tuskegee, Jefferson argued that "under Booker T. Washington, the Tuskegee conferences were less concerned with systematic research than with expedient local reform and interracial fence-mending."[37] Regarding the latter charge, it is clear in the declarations Washington offered after the first conference that interracial fence-mending was a goal. Of the ten declarations made at the inaugural 1892 gathering, five offered expressions of gratitude or desire for interracial cooperation and understanding.

Of those five, one declaration included an apology to Whites. The best example of Washington's attempts to mend racial fences was declaration number eight, which read, "we appreciate the spirit of friendliness and fairness shown us by the Southern white people in matters of business in all lines of material development."[38] Washington also expressed regret over the bind sharecropping placed on Whites.

> Third. Not only is our own material progress hindered by the mortgage system, but also that of our white friends. It is a system that tempts us to buy much that we would do without if cash were required, and it tends to lead those who advance the provisions and lend the money, to extravagant process and ruinous rates of interests.[39]

A discussion of Washington's conservative and conciliatory politics is not addressed here, and his attempts to benefit financially from his status as a Black man who White capitalists could do business with is easily found in the existing literature. Nevertheless, it must be stated clearly that in order for an institution like Tuskegee to exist in the American South at the dawn of the twentieth century it required nuanced and delicate dances between the races, given the often-deadly consequences that could befall Blacks deemed to be moving *too fast and too soon* for equal rights. That Washington desired improved race relations (even if they sometimes meant his own financial benefit) for a people who could be lynched for merely looking at a White woman should not diminish or tarnish his unintended role in establishing the first program of applied rural sociology. Instead, one can view this feat as a major accomplishment given the precarious state of Black American lives upon the arrival of the nation's first domestic terrorist organization, the Ku Klux Klan, and demise of the first American school of sociology, the Atlanta Sociological Laboratory.

Tuskegee and Black Sociology

After W. E. B. Du Bois's departure from Atlanta University in 1913 a void emerged in the institutional application of Black sociology. While the

Atlanta University conferences continued until 1924, the program of sociological inquiry started by President Bumstead and trustee Bradford that later expanded into the first American school of sociology under Du Bois was a shell of itself after his departure. There appeared in the moment to be no HBCU, nor HWCU for that matter, capable or interested in continuing Atlanta's program of disseminating accurate, timely, and scientific data on the condition of Blacks in America. One HBCU, however, did emerge to fill the Black sociology void. Ironically, it was Booker T. Washington's Tuskegee Institute. Despite its emphasis on vocational and agricultural education, the school, unwittingly, carried on the Black sociology tradition started at Atlanta. At first glance it seems improbable that Tuskegee could become the successor to Atlanta in the production of social science research on Blacks in America. Certainly, for those unaware of the school's rural sociological activities the idea that the Washington-led institution would become a leader in social science research would be considered anathema. However, when one examines this subject deeper, the idea that Washington provided such a platform at his institution becomes more plausible.

I noted earlier that Washington demanded the presentation of scientific facts, as best could be amassed, at his yearly conference. What resulted was the expectation that each year's gathering would include a one-day course in *practical sociology* where attendees learned the best practices in agriculture and business and employed that knowledge back in their home communities. Washington, by most accounts, was pleased with his day of practical sociology but was also aware of new and competing conferences taking place at Atlanta University and Hampton Institute. Although his yearly gathering started four years prior to the Atlanta effort, it is certain that Washington, as evidenced by his attendance at numerous Atlanta conferences, understood the importance and significance of the massive sociological undertaking by Du Bois. Washington was so enthralled by Du Bois's work and its potentially enlarged impact, both nationally and internationally, that he attempted to hire his future adversary away from the Georgia institution. In a 1932 interview, Monroe N. Work, as reported by Linda O. McMurry, confirmed that Washington wanted to bring Du Bois to Tuskegee and establish a sociological laboratory there.

> Washington had long harbored a vague desire to introduce sociological studies of some sort at his school, perhaps because a rival institution, Atlanta University, had such a program. Indeed, in 1899, [Washington] had asked Du Bois to establish a sociological research program at Tuskegee. Du Bois's decision to remain in Atlanta dramatically affected the course of history and left a void at Tuskegee.[40]

One is only left to wonder about the possible impact Du Bois would have made on sociology and the nation were Tuskegee's resources made available him, the most powerful Black American intellectual at the turn of the century. Equally curious is the tension that may have emerged between the two giants of Black American life had their ideological battle been waged within the confined space of Tuskegee, Alabama. Washington was unsuccessful, however, in securing the services of Du Bois. Nevertheless, Washington's desire to hire someone to collect sociological data remained. Nearly ten years after Du Bois's rejection of Washington's offer, the school decided to "hire a man to 'study the work of the school and graduates with reference to what they are doing for society, and to collect and classify data which will be of general interest and value'."[41] It was the latter charge for the person hired to this position that, unwittingly, positioned Tuskegee to become the second school of Black sociology.

Monroe N. Work

Monroe Nathan Work was born in 1866 in North Carolina and reared by formerly enslaved parents in Illinois during his youth. Saddled with the responsibility of caring for his aging parents, his pursuit of an education was delayed until he reached his early twenties. Although he began his education later than most, Work made up for lost time, as he obtained a high school diploma at age 26. Ten years later he obtained a bachelor's degree in philosophy at the University of Chicago and in 1903 took a master's degree in sociology at the same institution. Work's tenure at the University of Chicago was impacted by relationships with members of the first generation of Chicago School sociologists, including Albion Small, C. R. Henderson, and W. I. Thomas. These men viewed urban settings as laboratories that should be studied with the goal of developing strategies to address the pressing concerns of residents. Work shared this philosophy and wanted to direct his scholarly and activist ambitions toward improving the condition of Black Americans in cities. Work soon found inspiration and a kindred soul who engaged in the type of scholarship he valued. While the mentorship of the Chicago sociologists was significant, McMurry argued, "perhaps the greatest influence on Work during his years at Chicago was his research association with W. E. B. Du Bois through the Atlanta Studies."[42]

Work knew of Du Bois's groundbreaking sociological research at Atlanta University and "became involved in the Atlanta Studies while still a student in Chicago."[43] Attesting to the influence Du Bois's sociological laboratory wielded over the promising scholar, McMurry suggested that "Work's desire to continue [working with the Atlanta Sociological Laboratory] was probably a major factor in his decision to accept a position at Georgia State Industrial College in Savannah, [now Savannah State University]."[44] After taking his master's degree in 1903 Work accepted a position at the Georgia institution and between 1903 and 1917 wrote four essays that were published in the Atlanta University Study of the Negro Problems, making him another unsung member of and contributor to the Atlanta Sociological Laboratory. This was quite an accomplishment since Du Bois was the primary, and often singular, author of contributions to the Atlanta University publications.

Although Work's contributions to the Atlanta University publications were solid, one piece stood out. His 1904 contribution, "Crime in Cities," focused on the experiences of Black Americans and the criminal justice system. He examined crime data from the most populous cities in each region of the nation to ascertain if, as promoted at the time, Northern cities experienced increased criminal activity because of the heavy internal migration of Blacks from the South to the North.

Work presented data debunking the notion that the amount of crime committed by Blacks in the North was higher than that committed by Blacks in the South. This "urban coon" theory was grounded in the misnomer that Blacks in the American North were more violent than their counterparts in the American South and that crime in the American North had increased because of the mass migration of southern Blacks to cities like Chicago, Detroit and Cleveland and their inability to successfully adapt to their new urban surroundings.[45]

One can surmise that Work's participation with the Atlanta Sociological Laboratory, on some level, fulfilled his desire to engage in research on Blacks in America that affected their lives. It is also safe to surmise that the resources available for him to engage in his own brand of critical social science research at the Savannah institution were not as exhaustive as those available at schools like Washington's Tuskegee Institute and to a lesser degree Du Bois at Atlanta. This is why he embraced the opportunity to continue his engagement in sociological inquiry at the relatively well-resourced Tuskegee Institute when Washington called for him. Although Washington desired someone who could produce data for, and when necessary ghost author, his many national and international speeches, he was well aware of the sociological activity taking place at Atlanta University and wanted to introduce the discipline in full at his Alabama-based institution. While Work was fully capable of accomplishing the former tasks, it was the latter that most attracted him to Tuskegee. It must be noted here that the former responsibilities were largely performed by soon-to-be University of Chicago sociologist Robert Park, who came to Tuskegee in 1906 to be "the already renowned Tuskegee principal's private secretary, research analyst, [ghost writer], and amanuensis" for the next seven years.[46]

In 1908 Work was appointed Director of the Division of Records and Research. Although the former title did not interest him very much, Work was committed to engaging in research and teaching courses in sociology, as requested by Washington. Inspired by the opportunity for substantive scholarly inquiry at Tuskegee, Work's desire to employ sociology as a tool for the social uplift of Blacks in America had seemingly come full circle. In a speech he delivered while a student, Work discussed the liberating power of the young discipline. Reflecting on this speech some years later he revealed, "It was then . . . that I dedicated my life to the gathering of information, the compiling of exact knowledge concerning the Negro."[47] The gathering of data on Blacks in America is just what he did at Tuskegee. It is unfair to judge the scholarly merit of the junior scholar by Du Bois's stick, since Work did not fully engage in sociological research in the same manner as Du Bois and the Atlanta Sociological Laboratory. Instead, Work's role in continuing the tradition of Black sociology after the demise of the Atlanta Sociological Laboratory included the dissemination of *exact knowledge concerning* Black American life. In effect, with the establishment of the *Negro Year Book* in 1912, Tuskegee, under the direction of Monroe N. Work, became the leading clearinghouse in the nation for data on Blacks in America.

Negro Year Book and Anti-Lynching

In 1910 W. E. B. Du Bois left the faculty at Atlanta University and was within three years of relinquishing directorship of the Atlanta University studies. While this was occurring there was no coordinated attempt to transfer the Black sociology baton from one entity to the next. Nevertheless, waiting in the wings to fill the void of curating accurate and timely data on the condition of Blacks in America was Monroe N. Work with his annual publication, *Negro Year Book*.

It was almost by happenstance that the *Negro Year Book* came to be. Tuskegee was the recipient of a 1904 grant via the philanthropic generosity of Andrew Carnegie. The purpose of the award was to "disseminate publicity relating to the Negro."[48] Within a few years the majority of funds appropriated to Tuskegee were used for this purpose. However, by the early 1910s school officials noticed that a sizable amount of monies from the grant remained in their coffers. Washington came up with a way to use the funds. In celebration of the forthcoming fiftieth anniversary of the emancipation of Africans from enslavement, Washington called for the creation of a yearbook to celebrate seminal advances made by members of the race. Guided by Washington's vision, consultation from Robert Park and the leadership of Work, the first edition of the *Negro Year Book* was released in 1912 as "a permanent record of current events, an encyclopedia of historical and sociological facts, a directory of persons and organizations, and a bibliographical guide to the subjects discussed."[49] The range of topics covered by the *Negro Year Book* was extensive and included, but was not limited to, business, education, health, history, politics, racism, and religion. Arguably, the most important information included in the publications were data on lynching that, ideally, would be used in the efforts of Blacks and Whites to end the horrible practice dominated by the nation's leading domestic terrorist organization, the Ku Klux Klan.

The post-emancipation America experienced by the formerly enslaved Africans was, ideally, a time when the benefits of citizenship should have been pursued with joyous vigor. It should have, theoretically speaking, been a time when complete access to quality employment, education, and every other aspect of life were attainable. Instead, the post-emancipation world of Blacks in America quickly darkened as White America viciously snatched away dreams, aspirations, and opportunities for millions. What's worse, White America viciously snatched away the lives of thousands of innocent men and women because of their race. The forms of killings varied but one stood out because of its unique mercilessness: lynching.

From its inception, Work's *Negro Year Book* was, among other things, a catalog for accurate accounts of the inhumane and unjust lynching deaths of Blacks in America. In the overwhelming majority of cases the victims of lynching were denied due process. The first volume of the *Negro Year Book* included an account of the number, nature, and location of lynchings. Data from 1911 noted the lynching of 71 Black Americans and 9 Whites at varied locations around the nation including, but not limited to, Georgia, Idaho, Maryland, and Pennsylvania. The *crimes* for which persons were lynched, excluding the obvious accusation of rape, included acting suspiciously, quarrelling, using insulting language to a lady, and using abusive language. Similar accounts were recorded by Work over the next five years. It is not suggested here that Tuskegee was the singular, primary, or leading entity engaged in the collection of data on lynching at this time. The National Association for the Advancement for Colored People (NAACP), local newspapers, and anti-lynching organizations were also engaged in this work. However, Tuskegee is singled out as being the most reliable academic-based institutional clearinghouse of data on lynching. With the collection of scientific data on the number, nature, and locations of lynchings, proponents for its abolition hoped they could proactively engage elected officials and solicit their help in ending the practice.

In 1918 a national movement calling on Congress to pass anti-lynching legislation reached a crescendo. In April of that year Representative Leonidas Dyer of Missouri sponsored what became known as the Dyer Anti-Lynching Bill. Penalties for lynching at this time were determined by state and local officials. More often than not, murderers who chose lynching as their preferred method of killing received light or no penalties, especially if the person killed was Black. Dyer's bill sought to remove the charging authority for the crime of lynching from the state and local level to the federal government. In theory, since federal officials were physically removed from personal relationships and other social and political entanglements that may influence whether or not one was charged with the crime of lynching, the possibility that a person would be charged if they committed the act theoretically increased. Second, the Dyer Anti-Lynching Bill mandated penalties for lynching that included jail and fines. Moreover, these penalties were not only directed at the actual murderer but anyone who participated in the event and/or did not act proactively to save the life of the person not given due justice. This meant sheriffs, police, and court officials could be subjected to jail or fine too. Although the House of Representatives passed the Dyer Bill, the Democratic-led Senate filibustered the legislation. Despite the efforts of Work at Tuskegee and others, including Ida B. Wells-Barnett, to bring to America's attention the unconscionable horrors of lynching, the fight to establish federal penalties for the abhorrent practice failed repeatedly over the following decades. It is unconscionable to think a reasonable and simple act of passing legislation to save the lives of thousands of innocents was unsuccessful during Jim Crow. What's even worse is that, at the time of this writing, there *STILL* does not exist any legislation outlawing lynching.

The significance of Monroe Nathan Work and the *Negro Year Book* to science is not minimized because the United States Congress failed to pass anti-lynching legislation during this nation's period of Jim Crow segregation and domestic terrorism. Instead, the Tuskegee effort should be viewed as a means by which sociological data collection and analysis were used as tools to address real world conditions of the nation's most vulnerable population. Instead of simply theorizing on the condition of Blacks in America, Work gathered primary and secondary data to impact public policy. Work's engagement in Black sociology was, indirectly, a continuation of Du Bois's Atlanta efforts, yet the precursor to bigger manifestations of the burgeoning field.

Ida B. Wells-Barnett

In recent years there has been an effort to expand the canon of those considered to be early sociologists despite not having academic training in the field. Arguments in support of this position center on the idea that, in lieu of professional training and a degree in the field, the real-world activities engaged in by these persons were applications of sociology. Such was the case with Ida B. Wells-Barnett. This chapter would be incomplete if a brief note on her practical sociological efforts documenting and challenging lynching in America were not noted. Toward this end, below I briefly highlight Wells-Barnett's engagement with sociology via her anti-lynching campaign, which predated the Tuskegee-led efforts of Monroe Nathan Work.

Ida B. Wells-Barnett was born in 1862 in Holly Springs, Mississippi, and spent a considerable portion of her life a stone's throw away in Memphis, Tennessee. During her early years she observed first-hand how the lives of recently emancipated Africans were in constant danger. She was socialized into understanding the consequences that could befall those who attempted to live in the sun and beyond the Black codes. While she clearly understood the outcome of attacks on the lives of Black Americans, in many instances she knew of their innocence and the lack of due process afforded to those against whom accusations were made. Wells-Barnett's defense of victims of lynching, generally, and Black men accused of raping White women, specifically, placed her life in danger, constantly. In her own words, Wells-Barnett wrote:

> It was for the assertion of this fact, in the defense of her own race, that the writer hereof became an exile; her property destroyed and her return to her home forbidden under penalty of death, for writing the editorial which was printed in her paper, the *Free Speech*, in Memphis, Tenn., May 21, 1892.[50]

This incident did not deter Wells-Barnett from shining light on the abhorrent practice of lynching. Instead, it led her to publish a pamphlet, *A Red Record: Tabulated Statistics and Alleged Causes of Lynchings in the United States, 1892-1893-1894*, that I argue stands as her seminal sociological contribution. Although she is not credentialed, she certainly qualifies as a citizen sociologist.

Wells-Barnett's sociological efforts, in many ways, mirror the uncredentialed citizen sociologists that assisted in data collection for Du Bois and the Atlanta Sociological Laboratory. Because of the legitimate probability that even the most well-meaning white sociologist would not garner accurate personal data from Blacks during Jim Crow, the Atlanta Sociological Laboratory was compelled to employ citizen sociologists to engage in data collection. Du Bois defended utilization of this cadre of non-PhD researchers with the argument, as interpreted by this author, that:

> The repeated use of Atlanta University and other graduates and students enabled the volunteer/untrained researchers the opportunity to become proficient researchers through on-the-job training. Du Bois noted that "by calling on the same persons [as researchers] year after year, a body of experienced correspondents had been gradually formed, numbering . . . about fifty."[51]

Du Bois surmised that the repeated use of the same citizen sociologists as data collectors each year was the equivalent of one's practical engagement in the discipline, whereby repeated sociological practices would lead to competence, if not expertise. A similar argument is made here about Wells-Barnett. While not in possession of a doctorate in sociology, she was a citizen sociologist as evidenced by her repeated employment of the discipline's methodology (participant observation and primary and secondary content analysis) and theoretical analysis. The agitator for the human rights of Blacks in America expressed in *A Red Record* not only an understanding of the utility of the discipline in shaping the future of the race, but also comprehension of the limitations of existing scientific practices so clearly called out by Du Bois as "car-window sociology."

Wells-Barnett began her book referencing the discipline's engagement with analyses of societal behaviors and interactions related to the horrors of lynching and the fact that most Americans had grown immune to the barbaric practice against their fellow citizens.

> The student of American sociology will find the year 1894 marked by a pronounced awakening of the public conscience to a system of anarchy and outlawry which had grown during a series of ten years to be so common, that scenes of unusual brutality failed to have any visible effect upon the humane sentiments of the people of our land.[52]

It is clear she understood that one of the discipline's goals was to *make sense* of societal behaviors such that one could come to understand the ways a human group could be so dehumanized as to make their publicly advertised and actual death a societal event more than a call to action to end an abhorrent practice. What's more, Wells-Barnett understood, as did Du Bois, that data were needed to convince some members of the country that a problem existed and that her efforts were not simply those of one engaging in research soiled by racial favoritism. Instead, she wanted to penetrate the closed minds of *seemingly* reasonable Americans in the hope that her data would promote social change. Effectively, she was employing sociology as a tool in the liberation of Black people as mandated by Black sociology.

Wells-Barnett's content analysis of lynchings between 1892 and 1894 relied on tabulations comprised by White reporters. Again, similar to Du Bois's concern that the direct engagement of Black sociologists in social reform efforts would render their scientific findings void in the minds of White scholars, Wells-Barnett similarly sought to fend off denials of the fact that a high number of Black Americans were unjustly killed by this practice each year. Wells-Barnett explained:

> The purpose of the pages which follow shall be to give the record which has been made, not by colored men, but that which is the result of compilations made by white men, of reports sent over the *civilized world* (emphasis mine) by white men in the South.[53]

It is sad that many White Americans would only accept data and science from members of their own race—and only that of Black scientists if sponsored and promoted by the right individual or entity. It is sad that many White Americans could not be instantly repulsed by the lawlessness and violence bestowed on Black bodies because they questioned whether or not the data were believable since the author was Black. Wells-Barnett knew the inroad to making substantive impacts on anti-lynching legislation rested first on the basic acknowledgment that a problem existed. Certain that data from a Black woman banished from her hometown would be met with nothing but skepticism, Wells-Barnett insisted data from White reporters be used because:

> Out of their own mouths shall the murderers be condemned. For a number of years the *Chicago Tribune*, admittedly one of the leading journals of America, has made a specialty of the compilation of statistics touching upon lynching. The data compiled by that journal and published to the world January 1, 1894, up to the present time has not been disputed. In order to be safe from the charge of exaggeration, the incidents hereinafter reported have been confined to those vouched for by the *Tribune*.[54]

After using content analysis to document the number of persons killed via lynching and sketching a few graphic details of the barbaric process, Wells-Barnett drew a seemingly simple conclusion.

> The very frequent inquiry made after my lectures by interested friends
> is "What can I do to help the cause?" The answer always is: "Tell the
> world the facts." When the Christian world knows the alarming growth
> and extent of outlawry in our land, some means will be found to stop it.[55]

At a very basic level, her answer speaks to the idea that the discipline can
be used as a tool to improve the life chances and life outcomes of people if
the known facts (data) are presented to members of a society in a manner
they will embrace. Understanding the fact that data gathered by, for
example, a Black newspaper would not be convincing to a White audience,
Wells-Barnett employed the most effective data-gathering method to
accomplish her goal. Once in possession of *objective* data she could then
travel across the nation and engage Blacks and Whites on lynching and literally place into their hands information allies could use in their efforts to
end the practice. Today, this practice would loosely mirror and be labeled
"applied sociology." During her era, it was called survival.

Summary

Heretofore, the common (mis)conception of Booker T. Washington's
Tuskegee Institute simply construed it as an agricultural and industrial
institution that demonstrated little sympathy toward liberal arts or
the social sciences. A more nuanced assessment of Washington's school
suggests it unwittingly accepted the Black sociology baton after the demise
of the Du Bois-led Atlanta Sociological Laboratory. In so doing, Tuskegee
established the first program of applied rural sociology. It is not argued
here that Washington's efforts represented the same scientific rigor practiced by Du Bois at Atlanta University. At best, the scientific endeavors at
Tuskegee were elementary. At worst, the scientific endeavors at Tuskegee
were rudimentary. What is beyond dispute is that compared with the
quality of sociological inquiry performed at HWCUs of the era via sociology of the South and articles found in *AJS*, Tuskegee's efforts were on par.
Combined with the establishment of the nation's first program of applied
rural sociology was the school's attempt to impact public policy via its

dissemination of data on lynching. Although anti-lynching legislation was never passed, the idea that science should be used for the greater good of improving a group's social, economic, and physical condition in a society was cemented as a core principle of Tuskegee's Black sociology. While Tuskegee, seemingly, stumbled into its actualization of Black sociology, the actions of other early Black sociologists at HBCUs were more intentional.

CHAPTER 4

Fisk and Howard

Laying the Foundation

In 1902 Frank L. Tolman wrote a series of articles on the state of sociology in the United States. Tolman's three *American Journal of Sociology* (*AJS*) articles totaled nearly one hundred pages and was his "attempt to catalogue and to evaluate the present instruction of sociology throughout the United States."[1] His evaluation of sociology programs included HBCUs and HWCUs. Although the task undertaken was important insomuch as it provided the discipline a benchmark to evaluate its development in this nation, a major failing of his endeavor was that he did not offer substantive comparisons of departments of sociology against one another. Despite this limitation Tolman's effort was notable because it provided data on the number and types of courses taught at newly established HBCUs as well as newly established and long-standing HWCUs.

The most interesting finding of Tolman's study was data indicating that numerous HBCUs were engaged in the instruction of sociology in ways that were empirically similar to their HWCU peers. That Tolman reached the conclusion that a number of HBCUs were engaged in the instruction of sociology at levels equal to, if not greater, than many HWCUs was noteworthy for a number of reasons. First, HBCUs were relatively new and had not fully developed instructional or research capacity for the full implementation of the discipline as a tool for social change. However, as discussed earlier, the foundation for the development of sociology at HBCUs was firmly established, as evidenced by the amount of instructional time devoted to the young discipline. Second, HBCUs were

vastly underfunded when compared to HWCUs and, thus, unable to secure
the discipline's most accomplished talent, unlike their peers. This is not
to suggest that faculty at HBCUs were inferior by any means. Instead, it is
a fact that many top White sociologists of the era did not work at HBCUs.
Ultimately, it is instructive to note that the quality of sociological instruction at the nation's Jim Crow institutions did not differ greatly from institutions dedicated to the singular instruction of White Americans in an era
where resources were unequally distributed. Last, HBCUs at this time were
largely comprised of faculty and students who, according to the prevailing
scientific racism literature of the era, were considered intellectually and
biologically inferior to Whites. That the academic prowess of a people so
mis-defined equaled, and in some cases outmatched, those believed to be
of a higher intellectual branch of the human family spoke volumes about
the assumptions of the era and quality of scientific research conducted
in all branches of the sciences. It is unsurprising that Tolman recognized
Atlanta University as the nation's highest performing HBCU because of its
excellence in sociological instruction. It is true that the school's production of sociological research was greater than other HBCUs. However, it
was Tolman's recognition of a little-known and now defunct institution
that is worthy of a brief examination.

Roger Williams University was established in 1866 by the American
Baptist Home Mission Society in Nashville, Tennessee. Despite its nearly
parallel birth and development with American sociology, instruction in
the new academic field was not offered until 1900. By the early twentieth
century, according to Tolman, the school's curriculum included courses in
sociology that were similar to those found at any Black or White institution.
The principal courses in sociology offered at the Nashville-based institution included introduction to sociology and, unsurprisingly, specialty
classes on race. Similar to other HBCUs offering courses on the sociology
of race, it was very likely that officials at Roger Williams University were
intentional in the development of a curriculum that affirmed the humanity
of Blacks in America while simultaneously challenging scientific theories
supporting the biological and intellectual inferiority of the freedmen and

freedwomen. Roger Williams University, however, wasn't the only HBCU noted for offering a sociology curriculum similar to its HWCU peers. As indicated previously, Tolman also recognized Atlanta University.

Similar to Roger Williams University, Atlanta University's curriculum and courses in sociology were comparable to those offered at HWCUs. Its courses included titles such as Introduction to Sociology and Sociology of Race. Tolman's analysis of the program at Atlanta, unlike other HBCUs surveyed, was more substantive and mirrored similar and multiple conclusions reached for the HWCUs examined. Additionally, Atlanta was the only HBCU to have a summary analysis of its program in the three-article inquiry. Tolman's narrative of sociology at Atlanta University consisted of accounts from the school's catalog description of the program. Information retrieved from the catalog revealed that Mayo-Smith's *Statistics and Sociology* was a required textbook and that the requirements for graduation included *special library work* and the completion of a thesis. That the department was led by W. E. B. Du Bois was also mentioned. Just as important, the sociological research program of the Du Bois-led Atlanta Sociological Laboratory was recognized. It was reported that five Atlanta University studies had been completed and that the school was currently working on its sixth investigation. Although the idea that Du Bois's work at Atlanta had not received its deserved recognition because his contemporaries were, supposedly, simply unaware of its existence is debunked later, it is worthwhile to note that Tolman recognized the efforts of the Atlanta Sociological Laboratory shortly after its sixth year of existence.

In sum, Tolman's articles provided a general overview of the amount and types of sociology courses offered at a variety of institutions across the nation. A better window into the development of the discipline and the types and number of sociology courses offered in the early twentieth century was found in the work of L. L. Bernard. He examined the instruction of sociology at Black and White southern institutions. Bernard's study allows one to more accurately compare and contrast departments of sociology at HBCUs versus HWCUs.

In 1918, one year after the final *Atlanta University Study of the Negro Problems* was published, Bernard conducted a study on the instruction of sociology at southern institutions at the behest of the secretary of the National Conference of Social Work. Limited to southern institutions, Bernard's study comprised a more thorough examination of the instruction of sociology than Tolman's because of its expanded method of data collection, which captured information beyond that merely found in each school's published catalog. Similar to Tolman, Bernard examined school catalogs to ascertain the number and type of sociology courses offered. Fifty-six catalogs released prior to 1916 and 138 catalogs published between 1916 and 1917 were examined. The point of departure from Tolman's study was Bernard's request for information from 139 institutions covering 14 southern states on topics including their number of sociology instructors and highest level of education; type(s) of research conducted by individual faculty and, if applicable, the collective department; list of courses taught; and prerequisites for the school's introduction to sociology course. Data were requested from 139 institutions and only 25 returned the questionnaire. From these data it was surmised that the instruction of sociology at HBCUs in the South did not differ greatly from its instruction at regional HWCU peers.

Bernard specifically requested data on topics covered in introduction to sociology courses. He found that the topical areas covered at HBCUs did not differ significantly from HWCUs. The typical introduction to sociology course at each type of institution included coverage of theory, theory and practice, and fieldwork. In an additional level of analysis, Bernard teased out data concerning which schools were engaged in what could be described as applied sociology. This was assessed through the integration of course objectives concerning theory and practice and fieldwork. Bernard highlighted two institutions, Louisiana State University and Atlanta University, for their collaborative research efforts with non-university affiliated agencies and community partners, or engagement in applied sociology. It is noteworthy that collaborative interactions between Atlanta University and its neighbors began prior to Du Bois's arrival and continued throughout his tenure as director of the Atlanta Sociological Laboratory and his departure. That Bernard, in the highly racialized and violent era of domestic terrorism against Blacks in 1918, placed the applied sociological efforts of Atlanta University on the same plane as Louisiana State University was quite a feat for a school barely fifty years of age with much less resources. Similar to Tolman, despite the historical marginalization of the Atlanta Sociological Laboratory, this study provides evidence to suggest that White sociologists of the era were aware of the first American school of sociology's activities and significance as they were occurring.

Perhaps the most significant finding in Bernard's study was that HBCUs, unlike HWCUs, offered more instruction in sociology than history. This was noteworthy, since the now separate and distinct disciplines were normally housed within the same unit at most institutions during this era. The fact that HBCUs emphasized instruction in sociology over history reinforces the idea that these institutions viewed the discipline as a living entity and more relevant than history in addressing the immediate needs of a people less than fifty years removed from constitutionally sanctioned enslavement. The embrace of sociology at HBCUs at the expense of history was a direct function of the desire of Black sociologists, and in many cases their White allies, to use the discipline as a tool to improve the social, economic, and physical condition of Blacks in America. Unfortunately, the demise of Du Bois's Atlanta Sociological Laboratory created a vacuum in the implementation of Black sociology as a blunt scientific tool to address the needs of American Blacks. Although Monroe N. Work and the Tuskegee Institute filled the gap to some extent, they were ill equipped to engage in the type of work conducted by the first American school of sociology. Reasonable questions to ask are, "Could any institution replace the quality and quantity of engagement in Black sociology as practiced at Atlanta University?" and "Was there any sociologist who could, even unwittingly, embrace the challenge of engaging in a program of Black sociology?" The answer to both questions is yes. The baton of engagement in academically housed research directed at improving the social, economic, and physical condition of Blacks in the United States was theoretically passed from Du Bois, through Work, into the more than capable hands of George Edmund Haynes at Fisk University. While Du Bois's research at Atlanta was exemplary and foundational in the establishment of sociology as a legitimate scientific discipline, whether acknowledged or not, Haynes's sociology centered on an agenda championed by Bernard in his 1918 study: the nexus between theory and practice and fieldwork. This is known today as applied sociology.

Fisk University

Fisk University was established in Nashville, Tennessee in 1866. Nashville was thought to be an appropriate location for the American Missionary Association-backed school because it is centrally located in the corridor between northern and southern regions known during the Civil War as border states. The city was thought to be ideal because some believed it was more tolerant of northern sensibilities and carpetbaggers than towns located deeper in the South. The city's seemingly open embrace of its northern brethren was why the school's founders openly proclaimed "Nashville was 'a nostril' through which the state had 'long breathed the Northern air of free institutions'."[2]

Knowledgeable concerning Nashville's relative openness to interracial cooperation, but fully aware of their location *Up South*, Fisk's leaders worked feverishly to establish positive relationships with the city's White community. This was a primary objective upon the school's establishment because Fisk's founders were well aware of the anger and resentment of some Whites toward the promotion of education for Black Americans who, after graduation, would dare believe themselves equal to or better than Whites, if they already had not prior to earning their degree. The racial climate of the Reconstruction Era in America was so vile, even in Nashville, that it was not beyond reason that a White southerner so offended by the idea that a Black person would overtly assert their human equality would extend some sort of violence, and possibly death, upon the person(s) by whom he believed he was offended. In an effort to minimize the possibility of race-based violence at his newly established institution and against the students being educated there when they ventured beyond campus:

> [Fisk University] President Cravath and his associates moved among Southern leaders who entertained convictions different from their own, winning the respect and confidence of many without compromising their own belief in the fundamental equality of individuals before both God and man.[3]

Among audiences not keen on providing resources or opportunities for Black Americans to practice or gain agency over their lives, Fisk's founders allayed many of the more extreme and exaggerated concerns of their new neighbors. Nevertheless, the Ku Klux Klan, established two years prior to the school in a small town located only a short distance from Nashville, occasionally held marches near Fisk. For the most part, the efforts of the school's founders to establish a barrier between its students and dangerous White citizens was successful.

One must be mindful that many HBCUs established during this period, while tagged with the name "college" or "university," offered curriculums ranging from elementary school to college. To many Black Nashville residents, Fisk represented their first opportunity to become formally educated. The establishment of a tuition-free school to educate Blacks one year removed from passage of the 13th Amendment outlawing slavery was significant, since no such institution existed in Nashville prior to Fisk. That Nashville, with the state's largest Black American population at the time, did not have a system of free public education for its brown-skinned citizens may not have been a matter of concern for city leaders prior to the establishment of Fisk. However, it is quite possible that the relationship established between the school's leadership and the city's political and business leaders, or simply happenstance, brought this void to the community's attention, because within one year of Fisk's opening the city of Nashville opened two tuition-free public schools for Blacks.

The opening of two free public schools by the city relieved some of the responsibility of the instruction of Nashville's uneducated Black masses from Fisk and enabled its administrators and faculty to direct their efforts at college instruction. By 1869 the school ended its instruction in elementary education and Fisk began to offer courses in departments including high school, model school, commercial department, theology department, and college. Instruction in college work quickly consumed more of the institution's resources and when the school graduated its first class of college students in 1875 the amount of non-college instruction was reduced immensely. This enabled the school to develop and expand units that would soon become central to its mission.

Fisk Sociology

For many years Morgan College (now named Morgan State University) was believed to be the first HBCU to offer instruction in sociology.[4] Data uncovered recently, instead, indicate that the instruction of sociology at Fisk predated Morgan by one year.[5] Sociology first appeared in the Fisk University catalog in 1893–1894 when its instruction was listed as one area of study in an English course offered in the Theological Department. Although very little detail on the subject matter was provided, in the course description it was noted that "lectures will be given on this important science."[6] By 1895, two years after its infusion into the university curriculum, the instruction of sociology was expanded. Sociology was now listed as an area of study under the sub-discipline Pastoral Theology and it was noted that its instruction was now a component of an expanded number of courses. Although a standalone course in sociology wasn't developed for a number of years, what was clear was that its instruction at Fisk was grounded in the social gospel movement taking place at that time.

The social gospel movement was an effort by Protestant leaders and practitioners, many of whom were sociologists, to integrate Christian principles with academic research and knowledge to improve the life chances and life outcomes of all Americans. Supporters of this movement were found among the early administrators and faculty at Fisk. W. E. B. Du Bois, an 1885 graduate of Fisk, wrote about the influence of the social

gospel-inspired instruction and curriculum during his tenure as an undergraduate. It was clear that administrators and faculty affected the way he
viewed science in general, and sociology specifically, as a tool to be wielded
for the improvement of society. Du Bois acknowledged that school officials
"developed in me, and I am sure the majority of my fellow students, the
idea of the Negro problem as being an evangel, a gospel where chosen men
were trained and armed, and went out to take the leadership of the mass."[7]

Evidence of the school's embrace of a social gospel-based sociology
curriculum is partially ascertained by the fact it was housed in theology-
based colleges and departments. Moreover, the school's commitment to
the social gospel and its relationship to objective sociological instruction
and inquiry was clearly articulated in the 1895 catalog, where the course
description listed sociology as a sub-discipline of Pastoral Theology. The
teaching of sociology at Fisk was clearly aligned with the tenets of the
social gospel, since "the relation of the ministry to the social problems
of our times is made a subject of the lectures. The aim is to improve the
facilities for study and original work in this line."[8] Clearly, not only did
Fisk promote the social gospel-grounded instruction of sociology, there
was a push from the school's leadership to expand the area by combin-
ing the spirit of the movement with a young sub-area of the discipline,
applied sociology.

George Edmund Haynes and Applied Sociology

The first standalone sociology course at Fisk appeared in 1900. The course,
titled Sociology, was a requirement for students majoring in Classics and
Latin. The university's commitment to sociology was evidenced not only
by its first course in sociology, but also by the hiring of its first instructor of sociology, Herbert Adolphus Miller, who was a recent graduate of
Dartmouth College. Dartmouth and some of its Ivy League peers were
known for employing faculty and producing graduates dedicated to promoting and practicing the tenets of the social gospel. While a student at
Dartmouth Miller was exposed to and influenced by instructors promoting

the social gospel; it is possible that he carried a commitment to this philosophy to Nashville. However, while one cannot definitively determine the impact of the social gospel on Miller, it is clear, at least early in his career, that he was also influenced by the scientific racism theories of the era.

Just as important to Miller's intellectual development as the tenets of the social gospel was a sociology course led by Dartmouth professor, David Collins Wells. In this course, Miller was taught, via the book *Ethnology* by Augustus H. Keane, the belief that racial hierarchies existed and were determined by biological and intellectual characteristics of specific groups. Apparently Miller accepted this idea. After leaving Dartmouth, armed with scientific theories of the biological and intellectual inferiority of Blacks, Miller accepted a position at Fisk, where he was assigned to teach Greek and athletics. It is quite possible that prior to arriving at Fisk Miller had little to no substantive contact with Black Americans. This seems likely because while Miller was at Fisk, seemingly benefitting from the sociological concept of social distance, he learned that his undergraduate training on racial hierarchies and the inherent inferiority of Blacks was incorrect. His brief tenure at Fisk provided a corrective lens through which Miller came to better understand issues of race. Indeed, he learned he was the victim of racial mis-education at the Ivy League institution. Miller's tenure in Nashville lasted only three years, as he left to enter graduate school at Harvard. After completing graduate work, he went on to have a distinguished career in academia, but he never returned to Fisk. However, his hiring as the first instructor of sociology and the school's establishment of the first standalone sociology course signaled its commitment to the discipline and its liberating potential.

In 1909 George Gates was selected to serve as president of Fisk. The hiring of Gates was an important moment for the school's promising sociology program because of his commitment to the discipline. Although one cannot say it was a determinative factor in him getting the job, the fact that Gates's embrace of sociology mirrored the school's prioritization of the discipline up to this point is noteworthy. Prior to Gates's hiring Fisk offered three programs from which students could obtain the baccalaureate degree: Classics, Scientific Course, and Education. A history of Fisk notes that "Gates added sociology, a subject that came to receive much emphasis in black schools and one for which Fisk became internationally known."[9] The school's commitment to expanding the potentially emancipatory discipline continued into the second decade of the twentieth century with the hiring of George Edmund Haynes. Fisk's ascension to national prominence began with this important hire.

George Edmund Haynes was no stranger to Fisk. He took his B.A. from Fisk in 1902 when the school was affirming and strengthening its commitment to the instruction of sociology. After taking an M.A. from Yale in 1904, he later co-founded and served as the first executive director of the National Urban League (NUL). NUL, similar to the National Association for the Advancement of Colored People (NAACP), is a civil rights organization dedicated to improving the lives of Blacks in America. Departing from the NAACP, NUL's focus was principally, but not exclusively, on the condition of city folk. The organization's emphasis on urban issues mirrored Haynes's desire to engage in direct action to address city concerns. Haynes's vision for accomplishing this task included the establishment of an educational and research component within NUL that connected the theoretical and academic understandings of societal problems with the real-world needs of urban residents.

That Haynes was spearheading this effort while simultaneously completing the requirements for the Ph.D., which he took in 1912, was evidence of his drive and determination. It should be noted that Haynes's idea to engage in what we now call applied sociology was encouraged by an instructor during his doctoral years. Haynes's professor at Columbia University, Edward T. Devine, understood the young scholar's desire to make a tangible impact on the increasingly urbanized American society and encouraged him to combine his plan for training social workers, or applied sociologists, with academic research. Thus, when approached by Fisk to establish a social science department and training center for social workers, Haynes eagerly accepted the offer because it provided an excellent opportunity to implement his program of applied sociology.

Haynes's plan to develop an applied sociology program was captured in the writings of Fisk faculty member and early Black sociologist Preston Valien. According to Valien, "The primary aim of Dr. Haynes, in developing the department, was to formulate a plan of work which would bring the education of the students closer to the needs of the community."[10] The 1910–1911 university catalog clearly articulated the institution's commitment to applied sociology and why, vicariously, the institution's leadership sought out Haynes to lead the program.

> The study of sociology and the scientific approach to social problems is now established as a part of the college curriculum and Fisk is making every effort to keep abreast of this development. Especially is there need for thorough training in scientific methods of study of social problems and the development of the spirit of social service among Negro college youth.[11]

Looking to distance itself from social science uplift efforts at Hampton Institute and Tuskegee Institute along the lines of industry and agriculture, respectively, Fisk officials argued that

> the growing urban concentration of Negroes demands special study and the development of methods of social betterment to meet the problems attendant upon the increasing complexity of their life and conditions in cities, North and South. This urban situation can best be met by college Negroes who have had training in the social sciences and in practical methods of social work.[12]

Few institutions were better suited at this time than Fisk to engage in the expressed applied, or practical, sociology articulated by the school. The school's engagement in this brand of sociology included courses directly addressing issues of concern for city residents.

The courses offered at Fisk during this period were immediately applicable to urban life and included the titles Advanced Economics, Economics & Labor Relations, Elementary Economics, History of the Negro in America, Industrial History & Organization, The Negro Problem, Social Problems, and Sociology. In the Social Problems course students learned sociological theory during the first part of the semester then engaged in fieldwork in Nashville's Black community the second half of the semester. Since the requirements for this course included training in theory, research methods, and the application of the two in a fieldwork setting, Haynes very quickly realized the need to separate all three components from one course and develop specific courses for each. Essentially, Haynes was expanding the curriculum of his applied sociology program. Thus, "in order to facilitate the comprehension of material and information, Haynes, within five years [of his hiring], had replaced the Sociology and Social Problems course[s] with four separate courses: (1) Principles of Sociology, (2) Playground and Recreation, (3) Practical Sociology, and (4) Statistics and Methods of Social Research."[13]

Although Haynes was a faculty member at Fisk, he did not relinquish his leadership role in NUL. In fact, he continued to serve as the organization's executive director. Because of his dual positions he was able to connect the civic uplift ideals of NUL with the research training offered at Fisk. The result was the establishment of a NUL Fellowship Program at Fisk. This relationship provided non-Fisk student participants the opportunity to earn a certificate in social work training. In addition to taking the courses listed above, participants in the social work, or applied sociology, training program were required to complete fieldwork.

> The field experience required seniors to work in the field four hours per week for a thirty week period. Six additional hours were to be spent in the study of methods of statistics and social investigation, totaling ten hours per week for field involvement.... The field instruction program, was similar in content to other pioneering schools of social work in New York, Chicago and Boston.[14]

Participants in the NUL Fellowship Program were not required to work for the organization nor were other excessive demands placed upon them. After completing the program participants were only required to work for a social work agency at the location of their choice for one year. Prior to completing the program, however, each participant was required to engage in fieldwork at an approved local site. The fieldwork location where a good number of students employed their sociological training was Bethlehem House.

Bethlehem House

Prior to Haynes's hiring Fisk was committed to directing its faculty and student resources toward activities aimed at improving the social conditions of Black Americans in Nashville. The school's 1910–1911 catalog affirmed this commitment in its description of the mission of the department of social sciences.

> The time has come for the Negro college to become closely articulated with the community in which it is located. The further aim is to bring the University in closer relation with the conditions among colored people in Nashville and to seek the cooperation of other Negro colleges in developing this much needed phase of education.[15]

One way Fisk accomplished this mission was through a partnership with a local settlement home, Bethlehem House.

In 1907 Fisk graduate Sallie Hill Sawyer began her efforts to establish a settlement home in Nashville similar to Hull House opened by Jane Addams in Chicago, Illinois. Instead of directing its attentions to the needs of immigrants, Sawyer instead focused her settlement home on providing assistance and opportunities for Black women in Nashville. Her efforts resulted in the establishment of Bethlehem House in 1910. In 1913, Fisk entered into a formal relationship with Bethlehem House. Consistent with the desires of Fisk's founders to actively engage in positive and cooperative relationships with the city's White residents, Bethlehem House exemplified racial cooperation of the highest degree as its board of governance, staff, and volunteers from local colleges included Blacks and Whites.

Bethlehem House was critical in Haynes's applied sociology program because it was "a local settlement house in a Negro slum area . . . where the students could do their practical work in sociology."[16] The practical, or field, work engaged in by Fisk students was outlined in the school's 1914 catalog. In a course titled Social Service Training it was noted that the instruction provided was a

> thorough practical training for those who wish to prepare for service, volunteer or employed, as probation officers, settlement workers, kindergarten directors, executive secretaries of social betterment and civic organizations, institutional church workers, church and charity visitors, home and foreign missionaries and secretaries of religious organizations.[17]

Fisk's partnered training opportunity at Bethlehem House was a one-year program that was open to high school and college students as well as post-graduates. After completing the required social science training courses students received a certificate verifying their expertise in this area and that they were prepared to practice their craft in any number of social welfare settings. The partnership between Fisk and Bethlehem House was successful on many levels. The clearest example of the strength and effectiveness of this partnership occurred three years into their collaboration when Nashville experienced a disaster that put on display the talents of Fisk students via their social science training.

1916 Nashville Fire

In March 1916, according to legend, a young boy was playing with a ball of yarn at his home when, unexpectedly, it caught fire after landing on or near a stove. Unsure of how to put out the fire, he removed the ball and threw it into a nearby vacant lot. The result was a fire that destroyed the homes of over 300 Black and White families over a range of more than thirty blocks. The fire immediately drew the attention of local Tennesseans and those from afar because this area was considered one of the most well-to-do neighborhoods in Nashville. The fire also drew the attention of Haynes, his Fisk colleagues, and students.

While the fire was still raging Haynes and his Fisk colleague Paul Mowbray "'walked out Jefferson Street to the bridge and saw where the fire had been and place where it was then burning.' As they returned to campus, Haynes and Mowbray began an informal survey 'inquiring to the extent of suffering and loss of residents'."[18] Certainly, dismayed at the destruction he was witnessing, it is quite possible that Haynes viewed this tragic event as an opportunity to not only provide assistance to his fellow Nashvillians, but to put into action the training of his cadre of applied sociology students. At the behest of the Nashville Negro Board of Trade, "the accepted voice of black business and professional men in Nashville," Haynes spearheaded a plan of recovery for fire victims.[19]

Haynes received permission from Fisk President McKenzie to allow senior social work students to engage in relief work. Students from Fisk then participated in activities including the establishment of a headquarters the day after the fire to assess the needs of the victims, collecting data on the affected households (e.g., number, age, and condition of residents, etc.), conducting site visits to the temporary residences of victims for needs assessment, and developing plans for resource allocation and distribution. Although Black students from nearby institutions including Meharry Medical College, Roger Williams University, and State Normal School (now called Tennessee State University) participated in the recovery efforts, Haynes and his applied sociology students led the process. The students were so efficient in their assignments that "observers noted that many of the black students and teachers obviously had been trained for 'scientific work'."[20] Ultimately, Haynes and his students were noted as *domestic science experts* for their effective and needed services during the Nashville fire of 1916. It is without question that the response of the Fisk community to the Nashville Fire of 1916 assisted in the readjustment to normal life, as best possible, for the many homeless victims. In many ways this event embodied the importance and utility of the applied sociological training offered by Haynes and Fisk.

Applied Sociology or Social Work

A central theme in this discussion on the early instruction and practice of sociology at Fisk is the idea that it comprised one of the earliest institutionalized programs of applied sociology. It must be stated that no argument is presented here suggesting its status as *the first* such program. Instead, it is simply argued that this program of applied sociology existed during the discipline's formative years in this nation and should be recognized accordingly. An additional matter that deserves clarity is whether Fisk's program was indeed applied sociology or *merely* social work.

I argue that Haynes's program at Fisk was, indeed, an applied sociological effort and not a purely social work endeavor. Social work, as generally understood by today's conventions, is the application of social science theories and concepts to positively impact targeted communities. Sociology, as generally understood today, is employment of the scientific research method to study social phenomena. The point of departure between the two, and my reason for identifying Haynes's work as applied sociology, is that he actively employed sociological tools while engaged in research. When one employs the sociological method to answer a research question, and then uses the findings to affect a targeted group, then one is engaging in applied sociology. So the notion that Haynes and his students were simply engaging in social work and not applied sociology, even if they used the term *social work* themselves, is rejected here. This position is consistent with the social historical narrative on understanding the simultaneous and interwoven development of sociology posited by Patricia Lengermann and Gillian Niebrugge in their essay "Thrice Told: Narratives on Sociology's Relation to Social Work." Lengermann and Niebrugge write:

> The social history narrative treats the relation between sociology and social work as an ongoing social construction, created not by the autonomous development of abstract theoretical systems but out of the actions, relationships, negotiations, and associational inventions of individual, social actors in multiple social settings, of which the academy is only one.[21]

This understanding of the relationship between social work and sociology provides space for a better understanding of Haynes's role in the development of applied sociology in the United States. Added to this are several additional points that should be highlighted.

First, Haynes's academic training is in sociology: he took the doctorate in 1912 at Columbia. One little-known aspect of Haynes's academic training is that he earned his M.A. at Yale, where he took a class under the tutelage of the first person to teach a course on the discipline in this nation, William Graham Sumner. Sumner had quite an impact on Haynes via this class and other interactions. Years later Haynes recounted how Sumner encouraged his students to question all facts presented to them. Haynes said Sumner "taught us to subject any notions to rigorous tests of facts."[22] One manifestation of this charge from Sumner was exemplified in the performance of Haynes and his students after the Nashville fire of 1916 as they collected data and developed plans to address the many needs of the victims.

Second, although sociology was fast becoming a more integral part of university curriculums across the nation, with the exception of a few institutions, its instruction was housed in social science units as opposed to standalone departments. The establishment of social work as a separate discipline with foundational principles is normally noted as occurring in the early 1920s with the establishment of the American Association of Social Workers. As an aside, the American Sociological Association was established in 1905. Since both developing disciplines were generally housed within social science departments during this time it stands to reason there would be some overlap in the practice and understanding of each. In fact, the New York School of Philanthropy, established in 1898 as the first American school of social work, expected its students to engage with both disciplines. This point was made by Iris Carlton-LaNey, who wrote:

> In the early years of the twentieth century, the field of social work and the discipline of sociology were closely intertwined and students studying social work at the New York School of Philanthropy, for

example, were encouraged and expected to study sociology and/or economics at Columbia.[23]

Herbert M. Hunter penned, arguably, the most insightful argument concerning Hayne's sociological practice. In an article wherein an argument
was made for Haynes's status as a clinical sociologist, Hunter wrote:

> All in all, perhaps Haynes' legacy in American sociology should not
> be judged by his scholarly success alone.... He used his sociological
> training and skills to challenge the racial status quo in the United States
> in ways that were compatible with his own convictions. Haynes' career
> was exemplary of an earlier generation of professionally trained sociolo-
> gists who contributed to the discipline by applying their expertise rather
> than simply pursuing academic goals.[24]

Stated another way, Haynes, and countless other early Black sociologists,
were more concerned with engagement in (Black) sociology as a tool to
improve the lives of the masses rather than a venue for abstract pursuits
of theoretical scientific interests. Whether it was called applied sociology
or social work (it is called applied sociology here), the objective of the
scientific endeavor was to make a direct impact on *the least of these*. In so
doing, Haynes and the women and men of the applied sociology program
at Fisk were successful.

Black Sociology "Up South"

The majority of HBCUs are located in the Deep South. This is common-
sensical since the majority of Blacks in America, then and now, live
there and the need for such institutions, based on population density, is
greatest there. There are, however, a number of HBCUs above the Mason
Dixon line and within geographical terrain commonly referred to as *the
North*. This geographical area is referred to here, instead, as *Up South*. Up
South is a transitory region where slavery was eradicated prior to the 13th
Amendment. Despite this feat, the region remained not quite a space where
Blacks were spared denigrations of their humanity that accompanied

the slavery experiences of their Deep South brethren. Nevertheless, the prevailing thought of many Blacks, and some disillusioned Whites, living below the Mason Dixon line was that the social, economic, and physical inconveniences experienced by Up South Blacks were nonexistent at best, and negligible at worst. Contrary to this misnomer, Blacks living Up South in areas such as Delaware, Maryland, West Virginia, and Virginia understood clearly that their experiences bore little difference from their brethren in the Deep South. The degrees of difference in the mistreatment of Black Americans living in the Deep South and Up South were manifest. The bottom line concerning the experiences of both was the common goal to resist efforts to dehumanize Black Americans and place them in a permanent racialized caste system that bore out the scientific racism theories of the day. In many respects, the differences and similarities between the experiences of Black Americans in the Deep South and Up South were evidenced by their embrace and practice of Black sociology as a tool of liberation. However, its practice Up South could be construed as more theoretical than the brand practiced in the Deep South.

When slavery ended, one of the most important goals of the freedmen and freedwomen was the acquisition of an education. Book learning had been denied to enslaved Africans and they viewed its acquisition as an important step toward achieving the American Dream. The emancipation of five million persons created a demand for institutions of higher learning for Blacks in Union as well as formerly Confederate states. Washington, D. C., the nation's capital, embraced the opportunity to establish educational institutions for the freedmen and freedwomen. While geographically situated Up South, Washington was viewed by many postenslavement Black Americans as a place that provided opportunities for gainful employment and a space that was relatively safe from racial violence perpetuated by groups, including lynch mobs. Notwithstanding Atlanta, Washington was the most popular destination for Blacks seeking to transition from rural to urban life during this era. For Black Americans heading Up South, "Washington was the most attractive [place to relocate]. It was a 'promised land' to many freedmen, for it was the Capital of the

Nation—that is, of the North that had set them free."[25] Although the city did not eliminate slavery until 1862, it quickly embraced the idea that access to education was a human right that all citizens should be allowed to pursue. Accordingly, schools for the education of Blacks in America opened as early as 1863.

One school established for the education of Blacks in the Washington metropolitan area was Howard University. The founding of Howard, named after General Oliver Otis Howard of the Freedmen's Bureau, signaled the region's commitment to providing Blacks in America instruction in the liberal arts, as opposed to technical and vocational programs that were established simultaneously at other Up South institutions. The reader is reminded, as discussed previously, that early HBCUs at this time, and by necessity, included college preparatory programs where instruction at varied secondary grade levels was offered, to students ranging from traditional school age to the elderly. Regardless of age, there was a thirst by Blacks to obtain formal schooling, as many believed, incorrectly, it was a cultural capital that would lead to equality and equity in America's new social order. With a commitment to providing an education to whomever entered its doors, Howard's founding administrators were intentional in distinguishing it from other regional and national schools by emphasizing liberal arts rather than industrial training, like its sister institutions Tuskegee Institute and Hampton Institute. One caveat to the school's embrace of a liberal arts curriculum was its deliberate selection of administrators and faculty who would not impede the academic dreams and pursuits of the new freedmen and freedwomen.

Up South Social Gospel

Howard's desire to create and foster an institutional culture without views of Black Americans as inferior was evident through its meticulous selection of administrators and faculty. School officials were intentional in the selection of persons to work at the institution and, in some respects, developed a checklist for ideal candidates. In order to join the administration or faculty at Howard, "Every officer of the school had to be first a 'member of some Evangelical Church,' then subscribe to 'Republican-Protestantism,' and finally have a 'liberal education'."[26] The first criterion for joining the staff at Howard, similar to Fisk, was that applicants must adhere to a religious perspective that was influenced, in some manner, by the social gospel. The second criterion indicated school's administrators were looking for faculty attuned to the political sensibilities of the day of Black Americans that were favorable toward the Republican Party. Thus, support for the platform of the Republican Party that mandated Blacks in America, in word and deed, be treated no differently than Whites was a requirement. Another criterion was that the ideal Howard employee must wholeheartedly embrace instruction in the liberal arts in an era where Booker T. Washington's influence on White policymakers and his commitment to industrial education were formidable. Additionally, the final, commonsensical, vetting criteria mandated that one possess some type of liberal arts training as a minimum requirement for employment. As outlined in the following section, although a liberal arts education was required to gain employment at Howard, in the school's early years one's teaching assignment often had little relationship to their area of expertise given school officials' unwillingness to hire qualified candidates if they did not meet all the criteria identified above.

Similar to Atlanta University's promotion of the agency of Black Americans and a curriculum scrubbed of demeaning "scientific" accounts of its students, it was noteworthy that officials at Howard actively and intentionally created an environment conducive for the success of its students. In fact, school officials expected their students to assume positions of leadership and influence after graduation. This environment, again similar to Atlanta University, was led by the early White founders and supporters of the school. Howard University's first Black president Mordecai Johnson said during his inauguration speech in 1927:

> There has been a decided increase in the number of Negro scholars gathered on the several faculties, it being the purpose of the original white founders of the university to not merely train Negro men and

> women for practical life, but to train educational leaders who participate
> with them on a basis of uncondescending equality in the whole enter-
> prise of Negro education.[27]

It is equally noteworthy that the school's emphasis on the personal characteristics of the persons it employed directly impacted the quality of
education dispensed during its early years, for good and bad. Because of
the school's commitment to employing persons sympathetic to causes of
concern to and the uplift of Blacks in America its early years were replete
with teacher-subject area mismatches. The consequence was that a number
of faculty were assigned to teach classes outside their area of specialty.
According to Walter Dyson, "Special fitness for a position was considered
of little importance by the applicant [and the institution]."[28] Between 1867
and 1872 Howard allowed the mismatch of teacher and subject area so
long as the persons were committed to the principles articulated above.
In 1872, however, the institution recognized this disservice to its students
and mandated that faculty only be assigned to offer instruction in courses
within their area of specialty.

The Nation's University

Howard University is a unique educational institution for a number of
reasons. First, as of 2020, it is the only HBCU to offer the doctorate in
sociology in the United States. Also, Howard is unique because it is the
only American institution to receive annual Congressional appropriations.
The school's fiscal relationship with the federal government started upon
its founding. From its establishment in 1867 until 1872 the school received
funding via the U.S. Bureau of Refugees, Freedmen, and Abandoned Lands
(otherwise known as the Freedmen's Bureau). This source of funding,
however, was shortlived. After Democrats gained control of the federal
government, the Reconstruction Era effectively ended and Howard's
principal source of funding was eliminated. As a consequence, between
1872 and 1880 Howard, like most institutions, relied on tuition and philanthropic gifts from individuals and institutions including churches to pay

its expenses. The monies garnered from organizations such as churches and various social advancement clubs was not enough to adequately compensate for the amount lost due to the termination of funding via the Freedmen's Bureau. Howard officials, nevertheless, persisted in their efforts to, again, secure funding from the federal government to operate the school.

Under the administration of President William Patton, the institution experienced "the dark age in the history of the university" as the poor fiscal condition of Howard lasted "seven lean years."[29] Determined to improve the fiscal state of the institution, President Patton directed the bulk of his attention toward securing annual funding from the federal government. Two years after becoming president Patton successfully secured his first federal appropriation. The $10,000 guarantee, while much needed, was not enough to meet its many financial obligations and there was no guarantee of annual funding from the federal government. Funding from the federal government did not become an annual line item from Congress until the administration of President Mordecai Johnson.

By the time Johnson was installed as the school's president in 1926, its appropriation had increased to $200,000. Moreover, due to the vigorous efforts of two Congressional representatives, Louis C. Cramton (Michigan) and Daniel A. Reed (New York), Howard's appropriation from the Department of Treasury became an annual line item starting in 1928. Although it was not the intent of Congress to serve as a substantive and permanent financier of the institution, since 1879 its fiscal assistance has helped the school in its efforts, as outlined by school president Wilbur P. Thirkield, "to serve the urban Negro as Tuskegee was developed to serve the rural class."[30] With a permanent annual appropriation now allotted to Howard, the school became and continues to be the only federalized post-secondary institution in the nation. Fred J. Kelly articulated the significance of the fact that the Washington-based school is the United State's only *national* university:

> Howard is in fact a national university. Indeed, Howard is the only national university. Howard receives generous appropriations from the

Treasury of the United States, not as a District of Columbia institution, but as a federal government institution.[31]

With an annual appropriation secured from the federal government of the United States, it is not a stretch to suggest that school administrators and faculty may have been sensitive to this fact and, in certain instance, chose to self-censor or play the role of centrist in the politics of the day. Zachary Williams believes this to be the case, as he suggests, "Federal appropriations had a mixed impact on the scholarly development of the Howard intellectual community. Johnson, despite his dedicated strong-arm control of the institution, worked to balance both academic freedom and adherence to mandates set forward by the federal government in its allocation stipulations."[32] It would be naïve to believe that a Black institution would not consider the ramifications of engaging in works counter to the accepted norms of people upon whom one's financial dependence is predicated. This conundrum would only seem to become more dire during the waning years of Jim Crow, when the school found itself positioned between the United States Congress and its faculty and students, who desired more direct and substantive scholarship and agitation on issues like race. Continuing with Williams:

Muse highlighted the manner in which Howard "benefitted from federal Legislation" and examined whether racial, political or economic factors, or a combination thereof, determined the scope and dynamics of the institutional relationship between Howard and the federal government, and, by extension, the degree to which the federal government supported or impeded the development of black private education at Howard.[33]

It is clear that school officials were aware they should give some consideration to how the actions of members of its community could impact its bottom line. The question that lingers for me, and to which there is probably no determinative answer, is how this Catch-22 was internalized by the leader of the department of sociology.

While his intention was not known, one can surmise that the founder of the school's department of sociology was an astute tactician who was acutely aware of the political implications of matters regarding race and politics at the dawn of the twentieth century and that may have impacted the direction of the unit. Moreover, it is possible that he symbolized the school's precarious placement between the worlds of politics and education, similar to the University of Kansas during its effort to name its social science department, but with respect to sociology and politics.

Howard Sociology

Kelly Miller is one of the most unheralded early sociologists in the history of this nation. While he did not produce a massive number of scholarly products, his impact on the discipline can be measured in other ways. First, he provided leadership facilitating the establishment of Howard University's Department of Sociology while laying the foundation for what remains to this day, unfortunately, the only HBCU offering the doctorate in the discipline. Second, during periods of intellectual disagreement between early Black sociologists on divisive issues he was a moderating figure respected by all parties and astutely adept at conflict resolution. Here a brief overview of his life will be followed by an examination of his impact on the discipline.

Kelly Miller was born in South Carolina in 1862 and eventually ventured to Washington, D. C., to pursue an undergraduate education. In 1886, he received his B.A. from Howard University. Between 1887 and 1889 Miller broke ground as he became the first Black student admitted to Johns Hopkins University, where he majored in mathematics. Miller's tenure at Johns Hopkins lasted only two years, as he was compelled to leave school because of an offer of full-time employment at a nearby university. Miller left Baltimore without a graduate degree to accept an appointment to become a professor of mathematics at his alma mater, Howard.

Miller did not intend to develop a sociology program upon his hiring, but it is evident that he observed from colleagues around the nation how the new science could be used as a tool to not only investigate the social problems experienced by Blacks in America but to develop solutions to said problems. It was probably for these reasons that "in 1895 he recommended that sociology be added as an elective to the college curriculum."[34] It was also in 1895 that his title expanded from professor of mathematics to professor of mathematics and sociology. Miller served as a faculty member at Howard from 1890 to 1934, with the bulk of that time as a member of the department of sociology and with several stints in administrative positions at the university. In his roles both as Dean of the College of Arts and Sciences and department chairperson, Miller oversaw and/or participated in the establishment and development of sociology. According to Charles Jarmon:

> Sociology began at Howard University as a series of lectures in 1895 [led by Kelly Miller]. By 1903, although there is no department of sociology listed in the school's catalog, it does indicate the instruction of an elective sociology course for seniors in the college of arts and sciences. In this two-semester course students were required to read *Study of Society* by Albion Small and George Vincent and *Outline of Practical Sociology* by Carroll Wright. By 1913 the department of sociology at Howard offered two courses, Theories of Social Progress and Practical Social Questions, where "emphasis is placed upon present day social problems."[35]

The department's expansion over the next few years included growing the curriculum and using textbooks such as *An Introduction to the Study of Social Evolution* by F. Stuart Chaplin and *Principles of Sociology* by Franklin Giddings. Through each period of the program's development Kelly Miller was the one constant. It is hard to imagine anyone having a larger role in establishing and molding a department where they worked for more than forty years. His contributions to and impact on the discipline, however, extended beyond his institutional achievements. Accordingly, it is important to discuss Miller's status within the discipline.

Kelly Miller: Overfed on Optimism?

Kelly Miller has been described by the majority of his biographers as a "marginal man" who never planted himself firmly into any particular social group or position nor lent his voice decidedly to the major issues of the day. On matters of race, it has been argued that he did not establish firm relationships with Whites, given the mores of the era mandating nearly complete racial segregation, even Up South. His relationships were also fragile among non-White professional colleagues. His relationships with Blacks were tenuous because of his perceived middle-of-the-road, or middleman, posture on the major issues of the day. Moreover, that he often took unpopular or contrarian positions on matters of race when he did take a stance further complicated interactions with his Black peers. It can be argued that Miller's middle-of-the-road or nuanced stances were reflective of the position his institution was placed in. It is not a stretch to suggest that Howard University, because of its dependence on the federal government for needed financial assistance, encouraged or expected members of its university community to assume nuanced or neutered positions on sensitive matters that, if viewed negatively by members of Congress already predisposed to be unsympathetic to Black Americans, could cause irreparable harm to the school's bottom line if they acted in ways deemed disagreeable. I propose that Miller's moderate and nuanced leadership style, consistent with the precarious situation of the institution, indirectly affected his position on political and racial matters. Let us look at two examples.

The first example of Miller's nuanced leadership style is the role he played in the infamous ideological sparring between Booker T. Washington and W. E. B. Du Bois over the most appropriate type of educational pursuit for Blacks post-slavery. During this debate Miller planted himself firmly in the middle. He recognized Washington's status as the leading Black American political voice of the day and agreed with his position that the path to economic security and independence for Blacks in America was best achieved through rural efforts. Simultaneously, Miller greatly respected Du Bois's scholarship and activism and, as an administrator at a liberal arts college, understood the value of such programming and his institution's dedication to the social sciences. Despite showing more favor to Washington's educational philosophy than Du Bois's, Miller was harshly criticized by the Wizard of Tuskegee as he became increasingly frustrated by the Howard professor's lack of intellectual extremism. Washington once lamented, "[Miller] is mushy and cannot be depended upon for a straight out fight."[36] Instead, Miller sought to find common ground between Washington and Du Bois in the hopes the two giants of Black American life could form an alliance to collectively address the ills facing Blacks in America. It is possible that Miller could have taken a stronger stance in defense of Du Bois and in favor of the liberal arts. Such a stance, taken by, arguably, a representative of the most well-resourced HBCU of the era, may have placed Howard sociology in a position where the mission of the institution would have been more clearly aligned with the department, such that it could become a leader in the production of liberal arts research and scholarship just as Atlanta University had been. This may have put the school at odds with Congress, however.

Toward the end of his academic career Miller took a stance that distanced him from the majority of Blacks in America. The killing of innocent Blacks was well documented and at the turn of the twentieth century was one of the principal causes of death for the freedmen. One of the few attempts by Congress to address lynching was the Robert F. Wagner–Edward P. Costigan anti-lynching bill. A key component of this bill was the inclusion of penalties for sheriffs who failed to prevent inmates from being removed from jail and who were subsequently hanged. While no single piece of legislation could bring a complete end to the unjust killing of Blacks in America by lynching overnight, an argument can be made that any movement in that direction should be viewed favorably. Miller opposed the anti-lynching bill. His opposition was grounded in his contention that the bill would not completely protect the lives of Blacks in America. Any penalty coming from the federal government, according to Miller, would occur after the death of the more than likely innocent person. Moreover, the possibility that an all-White jury would produce a guilty verdict, he believed, was virtually zero. Thus, if there were no guaranteed protections, believed the Howard professor, then other solutions and legislation should be crafted.

One can surmise that Miller believed Blacks should be self-reliant when confronting violence against them by engaging in direct resistance against Whites. This, presumably, included the use of firearms. While this philosophy could be openly and brazenly espoused from the position enjoyed by a Black American living Up South, the outcome of Miller's recommendation would most assuredly lead to higher numbers of Blacks in the Deep South being killed if they were to embrace his idea. This was a missed opportunity for Miller to employ the resources at Howard pro-actively to challenge the abhorrent practice of lynching. With Howard uniquely situated as the nation's university, who else was better posi-tioned to engage in research and present it to Congress? Conversely, it is quite possible that the school's precarious fiscal dependence on Congress was reason enough to not engage in any forms of research that would endanger their bottom line. It is for these reasons that Miller and Howard, despite having more resources than the average HBCU, often occupied the "marginal man" space. Although Miller often took the middle ground on controversial positions, there is evidence that he used his platform as pro-fessor to develop a cadre of students to engage in social agitation.

Under Miller's leadership the department of sociology at Howard was never at the forefront of radical sociological protest of the atrocities confronting Black American life, unlike the leadership at Atlanta. One can surmise that Miller's personal posture of nuanced leadership contributed to the unit's muted impact on the discipline in the early twentieth century. It is also possible that he viewed his role differently than other early Black sociologists. Instead of being the leader of scholarly campaigns challeng-ing scientific racism, discrimination, and inequality, maybe Miller viewed his role as that of a facilitator. That is, he provided the necessary training and skills to his students so they could positively impact the world. W. D. Wright promoted this position when he argued that Miller's contribution to the radical cause of Black American liberation was twofold.[37] First, according to Wright, it is possible that Miller influenced the discipline through the instruction of Black students who then communicated the language and techniques of the liberating possibilities of sociology to their rural and city-dwelling brethren. Second, Miller's impact may have come by direct contact from and interaction with his students in their respective communities on the need for them to employ the sociological method and engage in direct activities to improve the social, economic, and physical condition of their people. Both types of impact emphasize the utility of universities as centers of deliberative conversations that lead to the development of strategies to improve the condition of the race.

Kelly Miller was not a prototypical sociologist whose impact can be measured by the quantity of his scholarly publications. Instead, Miller is best understood as "a strong intellectual presence . . . [who] proposed the idea of a National Negro Library and Museum at Howard . . . [and] functioned as a very visible public intellectual and debated the likes of V. F. Calverton, the socialist scholar and magazine editor. He also wrote a long-running daily column for the *Baltimore Afro-American*. Miller tried unsuccessfully to connect all black organizations under one umbrella movement he termed the *Negro Sanhedrin Movement*."[38] In many respects Miller is more accurately framed as a public sociologist whose contributions to the discipline may be considered greater than that of other early scholars if he is judged on the reach of his public engagements rather than the number of papers published and their contemporary relevance. This framing is important insomuch as it doesn't rank-order early Black sociologists based on the volume of works produced as much as it does on one's impact on the field—which includes laying the foundation for the first and only doctoral program in sociology at an HBCU.

Perhaps his greatest impact on the discipline, as suggested earlier, is his role in establishing the foundation that led to the creation of the doctoral program. More specifically, it can be argued that Miller's contribution also included the school's implementation of a positivistic focused curriculum whereby his skills as a mathematician could be combined with the emerging discipline to form a department grounded on quantitative applications of the science with specific regard to race. This idea is proposed by Morgan State College (now University) president D. O. W. Holmes in his eulogy for Miller.

> He was at first a teacher of mathematics and as such was very exacting. Those of us who were interested and followed him far enough realized that he could have been one of the greatest mathematicians of his day [had] he been willing to confine himself to the ivory tower of pure scholarship. But he saw early in his career that the greatest need at that time in Howard University and in all colleges for Negroes was the awakening of the students to a realization of the problems of the race and an interest in their solution. To this end, there being no sociology in the curriculum, he skillfully mixed, in their classes, a study of race problems with mathematical problems in such a way that when a course was completed all the students were keenly conscious of the American social situation.[39]

When examining Howard's inclusion into the Big Four of Black sociology one must be mindful not to whittle down the significance of a unit to its number of scholarly products. Instead, a more holistic understanding of its significance should be embraced and include the financial and fiscal resources procured to support a unit dedicated to the principles of Black sociology.

Kelly Miller is an important figure because of his establishment and stewardship of the department of sociology at Howard University. It is worth questioning, however, if the development of a more impactful program of Black sociology was squandered under his tenure. If he were not a marginal but more forceful figure could the department have produced scholarship leading to the faster demise of American Jim Crow, lynching, and any other number of inequalities facing Blacks in America? When viewed alternatively, it is possible that the school's status as the nation's only federally funded institution served as a hindrance to a more progressive scientific agenda. One must not forget that the school did not begin receiving funds annually until 1929, roughly five years before Miller's retirement. It is quite possible that the school's financial well-being may have been compromised if a program of research and racial agitation, such as that practiced by Du Bois in Atlanta, been attempted at an institution that was desperately seeking funding from the federal government. What's more, had Miller attempted to engage in such controversial research toward the end of his career it is reasonable to ask if the school's acquisition of top Black American scholarly talent across disciplines on campus would have been unwittingly compromised.

All things considered, it is possible that Miller's moderate posture made it difficult for him to truly promote a progressive vision that squared with the mission of the university as it delicately balanced its research products against federal financial assistance. Moreover, because of his perceived lack of consistency, it is possible that faculty may have balked at their boss's stance on institutional questions concerning their potentially radical racial research. Such vulnerability and unawareness may have encouraged some to err on the side of caution. August Meier appears to sum up the problematic nature of his leadership style and its impact on those around him when he wrote:

> Miller had a pragmatically shifting emphasis when he felt it wise. A "straddler," he had withstood criticism from both sides and moved along with the main trends in Negro thought, from verging on calculated conciliation of the white South in 1889–1899, to a new militance a dozen or so years later.[40]

While Miller's straddling could be construed as problematic, again, an argument can be made that he, as did Booker T. Washington, was simply navigating as best he could the political climate that allowed the most progress to be gained within what they viewed as a limited menu of choices.

Summary

After the demise of the W. E. B. Du Bois-led Atlanta Sociological Laboratory, the state of sociological instruction and practice at HBCUs was not distinguishable from that practiced at most HWCUs. Records from the era indicate that amount of time allocated to the instruction of sociology at HBCUs exceeded that at HWCUs. Although the demise of the Atlanta Sociological Laboratory was a significant blow to Black sociology, the void left by Du Bois's school was filled via the work of Monroe N. Work at Tuskegee, the applied sociological efforts of George E. Haynes at Fisk

University, and leadership provided by Kelly Miller at Howard. The stage
was now set for the greatest era of Black sociology to emerge, thanks to
the foundations established at the Big Four: Atlanta, Tuskegee, Fisk, and
Howard. The period, roughly speaking, from 1930 to 1960 is described in
the following chapter as the Golden Age of Black Sociology. It was in this
period that the foundations established at these institutions bear substantive scholarly fruit as the first major era of the production of Black
sociologists emerged.

CHAPTER 5

The Golden Age of Black Sociology

Black sociology experienced a golden age from 1930 to 1960. This period is labeled such because it comprised the apex of sociological practice, instruction, and leadership at HBCUs. The array of talented Black sociologists working at HBCUs at this time was undeniable and a good number of them made lasting impacts on the discipline. During this period the impact of Black sociologists at HBCUs on the discipline extended beyond their segregated workplaces, as a number of them garnered recognition from White colleagues and organizations for their scholarly contributions. Simultaneously, Black sociologists began to assimilate into formerly homogenous professional sociology organizations and spaces. Foremost among Black sociologists and HBCUs making such an impact on the discipline were Charles S. Johnson at Fisk and E. Franklin Frazier at Howard, the primary leaders of Black sociological thought during the Golden Age.

The Race Relations Department at Fisk University

After George Edmund Haynes's departure in 1918 the sociology program at Fisk was no longer one of the nation's leaders in applied sociological inquiry. The program and curriculum that Haynes so deftly guided continued to exist, but its products were decidedly less influential. In many respects the unit devolved into a typical sociology program with a primary focus on classroom instruction until 1926. In that year Fisk hired Thomas Elsa Jones as president. Having taken the Ph.D. in sociology the same year,

Jones became the youngest college president in the nation. After less than one year on the job, Jones conceived of a plan to increase the profile of the school's sociology program.

In a letter to Eugene Kinckle Jones of the National Urban League requesting to hire Charles S. Johnson away from the civil rights organization, President Jones wrote, "As you have doubtless heard, Fisk is establishing a department of social science which should be able to render very important service to the Negro race and to America in general."[1] It is clear that President Jones's desire was for his degree home to play a prominent role in addressing issues concerning race and racism. The school's 1928 catalog reflected this vision:

> The specific aims of the department are to effect a productive working relationship between teaching and research activities in the social science field; to stimulate and support research projects which offer promise of contributing to the store of useful knowledge in the social sciences, to provide a field of training for students in active social practices; to seek out and to encourage productive scholarship; to assist, thru its inductive handling of social materials, in converting social theories into a basis for social action. The interests of the department are thus related to the community.[2]

This passage suggests that the department was again committed to engagement with applied sociology. In order for the unit to reach its highest potential President Jones doggedly pursued Johnson to spearhead this effort because he believed the young scholar to be the most qualified and capable person to help him accomplish his goal. President Jones was so impressed by the scholarly potential and skill set of his primary target that he declared, "I have been searching the field for months and find no one who can take Mr. Johnson's place."[3] The immediate prospect of hiring Johnson away from NUL was bleak, as neither the organization nor Johnson were overly excited about the opportunity. Within a few months, however, Johnson had a change of heart. In the spring of 1928, he accepted the offer to join Fisk and began his appointment that fall.

When Johnson arrived to Fisk he made an immediate impact with the establishment of a graduate program in sociology. The focus of the program, in addition to imparting sociological knowledge and skill, was engagement with the Black American community that would lead to its social, economic, or physical improvement. Similar to the community-based participatory research posture of today, Fisk faculty and graduate students did not enter Black communities intent on dictating to residents what their major problems were or *telling them* how best to solve those problems. Instead, they conducted surveys of communities to learn directly from residents what the major issues affecting them were, and then worked collaboratively to study the problem and develop requisite policy proposals. For many graduate students the survey served dual purposes. "The graduate theses not only fulfilled the requirements for graduation but the materials covered have, in many instances, served as basic data in planning for the improvement of the conditions of social and economic life of Negroes in Nashville."[4] In one respect, President Jones achieved his goal of establishing a unit to engage in the application of sociological knowledge to real-world conditions. However, in the midst of Jim Crow segregation and violence toward Blacks in America, particularly in the Deep South, there emerged a need for the development of another type of applied sociology program, with respect to race relations.

Race Relations Department

During the early 1940s World War II was nearing its end. While Black men in America were denied combat service to their nation in World War I, World War II presented an opportunity for the nation's supposed second-class citizens to not only participate but demonstrate their intellectual acuity, physical stamina, and overall bravery. Many Black men believed their willingness to shed blood in defense of their country would result in improved relations between the races upon their return. Sadly, this did not occur. All too often Black servicemen with the audacity to flaunt their equal-ness in the presence of White Americans by publicly wearing their military uniforms were beaten and, in many cases, killed. That they placed their lives on the line for American values and the idea of freedom was meaningless to throngs of racist White Americans who believed them to be at that time and forever more, *"nothing but a nigger!"* These servicemen were only experiencing the racial climate their fellow Black American peers faced in their absence. Around the nation relations between Blacks and Whites were antagonistic but there were some individuals and organizations committed to improving that relationship. The American Missionary Association and Fisk University were two entities that attempted to alleviate tensions between the races via the school's applied sociology program.[5]

Members of the American Missionary Association (AMA) were crucial participants in the establishment of Fisk University in 1866. Nearly eighty years later AMA maintained a relationship with the school and agreed to collaborate with it to address race relations in the United States. It is certain that AMA was aware of the school's applied sociological efforts and believed, as the school's most famous alumni W. E. B. Du Bois once did, that increases in educational levels and contact among *the better classes* of Blacks and Whites would result in improved relations. Moreover, both entities may have been aware of a glaring void in academic scholarship in this topical area that could lead to the development of social policy. In a ten-year retrospective account of the Race Relations Department, Herman Long proposed that social science in general, and sociology specifically, had failed to develop an applied study of race relations.

> Although there had developed a body of knowledge in the field of social sciences which had given valuable insights as to the dimensions of the problems with which we were to deal, and as to the nature of the populations involved in them, *there had been practically no effort to shape this body of knowledge and information into the definite structure of an agency program* (emphasis mine).[6]

Yes, sociologists of the era were conducting studies on race. However, Long argued there existed, for example, no Hull House program for race relations in the nation. To fill this void, "it became the task of the Race

Relations Department [at Fisk University] to discover a way of rendering services to the communities in need of them, and making a dent in the armor of segregation and discrimination, long established in countless social practices as ways of meeting the racial problem."[7]

Charles S. Johnson led the Race Relations Department and was an important figure in the discipline for a number of reasons. However, it is important to note two points here. One, the intended goal of this section is not to focus on the singular and well-documented scholarly achievements of Johnson as a superstar sociologist. Other such efforts are found in the voluminous number of writings on Johnson. Second, the goal of this section is, similar to the discussion on the Atlanta Sociological Laboratory, to highlight the collective efforts of Black sociologists at an HBCU who made substantive impacts on the discipline and in their respective communities, but who are not well known or who are completely unknown. That said, because of the absence of full lists of participants, not every person who contributed to the Race Relations Department, whether faculty, undergraduate, graduate student, or citizen researcher, can be identified. Instead, a short account of Black sociologists and nonsociologists who contributed to the department's works at Fisk during Johnson's early years are noted. This list reads like a who's who of top scholars in their respective fields, and includes Horace R. Cayton, Bertram W. Doyle, John Hope Franklin, Horace Mann Bond, E. Franklin Frazier, James Weldon Johnson, and Mark Hanna Watkins. The activities of the department demonstrate the school's commitment to a Black sociology agenda, as the impact of the Race Relations Department extended far beyond Nashville and into communities from coast to coast in areas such as community studies, education, and public policy.

Community Studies

A primary objective of the Race Relations Department (RRD) was to "represent grass-roots action whose effects are immediate and direct."[8] It was important to this unit that knowledge connected with action, such that the needs of local residents were met. As indicated previously, members of this unit did not enter Black communities assuming they would dictate to its residents what their problems were and how they would *save* them. Instead, the RRD went to great lengths to not only listen to members of the community but also to develop social bonds. In total, the number of communities impacted by this unit within its first ten years numbered close to thirty. In each community it was important that the RRD accomplish several important tasks. First, engagement with members of the community lasted from one to two years. Instead of parachuting into the field and then helicoptering out after a *car-window sociological study*, these researchers were interested in establishing real and long-term relationships with residents that could prove fruitful for both parties. A second important task for each community study was the accumulation of fact-based data upon which to answer the stated research question. Third, based on the results of the actual study, data were placed into the hands of local community organizations and grassroots activists. This posture was taken for reasons similar to those practiced by Du Bois and the Atlanta Sociological Laboratory. Fisk researchers clearly understood their role was not that of active agitators. Their role was to supply the data needed for community members to improve the social, economic, and physical condition of their community themselves. The last task for the RRD was to "give to the community a set of objectives against which progress can be measured over a long period of time."[9] So, not only did Fisk researchers establish long-term relationships with community members, conduct investigations and translate to community members how to effectively fight for change, they provided the means for residents to measure the effectiveness of the study such that they could hold the powers that be accountable. This is the essence of what we now call community-based participatory research. Below are a few examples of the products of RRD's community studies.

The intensity of these studies ranged from seemingly minor investigations of neighborhoods to life-changing in-depth city-wide studies. For example, the RRD was invited to conduct a community study in Minneapolis. This request was made because White residents noticed an increase in the number of Black Americans moving into the city as a result of the Great Black Migration. This happening caused a degree of *racial hysteria* because some White residents believed the demographic change meant chaos would soon reign and the city would be changed for the worse, forever. Data produced by Fisk researchers allayed the concerns of White residents that companies and jobs would flee the city, that the crime rate would increase and that racial tensions would rise. According to RRD, "it is safe to say that the survey was a major factor in preventing the spread of racial hysteria into open conflict occurring with the immigration of Negroes from the South."[10] Another successful community study, arguably the most successful one conducted by the RRD, also took place in Minneapolis. Residents requested data on housing discrimination grounded in the idea that Blacks and Whites should not live in the same neighborhood because of the possibility the property value of White-owned homes would decrease substantially. Again, the RRD conducted a study and presented data indicating there was a negligible loss of property value for home sellers in integrated neighborhoods. Because of the efforts of Fisk researchers several neighborhoods in Minneapolis were opened to individuals based on their ability to pay the mortgage, not on their race. This particular effort resulted in a national award to city officials for their proactive actions to improve race relations.

Education

The efforts of Fisk social scientists also included engagement in educational programming directed at improving race relations. The school, however, did not seek to duplicate formal attempts at directly confronting inequality in education, as this space was ceded to national organizations with well-funded legal divisions like the NAACP. Instead, the RRD focused its efforts on:

> (1) direct services to schools which were seeking a more full integration of Negro and white students and re-shaping their educational programs to do a more effective job of getting across democratic concepts; and, (2)

to public education, covering the continuous job of training and orient-
ing community leaders in intergroup relations and the preparation and
dissemination of materials designed for mass public education.[11]

Evidence of success for the former objective is found in results procured
from the Michigan cities of Detroit and Ypsilanti, where Fisk faculty
were influential in a range of matters from "the placement of teacher
personnel to the selection of special units of study in the curriculum,
and to a program of orientation of parents and teachers."[12] Although its
direct service to schools was notable, perhaps Fisk and the Race Relations
Department were probably best known for the latter objective.

In 1943 Fisk established the Institute of Race Relations (also called
Race Relations Institute). The Institute hosted yearly meetings where the
best practices in bi-racial cooperation were conceived, tested, and plans
for implementation designed. Drawing on its history as a space where
racial cooperation was important, even if notions of the intellectual and
biological inferiority of Black Americans were disguised by visitors, school
administrators embraced the opportunity to host such an event. Instead of
shrinking at an opportunity to make an impact on American society on such
a sensitive topic, school officials, during the volatile era of White domestic
terrorism against Blacks in America, viewed this as an opportunity to
carve out areas of mutual agreement and possibilities for racial advancement. Toward this end a yearly institute was held and included high-
ranking interracial attendees. According to Long's unpublished history
of the department, "[The Institute] served and continues to serve, as a
meeting ground for practitioners in the field, as a basis of annual evaluation of departments and as a clearing-house of experience tested in day-to-
day activities of communities."[13] The yearly gathering was successful and
by its tenth anniversary was purported to have accommodated over 1,300
community leaders representing more than thirty states. The Institute was
so successful that communities around the nation began holding similar
meetings. These meetings soon took place in cities such as Baltimore,
New Orleans, Richmond, and St. Louis. The lasting impact of the meetings
at Fisk and beyond was described by former director Herman H. Long:

"The value of these city-wide institutes was that they provided a basis of enlightening public opinion on racial issues at a time when the discussion of such issues in the Deep South was frowned upon."[14] While Long, seemingly, downplayed the significance of the institutes, the information disseminated for public consumption regarding race relations was very important.

Another component of the RRD's mission was the dissemination of educational materials to provide accurate data on matters concerning race. In its first five years the department released more than fifteen thousand posters, twenty-five thousand cards, and three thousand five hundred calendars to assist in its efforts to educate Americans about race relations. Perhaps its most effective publications were pamphlets addressing specific race-related issues. One pamphlet, titled *Segregation*, was designed for Black Americans and their allies and identified ways the legalized separation of persons by race could be challenged and eventually eliminated. A companion pamphlet, titled *Integration*, targeted the same audience and focused on strategies other American groups had used to become integrated into the society, as well as suggesting best practices for similar achievements by likeminded collectives. Perhaps the most influential pamphlet during this era was, *If Your Neighbors Are Negroes*. This publication was published four times and more than twenty thousand copies were distributed. The publication included data refuting the notion that the integration of Blacks into White neighborhoods caused irreparable harm to Whites. Department officials argued that the pamphlet:

> was designed primarily to deflate the idea that the presence of Negroes in otherwise white neighborhoods automatically lowered property values, using figures actually taken from a reliable real estate journal showing that frequently quite the opposite occurs.[15]

Most of the activities conducted by the RRD at Fisk were grounded in Black sociology as conceptualized earlier. However, Fisk, more than the other schools discussed, probably maintained the strongest embrace of an important component of Black sociology, the development of social/ public policy.

Members of the Race Relations Department did not believe they should be active promoters of public policy. Instead (and similar to Du Bois's efforts at Atlanta), they viewed their role as objective social scientists who simply presented data to stakeholders who could, if they so decided, use the information to address the social, economic, or physical condition of their community. To this point, the department acknowledged, "Since the department is not a direct lobbying agency, a good portion of initiative in these matters has to be left with organizations which are at the present time free to act."[16] Two specific areas they addressed were segregation in interstate travel and housing discrimination.

Despite the fact that Blacks in America purchased tickets at the same price as Whites for public transportation, both inter and intra-state, during Jim Crow they were confined to segregated seating. Looking to create equality in public transportation, the RRD conducted a study of railroad companies to document the treatment of its Black passengers. The emphasis on interstate travel was a direct challenge to the Interstate Commerce Act that prevented companies from causing *undue burden* to its patrons. That Blacks in America paid the same price for a ticket and were not allowed the freedom of mobility in interstate travel was viewed by the department as an unfair burden for which they should take action.

> Our findings revealed discrimination in the amount of space allotted to Negro passengers, and exclusion from through-train services which were provided exclusively to white passengers; it indicated clear differentials in the quality of seating and coach accommodations provided for Negro passengers; it showed definitely the use of subterfuge in reducing the number and segregating of Negro passengers on reserve seat trains traveling through the South; it revealed a general pattern of rigorous application of racial codes, resulting in forms of violence against Negro passengers, loss of life and incarceration. These findings are now in the hands of the two committees on interstate commerce within the Senate and the House.[17]

Again, it is noted that units engaged in Black sociology understood their role as objective social scientists who placed into the hands of stakeholders the data necessary to address their specific social problem. Although the ban on segregation in interstate travel did not come to fruition until the 1960s, this example is representative of the school's employment of sociology as a tool of liberation for Blacks in America. The impact of the department's research was more immediate in its study on housing discrimination.

The RRD sought to assist the efforts of civil rights organizations to eliminate discrimination in housing. Toward this end, a study of racially restrictive covenants was conducted in Chicago, St. Louis, and Cleveland. Racially restrictive covenants were the means by which non-Whites were prevented from buying homes in certain largely White neighborhoods. The net result of racial covenants was that neighborhoods remained seg-regated. The Fisk study was "designed to discover the extent to which land areas and the various instrumentalities within the community, official and unofficial, were responsible for perpetuating these prac-tices."[18] Researchers discovered, unsurprisingly, that Black Americans were prevented from acquiring property in very large proportions of each city studied. The department produced a book, *People vs. Property*, and Charles H. Houston, noted civil rights lawyer and mentor of the first Black American member of the United States Supreme Court, Thurgood Marshall, used it in his argument before of the nation's highest judicial body challenging racial restrictive covenants.

> The findings of this study became an official document which the Court considered in its hearings of race restrictive covenants cases. When the case was won in the interest of eliminating court sanctions for restrictive agreements, Attorney Charles H. Houston generously sent to our depart-ment a word of congratulation for our part in aiding this victory for dem-ocratic and Christian policy. This was a case of an immediate and a direct impact upon national policy by a practical research project planned by the Race Relations Department, making research an instrument in the hands of lawyers speaking before the tribunal.[19]

The real-world impact of the scholarly efforts of sociologists and social scientists at Fisk were impressive and, unfortunately, continue to not be properly recognized in the discipline of sociology. What tends to occur in this discipline, and the academy at large, is that a single superstar sociologist is identified and given credit for accomplishments made from the sweat and labor of many others. In this section Charles S. Johnson was purposely not singled out as the singular producer of the research products of the Race Relations Department at Fisk University as this was a team effort by the persons listed earlier and others whose names are lost to history. Johnson did effectively lead the department and conduct groundbreaking studies for which he is recognized in the discipline. Also noteworthy is that he became the school's first Black president in 1946. However, sociology at Fisk, as well as the other schools discussed herein, extended beyond the superstar names we are all familiar with and included many persons whose names we will never know but who made contributions to the mission of the school and Black sociology in ways that remain influential.

Is Sociology Safe at HBCUs?

This era is not called the golden age of Black sociology simply because of the tremendous quality and scope of sociological research conducted at Fisk and other leading HBCUs. This era is referenced this way because it also represented a period when the instruction of sociology at HBCUs was comparable to, if not better than, that at HWCUs. This was an astounding accomplishment given the limited resources and challenges to their very existence by many of their fellow White citizens. Evidence of the quality of instruction in sociology at HBCUs was found in the research of a couple of notable scholars.

In 1933, Fisk sociologist Bertram Doyle authored quite possibly the first study examining the quality of instruction of introduction to sociology courses at HBCUs. This study "was undertaken under the auspices of a committee representing the American Sociology [Association]" and signaled that organization's interest in gauging the development of the discipline during Jim Crow segregation.[20] Of the 55 institutions Doyle contacted, 26 returned questionnaires. Of the total returned 22 were rated

"A" (4) or "B" (18) level institutions. Among the noteworthy findings was that 35 sociology teachers possessed the master's degree and only 3 in the entire sample had taken the doctorate. The textbooks used were consistent with those selected by faculty at HWCUs and included *Social Organization* by Charles Cooley, *Folkways* by William G. Sumner, and *Social Change* by William Ogburn, among others. A fascinating but not unexpected finding by Doyle was that the most commonly used journal and magazine by HBCUs were Black outlets, *The Journal of Negro History* and *Opportunity* magazine. These two publications combined were cited more than ten times among the sample while *American Journal of Sociology* was cited by four schools and *Social Forces* by one. Relatedly, Doyle reported that Black sociologists, including Charles S. Johnson, E. Franklin Frazier, and Kelly Miller were listed as persons with whom introduction to sociology students should be aware of, as much as the equally highly ranked William Sumner, Charles Cooley, and Franklin Giddings. Doyle's conclusion was decisive:

> The most obvious conclusion is that the introductory course in Negro colleges and universities is characterized by its resemblance to the course in other colleges and universities. If it differs at all, it appears to be in the attention paid to concepts referring to the status and condition of the Negro in America, in the use of Negro journals as collateral references, and in referring to Negro authors. But whatever the similarities and differences, one conclusion appears reasonable; viz., *the introductory course in sociology in Negro colleges and universities is safe for sociology.*[21] (Emphasis mine)

More than a decade after Doyle's study, early Black sociologist Joseph Sandy Himes expanded the literature on the instruction of sociology at HBCUs to cover the activities of departments. In his examination Himes found that sociology was taught at all 101 existing HBCUs. Similar to Du Bois's finding with the Atlanta University studies roughly fifty years earlier, the instruction of sociology at HBCUs was a substantive part of each curriculum and was only outranked by history. This was counter to HWCUs, where instruction in sociology was outranked by economics, political science, and history. The obvious explanation for the interest in sociology at HBCUs was its utility as a tool to improve the social, economic, and physical condition of Blacks in America. It is heartening to note an increase in the number of sociology teachers, as Doyle's study listed nearly 50 and Himes counted 199. Additionally, whereas Doyle's 1933 study cited 3 as possessing the doctorate, by 1949 this number increased to nearly 40, with 30 having training in sociology or the social sciences in general. Similar to Doyle, Himes concluded that sociology as an institutionalized practice was not being harmed via its instruction at HBCUs.

Whereas Doyle examined introduction to sociology courses and Himes focused on departments, E. Franklin Frazier's 1933 inquiry covered graduate instruction at HBCUs. His study was guided by a simple question, "Should HBCUs engage in graduate work?" Frazier's answer to this question was, yes, HBCUs should engage in graduate work, but only at a select number of institutions. According to Frazier, there were "four schools which are seriously undertaking graduate work [and] seem to be adequately meeting the demand for graduate work in Negro schools, there does not appear to be any reason why other Negro schools should undertake such work."[22] It was his opinion that graduate work at HBCUs should only take place at Atlanta, Fisk, Hampton, and Howard. Unfortunately, his study was not grounded in any tangible data but in *objective facts* as understood by Frazier and his colleagues. Frazier noted, "in undertaking this task, the writer has not relied solely upon his experience as a teacher of undergraduate and graduate courses and as a student in two universities in the North and one in Europe, but he has discussed the question with competent persons who are engaged in giving graduate work in Negro schools."[23] Based on these data sources he offered a number of reasons why graduate education at HBCUs should be limited to those listed above.

First, he argued that the relatively new institutions devoted to the education of Blacks in America should focus the bulk of their energies on developing and maintaining curriculums deserving of university status. As discussed in Chapter 1, when most, if not all, HBCUs were established they included the words "university" or "college" in the hopes of what they would eventually become, not what they currently were. By the early twentieth century many HBCUs continued to offer healthy amounts of secondary instruction. It was Frazier's belief that institutions that had not yet achieved legitimate university status should not burden themselves with graduate work. Instead, they should solidify themselves as legitimate institutions of post-secondary education first. This included maintaining fiscal stability and growing resources, including library and scientific laboratory facilities.

Second, Frazier believed the establishment of graduate programs at HBCUs would have deleterious effects on the admission of Blacks into advanced graduate programs at Northern schools. Part of his concern stemmed from the fact that a common practice at this time was the denial of graduate school admissions to Black students at HWCUs and their de facto consignment to segregated educational spaces because of racism. Instead of being forward thinking, the majority of HWCUs encouraged Blacks in America to attend HBCUs or schools with existing substantive numbers of Black students such that the literal integration of Black student bodies into White spaces would not occur, especially in fields where close physical contact among students was the norm. Frazier offered an example of this concern. "Home economics is another field in which more or less personal and intimate relations have caused some opposition to the full participation of Negro students in class requirements."[24] Stated plainly, the establishment of graduate programs at HBCUs would enable well-resourced HWCUs, particularly those in the North according to Frazier, to deny admission to Black students grounded on the argument they could attend a similar program but within a homogenous setting. Thus, HWCUs remained practically lily white.

Another consequence of denying Blacks admission into HWCUs, according to Frazier, was the possibility students would be compelled to attend *inferior* HBCU graduate programs. Again, while there was evidence that the instruction of sociology at HBCUs was safe for undergraduate programs, Frazier believed this to not be the case for the majority of schools offering graduate instruction in the discipline. It appears he believed those of exceptional ability who were forced to enter *select* graduate schools at

HBCUs would be prepared as well as anyone in the country if they were exposed to capable faculty such as those at Atlanta, Fisk, Hampton, and Howard. However, for those who entered graduate programs at HBCUs ill-equipped to offer graduate work they would depart those institutions as deficiently trained graduates, Frazier believed, who would be a stain on the race's efforts to create and sustain excellent programs of graduate study.

Third, Frazier believed "graduate education in Negro schools will further the educational segregation of the races and encourage a double standard of scholarship."[25] An argument can be made that the establishment of graduate programs at HBCUs would maintain segregation in education because this era of intense domestic terrorism, racial hostility, and violence experienced by Blacks in America may have led them to prefer attending schools with harmonious and supportive environments that could not be found on most HWCU campuses. Nevertheless, the idea that such programs should not be established simply for fear that the existing folkways and mores of America's separate and (un)equal society may be strengthened is nonsensical. Moreover, the idea that HBCUs would produce substandard scholarship, which was the suggestion given Frazier's comments regarding *a double standard of scholarship*, appeared to be a repudiation of the tremendous works of sociology performed by non-doctoral practicing sociologists and citizen researchers who participated in groundbreaking research at schools such as Atlanta, Tuskegee, and Hampton.

Fourth, Frazier reasonably and accurately noted deficiencies in the faculty and research facilities at HBCUs. While observing an increase in the number of trained doctoral faculty at HBCUs, Frazier insisted that until a critical mass of appropriately trained persons was secured by these institutions, they should not offer graduate instruction. Relatedly, he noted that faculty who were research-driven should be provided the most appropriate resources available to carry out their work. Overall, Frazier believed "Negro schools are not equipped either from the standpoint of faculty or research facilities to give adequate graduate work."[26]

Frazier believed graduate work should be performed at select HBCUs like Atlanta, Fisk, Hampton, and Howard because they "are seriously undertaking graduate work [which] seem[s] to be adequately meeting the demands for graduate work in Negro schools, there does not appear to be any reason why other Negro schools should undertake such work."[27] Frazier's stance was bolstered by the existence of strong infrastructure for teaching and research at these institutions as well as faculty capable of executing graduate work. Although he listed four schools as suitable to perform graduate work at HBCUs, it is without question he believed Howard was the dominant institution of the group and the exemplar of excellence for departments of sociology at HBCUs. This argument was based, in part, on the fact that Howard established its graduate college earlier than many (1927), was financially stable, and boasted a roaster of talented and distinguished scholars across the college curriculum. Frazier, in his own words, argued "Howard University is the only Negro institution of higher learning equipped at present to give graduate work on a large scale. It holds this unique position because of the character of its faculty, its laboratory and library facilities, and its location in respect to other institutions which may be drawn upon for purposes of research."[28] It is difficult to refute the proposition that America's national university stood, at this time, as the leader of graduate education for Blacks in America. It is equally difficult to refute the proposition that during the golden age of Black sociology Howard was not its intellectual and infrastructure touchstone.

A Commitment to Excellence in Research and Infrastructure

Howard University was the intellectual and infrastructure touchstone of HBCUs during the golden age of Black sociology because of the high number and quality of scholars and scientists on its faculty as well as its commitment to establishing top-notch research laboratories while providing the requisite resources.[29] My conceptualization of Black sociology includes scholars in related disciplines who engaged in works that challenged existing theories of Black inferiority and conducted research that had public policy implications. During the middle twentieth century, members of the faculty at Howard that fell under this broad conceptualization included , but was certainly not limited to, such well-known and accomplished persons as Charles Drew (known for groundbreaking works on blood plasma), John Hope Franklin (historian), Ernest E. Just (biologist), Alain Locke (first African American Rhodes Scholar), and Ruth Ella Moore (first African American woman to take the doctorate in bacteriology), among others. It is unquestionable that Howard's roster of faculty across all disciplines was unmatched during this era.[30] What's important to note here is that the creation of an institutional cohort of strong scholars at Howard was not accidental but an intentional outcome envisioned by an early leader of the school.

> There was the vision of Howard University's first black president, Mordecai Wyatt Johnson, who assumed the presidency in 1926 and held tenaciously to building the greatest concentration of black scholars at any one institution of higher learning, encouraging them to use their talents to address the critical issues confronting black Americans everywhere.[31]

The combination of federal funding, philanthropic gifts, and other fundraising activities provided the school resources to procure the most talented cross-section of scholars in the nation. Just as impressive as its general faculty was its collection of sociologists and social scientists led by E. Franklin Frazier.

E. Franklin Frazier arrived at Howard in 1934 after stints at several institutions. Although he did not take the doctorate until 1931, Frazier began his career as an instructor of sociology at Morehouse College in Atlanta in 1922. Never one to shy away from controversial and intense issues including race and racism, he was often outspoken against these matters in a town that had not too long ago experienced a massive race riot where the estimate of Blacks killed was around 100.[32]

In an essay critical of southern Whites, Frazier theorized that the cause of race hatred by Whites toward Blacks in America was attributable to a mental condition. "In the June 1927 issue of *The Forum*, [Frazier argues] that certain symptoms of racial prejudice were in no wise different from the symptoms of insanity."[33] In an era where many, if not most, Whites believed Blacks were biologically and intellectually inferior, that a Black man had the gall to make such a pronouncement was anathema, if not downright suicidal. Frazier made this public statement in a community that did not shy away from attempting, and many cases succeeding, to keep *Negroes* in their place. It is almost certain Frazier knew the dangers of living in the region and that at one time members of the White community had forced Morehouse's immediate neighbor, Atlanta University, to *teach around sociology* because of their fear of an educated and motivated Black population. Within this racial milieu it was unsurprising that "he was forced to leave" Atlanta under the threat of death.[34] Over the next two years he worked as a research assistant at the University of Chicago and under the guidance of members of the renowned Chicago School of Sociology. Then, in 1929, he accepted an invitation to join Charles S. Johnson's department of sociology at Fisk. It was during this period that Frazier had a front row seat to witness how to build a department and lead an institution, through his observations of Johnson, who later became the first Black president of Fisk. Although his relationship with Johnson was tenuous, Nashville provided experiences that he could use as the leader of Howard sociology to make the department an influential and important player in the discipline.[35] Frazier's time at Fisk was short-lived; he only spent five years there. In 1934 he left Nashville to join the faculty at Howard where he led one of the strongest departments of sociology, HBCU or HWCU, in the nation.

E. Franklin Frazier and Graduate Education

E. Franklin Frazier was one of the most accomplished sociologists this nation has produced and his canonical status in the discipline is cemented for a number of reasons. The most obvious is his classic book, *The Negro Family in the United States*. One of the earliest scientific accounts of the Black American family, *The Negro Family in the United States* posited the deficits experienced by Blacks as caused by structural factors instead of attributing them to individual failures or racial inferiority. This idea was fully captured in an essay Frazier penned some years later where he argued:

> The deviations in the character of the Negro family from the dominant American patterns have been owing chiefly to the social isolation and economic position of the Negro. As the Negro acquires education and enjoys greater economic opportunities and participates in all phases of American life, he is taking over the American patterns of behavior characteristic of different classes and regions. His family life increasingly conforms to the American pattern, which is becoming a part of his cultural heritage.[36]

Although the book faced criticism from Black scholars for suggesting that Blacks in America possessed no culture other than that learned during enslavement, its wide popularity propelled him to become an influential scholar and intellectual. This popularity later resulted in his election as president of the Eastern Sociological Society in 1944 and then to becoming the first Black American president of the American Sociological Association.

Frazier clearly stood out among sociologists at Howard and the argument made here is not that this school was the epitome of departmental excellence simply because of its collection of scholars. Instead, the argument made here is that Howard stood out as a leader among departments of sociology at HBCUs because of the school's commitment to excellence and its infrastructure, which enabled it to establish a doctoral program in sociology in 1972. To this day, sadly, Howard stands as the only HBCU in this nation to carry this distinction.

Graduate education at Howard dates back to 1867 when school officials declared students could receive a "*second degree* upon the presentation of a thesis and one year of advanced graduate study at the University."[37] Between 1867 and 1889 there was a bit of flexibility within one's understanding of the presentation of a thesis. During this era, one was allowed the option of presenting the thesis orally or in writing. After 1889, the Committee on Graduate Studies mandated that students submit a written thesis in order to successfully complete degree requirements. The school formally established a graduate school in 1927 and in 1935 Frazier developed a graduate program in social work. Over the next few decades this program thrived as its enrollment continually grew and its research impact was felt.

In his article examining graduate education at HBCUs, Frazier argued that, while schools including Atlanta and Fisk were safe for graduate instruction in sociology, his institution was uniquely situated to be the leader among this group. In addition to boasting a larger enrollment than other institutions, Frazier offered additional reasons why:

> Howard University is the only Negro institution of higher learning equipped at present to give graduate work on a large scale. It holds this unique position because of the character of its faculty, its laboratory and library facilities, and its location in respect to other institutions which may be drawn upon for purposes of research.[38]

With respect to its physical plant, the school was busily building new dormitories to house an increasing number of students, adeptly using its funds to bolster the physical sciences and establishing a medical school where future generations of Black students were trained to enter the profession. The development of an infrastructure appropriate to a leading university was also intentional, and was stated by President Johnson who made this a priority upon his hiring. During his inaugural speech Johnson indicated he "wanted to improve both the faculty and the facilities of Howard so that it could 'compete with any liberal arts university in America'."[39] It was the strong leadership provided by President Johnson that laid the foundation for Howard's success in the mid-twentieth century, as he made clear during his inaugural address his intentions to house the greatest collection of intellectual talent in the nation and provide them the resources and facilities needed to accomplish their scholarly goals.

More germane to the social sciences, however, was Frazier's suggestion that Washington, D.C., was a more desirable setting than other

leading HBCUs for graduate work because of its attractiveness as a sociological laboratory and the quality of its existing faculty. In one respect, the
commendation he attributed to the graduate program at Fisk could also
be applied to Howard if one keeps in mind that Frazier's argument was
not that graduate instruction should not take place at other HBCUs, but
that Howard was best suited to take on the task at a large scale. According
to Frazier, "The graduate work which is undertaken by the department
of sociology has been due to the fact that students have applied to Fisk
to work on specific problems under professors engaged on research
projects."[40] The professors that would compel graduate students to attend
Howard included Kelly Miller, E. Franklin Frazier, Abram Harris Jr., and
Ralphe Bunche, among others. While this collective is known for advancing
the "Howard School of Thought" that challenged and criticized old-school
Black academic leaders for not being in touch with the current trends in
advancing the rights of Blacks in America, without question they were
influenced at some point in their early careers by an old-school and still
leading academic of the era. Williams argues that:

> Howard public intellectuals were indeed members of Du Bois's talented
> tenth. In fact, many members of the community—Alain Locke, Ralph
> Bunche, E. Franklin Frazier, Rayford Logan, Abram Harris, for example—
> were to some degree students of Du Bois, following in his intellectual
> footsteps, and taking their lead from his life example and career.[41]

If this was indeed the case, imagine how strong this cadre of scholars would
have been had the university decided to prioritize hiring faculty in its
social science program at the expense of the physical sciences and medical
school. The school missed an excellent opportunity to hire one of the
leading sociologists of the day and architect of the first American school of
sociology a few years after it hired Kelly Miller. "In 1896, a young scholar
recently back from Germany, W. E. B. Du Bois, applied for a position on the
faculty of [Howard] University. For some reason he was not employed."[42]
The explanation for Du Bois's rejection rests in the school's prioritization
of hiring an architect instructor over other disciplines. One of the great

mysteries of the discipline is how Du Bois's hiring at Howard would have impacted the discipline when, combined with the talent already assembled and sufficient resources placed behind his efforts, he would have been positioned to potentially fulfill his proposed plan for a one hundred year study of the Black American experience. Despite the missed opportunity to hire Du Bois, the department was primed to greatly impact the discipline given the advantages identified earlier. Unfortunately, for as much as members of the department were able to accomplish individually, the collective impact of the unit was stunted during Frazier's tenure of leadership.

It is clear from his published writings that Frazier wanted to build upon the strong infrastructure laid by Howard administrators and establish a department to rival any in the nation. Unfortunately, his vision for a formidable department did not fully come to fruition for two principal reasons. Although Frazier had the talent as a social scientist to produce significant works for himself, as mentioned earlier, the university did not prioritize the department of sociology despite its acquisition of talent and resources. According to Platt, "Within the university, sociology was not a priority; the available limited funds were invested in the schools of medicine and dentistry."[43] The school was determined to make an impact in areas beyond sociology. This included its law school, once led by Charles Hamilton Houston, architect of the *Brown v. Board of Education* court case, and Thurgood Marshall, Howard graduate and the first Black American to serve on the United States Supreme Court. It is hard to quarrel with the school's decision to place its resources principally into areas leading to immediate and direct impacts on the Black American community. But, again, as with the opportunity to hire Du Bois some years earlier, one can only imagine the school's sociological products had the discipline been a higher priority and included the hiring of an up and coming scholar with a tireless commitment to the new science.

The second reason Frazier's vision did not come to fruition was more personal than institutional. He was an excellent academic but seemingly did not possess the requisite leadership skills to take the department higher. Again, Platt is insightful when he notes:

> Though Frazier was successful in upgrading Howard's sociology depart-
> ment, he was not an effective bureaucrat. He did not have the temper-
> ament or diplomatic skills necessary in academic politics. He disliked
> administrative work, had little patience for departmental infighting,
> and was not skilled at fundraising. To his disappointment, he was never
> able to turn sociology into a high powered graduate department with a
> serious doctoral program and substantial research agenda.[44]

Often academics do not embrace the mundane and odious tasks associated with leading a unit or institution. For many, having effective people
skills and bureaucratic skills does not come naturally. That Frazier was
not an effective university politician should not diminish the fact that
he helped establish the foundation for the eventual development of a
doctoral program at Howard. In fact, it stands to reason that his efforts
at the school, sans effective administrative leadership stylings, are a main
reason they established a doctoral program. Platt proposes that

> Frazier's main contribution to Howard's sociology department was in
> the area of curriculum development and educational standards. "When
> I came to Howard University," he recalled in 1948, "I reconstructed the
> entire curriculum" and increased student enrollment from about two
> hundred in 1934 to about two thousand fourteen years later.[45]

Building upon the infrastructure at Howard and his development of a
rigorous sociology curriculum, Frazier's impact on Black sociology is
noted here as being, in addition to his singular academic works, the
primary building block upon which the doctoral program was eventually built as his vision for the department included the development of
a cadre of Black sociologists in possession of the doctorate degree who
would be guided by the principles of sociology in their attempts to criti-
cally study and attempt to change the world around them. " 'The Frazier
style,' observed a former student, 'was to give the student the shock treatment to command his attention, for he wanted the student to understand
that the objective of sociology was to provide a realistic analysis of the
world about him'."[46] While not covertly advancing the principles of Black
sociology, one finds in the sociology program at Howard under the tenure

of Frazier a posture that embraced direct study of the pressing scientific questions that surrounded race at that time. As we look back, we can only imagine the impact on American sociology had the school provided additional resources for the department, had Frazier been a more strategic and political leader, and had the school prioritized hiring the discipline's most accomplished scholar. Assuredly, the sociological canon would look different. Although Howard did not offer employment to Du Bois, another institution with a strong interest in developing its sociology program did, Atlanta University. During his first tenure at Atlanta Du Bois established the first American school of sociology. Upon his return twenty years later, he attempted to revive his sociological laboratory.

The Phylon Institute

There can be no true golden era of Black sociology without W. E. B. Du Bois. Thus, it is provident that his return to Atlanta University occurred at the dawn of the ascension of sociological excellence performed by a cadre of individual sociologists and departments of sociology at HBCUs. Du Bois's first tenure at Atlanta ended because of the financial burden the school experienced when influential White philanthropists withheld financial gifts from the institution because of the Atlanta Sociological Laboratory's piercing scientific reports on race and racism in America. The research program Du Bois led at the turn of the twentieth century penetrated the souls of sociologists and non-sociologists alike who believed in the intellectual and biological inferiority of Blacks in America. His proposals for change were deemed anathema in Jim Crow America and Atlanta University became collateral damage in White America's response to his research. Added to this scenario is the fact that the leading Black American political voice of the era wielded his influence against Du Bois to limit his access to resources to conduct high-quality research. According to Du Bois:

> There came a controversy between myself and Booker T. Washington, which became more personal and bitter than I had ever dreamed and which necessarily dragged in the University. . . . I did not at the time see

the handwriting on the wall. I did not realize how strong the forces were back of Tuskegee and how they might interfere with my scientific study of the Negro.[47]

After learning of an instance where Washington was queried by a White philanthropist on whether or not to provide funding for a Du Bois-sponsored project and the Wizard of Tuskegee decided to not approve the effort, Du Bois tendered his resignation. In his 1910 resignation letter from the faculty at Atlanta Du Bois wrote, "I insist on my right to think and speak; but if that freedom is made an excuse for abuse of and denial of aid to Atlanta University, then with regret I shall withdraw from Atlanta University."[48] It is unsurprising that the sociology program at Atlanta University did not maintain the high level of research inquiry after the departure of the founder of American sociology. During its hiatus from sociological relevance Tuskegee, Fisk and Howard filled the void. After Du Bois's return to Atlanta the program became relevant again. But, unlike his first tenure, Atlanta did not wield influence as the leading department of sociology at an HBCU or in the nation.

More than twenty years after the demise of the Atlanta Sociological Laboratory, President John Hope decided to revive the first American school of sociology. Sensing that Du Bois's rocky tenure with the New York City-based NAACP was nearing its end, President Hope invited Du Bois back to Atlanta to restart his sociological laboratory. This was an opportunity Du Bois relished because he didn't want to resign from the school twenty years prior. "I may say frankly that if there had been any reasonable prospect of the continuing support of my work with the Atlanta Conferences, I should never have left Atlanta University even though the salary offered [at the NAACP] in New York was exactly twice as large as that I was receiving [in Atlanta]."[49] What most bothered Du Bois about his forced exile from Atlanta was the void it created for quality scientific research on Blacks in America and the opportunity it provided White sociologists to now mine an area many previously believed was unworthy of study and already replete with *believable* shelves of books on scientific racism. Du Bois lamented:

> I have always regretted that the work had to stop when it did and that a
> period of nearly twenty years went by when leadership in the social study
> of the Negro passed from the Negro's own hands here in Atlanta to the
> hands of white people in North Carolina and many Northern institutions.[50]

Clearly, Du Bois viewed his return as an opportunity for Atlanta and other
HBCUs to tilt the balance of power in research on Blacks in America back
to those institutions.

Despite his best efforts, the reimagined program of sociological
research at Atlanta, now called Phylon Institute, did not come close to
matching the excellence Du Bois produced during his first tenure as his
efforts only resulted in three meetings. The objective of the inaugural
1941 conference, according to Du Bois, was to gather leaders representing a wide variety of HBCUs together to "plan the American Negro's path
to economic independence under the guiding leadership of a Talented
Tenth."[51] As advertised, the paper presentations centered on best practices for Blacks in America to improve their economic condition. While
this was an important topic, the research significance of the presentations
was nil. Unlike the first era of Du Bois-led studies, "no resolutions were
adopted, nor was any attempt made to come to formal conclusions."[52]
In 1943 and 1944 Du Bois held meetings that more directly addressed
the establishment of research relationships between land-grant HBCUs.
Similar to the 1941 effort, these meetings failed to produce substantive
sociological products. It is possible that had Du Bois remained on faculty
beyond 1944 the meetings may have developed into what he envisioned
upon his return. Unfortunately, because of a spat with school administrators, Du Bois's tenure at the school was, once again, abruptly ended.

When President Hope brought Du Bois back to Atlanta it appeared
they had an unwritten understanding that the renowned sociologist would
remain on faculty until he chose to retire. Unfortunately, President Hope
died shortly after his arrival and Du Bois became embroiled in a power
struggle over who should become the school's next president. Du Bois was
not new to professional disagreements but did not believe this particular
dust-up would result in his firing. As he came to understand the matter:

> In 1939 the university instituted a system of rank and tenure.... The
> University, in 1939, gave Dr. Du Bois a five-year appointment which
> expired June 30, 1944. At this time Dr. Du Bois was "seventy-six years
> of age, eleven years beyond retirement age." However, Du Bois was not
> ready to retire. President Rufus Clement recommended Du Bois's retire-
> ment to the Board of Trustees and the Board agreed.[53]

Du Bois's understanding of his retirement was that it stemmed from a
political disagreement between President Clement and himself over his
lack of support for the young administrator. Moreover, in an effort to
place his institutional stamp on the school he needed to remove, arguably,
its most famous member. According to Du Bois:

> Neither Miss Reed nor President Clement said a word to me about retire-
> ment; but at the meeting of the Board of Trustees in 1944, Miss Reed
> proposed *that I be retired* [emphasis mine]. President Clement seconded
> the motion and apparently with little or no objection the Board passed
> the vote. Presumably most of the members assumed the matter had been
> discussed with me and had my agreement. No pension was mentioned.[54]

Summary

1930 to 1960 is recognized as the golden age of Black sociology because it
comprised the apex of sociological practice, instruction, and leadership
at HBCUs. With an increase in the number of trained Black sociologists,
Jim Crow segregation in the United States allowed for the assembling of
talented cohorts of scholars at HBCUs whose works exemplified some of
the best in the era. Charles S. Johnson's leadership of the Race Relations
Institute resulted in, arguably, the discipline's most impressive program
of sustained and institutionalized applied sociology. While not as influential in the discipline with respect to its output of research projects in comparison with Fisk or the Atlanta Sociological Laboratory, Howard stood
out in this era because it housed the most impressive collection of social
scientists and sociologists in the nation. That the school's ambitious sociological and social science goals were bolstered by an administration that

provided requisite infrastructure and financial support spoke volumes about the confidence it had in the members of that unit and their desire to become one of the nation's leaders in sociological training of Black Americans. Although W. E. B. Du Bois failed to recapture the glory years of his first tenure at Atlanta University that resulted in the establishment of the first American school of sociology, he did reignite a culture of collaborative social science research at HBCUs, particularly land-grant institutions. Ultimately, the Phylon Institute was not successful when compared to the Atlanta University studies, but it provided a platform for Black sociologists and social scientists at HBCUs to employ their scholarly talents for the benefit of their respective communities.

It is not hyperbole to suggest that Jim Crow segregation facilitated the creation of talented cohorts of Black sociologists at HBCUs. It is quite possible that a number of those individuals would have chosen to seek employment at HBCUs even if the option of working at HWCUs had been available. However, it is factual that once the integration of higher education institutions began, most HBCUs lost their battles to attract top sociology talent. The era of integration, I argue, led to the decreased significance and impact of HBCUs on the discipline in general and to the death of Black sociology as previously practiced and understood.

CHAPTER 6

Whither Black Sociology?

It is fitting that the death of W. E. B. Du Bois signaled the close of the golden age of Black sociology, if for no other reason than he was the person largely responsible for its beginning. Collectively, the deaths of Du Bois in 1963, E. Franklin Frazier in 1962, and Charles S. Johnson in 1956 were turning points in the institutional practice and application of Black sociology at HBCUs. These men were not only leading American scholars, but in the cases of Johnson and Frazier, Black Americans at HBCUs who elevated their sociology programs to high levels of achievement and accolades from the mainstream White sociological community. The deaths of these men did not result in the closure of departments of sociology at HBCUs. However, the deaths of these men did represent the end of the institutional practice of Black sociology because this was the final moment in this nation's history when the most accomplished Black sociologists were nearly exclusively employed at HBCUs. Whereas Atlanta, Fisk, and Howard were viewed as desirable places of employment for many Black sociologists because of the presence and stature of these men, their departures combined with advances in the Civil Rights Movement to make HBCUs less desirable destinations for future leading Black sociologists. The impending decrease of highly talented Black sociologists employed at HBCUs marked a defining moment in the transition from the golden age of Black sociology to the dark age of Black sociology.

Dark Age of Black Sociology

The 1954 *Brown v. Board of Education* decision ending state-sanctioned segregation in education was momentous. Inequities between Black and White public schools were substantive, problematic, and documented by the pioneering Atlanta Sociological Laboratory as early as 1900. At the turn of the century Du Bois's school uncovered gigantic disparities in teacher pay, school funding, and facility maintenance, or lack thereof, that should have rendered the most objective reader of the report embarrassed and dumbfounded with the racialized findings.[1] It was for these and a host of other reasons the Supreme Court ruled that separate and (un)equal public education was a stain on this nation's reputation and character and should be washed away *with all deliberate speed.* The speed employed by school districts varied by state and region. Eventually, nearly 25 years later, the court's mandate was met across the nation. Certainly, the decision to elim-inate segregation in public education was the correct call. However, one must also recognize that the Brown decision had an unintended conse-quence that contributed to the onset of the dark age of Black sociology.

At the onset of the golden age of Black sociology only 30 Black Americans held a doctorate in the discipline.[2] Of this number, "Some were dead and others were engaged in other institutions or other professions."[3] It is safe to assume that most, if not all, Blacks with the doctorate in sociol-ogy and working in academia were employed at HBCUs. One can make this argument given the rigidity of America's racial caste system and denial of employment opportunities to Blacks within most White institutional and informal spaces, save *so-called* menial labor. By default, then, the primary employer of Black sociologists working in academia were HBCUs. The best and brightest Black minds were funneled into universities, departments, and programs where they collectively grappled with topical social issues of the day while simultaneously influencing the discipline as it molded itself. It was in these unapologetically Black spaces that future generations of sociologists and college graduates received training from giants like Du Bois, Frazier, Miller, and Johnson. Referring to the previous chapter, the stockpiling of talented Black scholars at a limited number of HBCUs to perform first-rate graduate work was championed by E. Franklin Frazier. He touted the institutional resources and scholarly accomplishments at Atlanta, Fisk, Hampton, and Howard as evidence of the development of strong graduate programs at HBCUs that rivaled most, if not all, HWCUs. In effect, it was because of Jim Crow segregation that HBCUs became the home of influential, albeit largely ignored, sociology programs and accomplishments.

The stockpiling of talented Black sociologists at HBCUs was virtually mandated during Jim Crow and catalogued by Joseph Sandy Himes, Jr., in his study on teachers of sociology at HBCUs. Himes estimated that "In the aggregate [there is a] total of 249 teachers of sociology in the country's 101 Negro institutions of higher learning. This means that there are, on average, about two and a half teachers of sociology per institution."[4] Of the 249 sociology teachers at HBCUs, "All these teachers are not Negroes. A considerable number of white teachers of sociology are employed in the Negro colleges" (303). Since there were no hard data on the number of Black sociologists in possession of the doctorate Himes could only estimate the total number teaching at HBCUs. Himes concluded, "A considerable number of Negro students have received doctor's degrees in sociology since 1943 [the year of Greene's study], but the exact number is unknown. On the basis of these fragmentary data one may venture the judgment that at best hardly more than half of the 78 teachers of sociology with earned doctor's degrees are Negroes with doctorates in sociology. The others are, as we have already seen, white teachers, or Negro teachers with doctorates in fields other than sociology."[5]

When James E. Conyers published his study, he found there had been an increase in the number of Black American holders of the doctorate in sociology since the 1940s. More germane to this inquiry is that he collected data that allowed for a detailed and informed discussion on the impact of the *Brown* decision on departments of sociology at HBCUs. I argue that the *Brown* decision, partly, led to the onset of the dark age of Black sociology because of the *brain drain* of top Black American talent that no longer saw employment at HBCUs as their only viable option. While Sandy Himes projected in 1951 that around 40 Black Americans held the doctorate in sociology, by 1968 Conyers counted 121. Moreover, Conyers collected data from this group on a number of topics such as family history, education, and current employment status. Although there are no supporting data, it is safe to conservatively assume that pre-*Brown* 95 percent to 100 percent of all Black sociology teachers in this nation were employed at HBCUs. According to Conyers, fourteen years after *Brown*, "Only about 49, or about 40 percent, [of Black Americans] are employed at predominately Negro colleges."[6] The decrease in Black sociology teachers at HBCUs and their increase at HWCUs, I argue, was directly related to the *Brown* decision. During this era HWCUs began to admit Black students into their institutions in increasingly higher numbers. The *Brown* decision and other challenges to segregation in education led to admissions policies that not only increased the presence of young Black faces in formerly lily-white spaces but, resultantly, strategic decisions by HWCU administrators to bring onto campus Black faculty to not only engage in dynamic research but serve as mentors to Black students. Whereas HBCUs were, theoretically, the only viable employment option for Black sociologists in academia pre-*Brown*, the need or desire to construct a diverse (even if only symbolically diverse) faculty at HWCUs provided tremendous professional opportunities for members of a race considered not long ago to be biologically and intellectually inferior to Whites.[7] Add to this scenario the fact that many, if not most, HWCUs were able to offer financial and research packages as well as access to physical resources that could not be matched by many HBCUs.[8] When one considers all factors, it is no wonder that the number of Blacks working at HBCUs decreased from nearly 100 percent pre-*Brown* to about 40 percent around 1970. The *Brown v. Board of Education* decision and the deaths of Du Bois, Frazier, and Johnson, I ultimately argue, coalesced to lead to the exodus of talented Black sociologists from HBCUs to HWCUs and the institutional death of Black sociology at HBCUs.

It must be stated as clearly as possible that my argument is not that HBCUs were void of talented Black sociologists after the *Brown* decision and integration of HWCU campuses. There were, and remain, many talented Black faculty at HBCUs, many of whom could obtain employment at an HWCU if they so desired. My primary argument, however, is that a critical mass of highly talented Black sociologists were no longer *exclusively* funneled to or choosing to work at HBCUs and, thus, these spaces were no longer able to develop influential institutional programs of Black sociological research as they had in previous generations. Regardless of the reason, what we saw in the years after *Brown* was a *brain drain* of HBCU talent by HWCUs because Black Americans now had opportunities to take their talents to spaces that were previously not open to them. Indeed, the *Brown* decision opened the door to greater professional opportunities for Black sociologists at institutions with vastly larger resources, financial and otherwise, than those available at HBCUs. Because of the ability to access resources that allowed them to achieve their professional and personal goals it stood to reason that when given the choice they would decide, in most cases, to have greater access to said resources. The challenges of working at under-resourced HBCUs during a period when opportunities were opening for Black sociologists at HWCUs was expressed by the first president of the Association of Black Sociologists, James E. Blackwell.

> [During segregation Black sociologists] were compelled to work in HBCUs which, in general, occupied a subordinate if not extremely tenuous position in higher institutional hierarchy. As is the case in most institutions primarily devoted to the teaching enterprise, professors were constrained by enormously heavy teaching loads which, in turn, depleted time and opportunities for research, or when they did have such opportunities, travel funds were so restricted and disproportionally distributed that they often attended professional meetings at their own expense.[9]

The demise of Jim Crow segregation meant a good number of the most talented and research-driven Black sociologists were no longer choosing to work at HBCUs. This, combined with the deaths of established early and prominent Black sociologists, caused the institutional demise of Black sociology. Although this process was complete by the early 1960s, I propose that another variation of the substantive area of study (re)emerged at HWCUs prior to the end of that decade.

Black Studies or Black Sociology?

The traditional narrative on the origin of Black Studies suggests it emerged from the protests of Black college students seeking greater curricular representations of their race at HWCUs.[10] This narrative, while fashionable, minimizes the rich history of the development of Black Studies in the United States pre-emancipation, while overstating the idea that its academic origins did not emerge until the 1960s. Part of the problem with articulating an origin of Black Studies in the United States concerns which version one chooses to privilege. I highlight two representative and varying perspectives on the discipline's origin. The first is posited by Lawrence Crouchett who argued the Black Studies legacy included pre-emancipation attempts of educated Blacks to make their peers knowledgeable on matters of importance, post-emancipation efforts of Black historical societies committed to collecting historical and statistical data on the race, and, ultimately, the discipline's infusion into university curriculums at HBCUs and HWCUs.[11] Regarding the latter, Carter G. Woodson found in 1919 that, while no southern HWCUs offered courses on Black American life and history, Harvard University, Ohio State University, Stanford University, University of Chicago, and the University of Nebraska offered at least one course on the topic; presumably from a deficit perspective.

The second perspective on the origin of Black Studies is posited by Maulana Karenga. According to Karenga, "If we speak of Black Studies as a self-defined and organized discipline in the university, then we must place its origin in the 1960s."[12] This understanding of the discipline's origin directs one to the efforts of Nathan Hare and students at San Francisco State University where, after many tumultuous months of protests, the first Department of Black Studies was established in 1969. Karenga's understanding of what Black Studies should be was not limited to the formal establishment of a department. Like any area of scientific inquiry, Black

Studies, according to Karenga, should be governed by specific objectives and guiding principles that combine with an institutionalized academic presence to represent its tradition. I argue that the principles of Black sociology are not dissimilar from those outlined below by Karenga concerning Black Studies. If this is true, then even by Karenga's benchmark the intellectual and institutional foundation of Black Studies predated the 1960s and was represented by the works conducted by Du Bois and members of the Atlanta Sociological Laboratory. The objectives, or principles, of Black Studies presented below by Karenga represent the most detailed to date and are generally accepted as dogma since he is considered one of the founding fathers of the discipline.

Karenga's first objective of Black Studies is that the entire diasporic African experience be included in the curriculum. Simply because the discipline originated in the United States does not mean the experiences of non-American Blacks should be minimized at best, or excluded at worst. This objective is embraced and promoted within my conception of Black sociology, as it is recorded that Du Bois's curriculum at Atlanta University included courses on the Black experience beyond the United States.[13] Second, there should be the creation of research emphasizing intellectual and political emancipation. Similar to the tenets of Black sociology, this objective promoted agency and the idea that engagement in science should not be a passive endeavor, but one that results in positive impacts within the society. Third, Black Studies faculty should focus on engagement in research that impacts the community, not engagement in research for one's selfish purposes. Again, this is a primary principle of Black sociology. Fourth, there should be positive engagement with the local community. Records from Atlanta, Fisk, and Tuskegee indicate that the practice of engagement with one's local community was entrenched within these units that unknowingly were engaged in a collective activity known as Black sociology. Karenga's last objective encouraged adherents to continue efforts to "reaffirm [Black Studies] . . . as a discipline essential to the educational project and to any real conception of a quality education."[14] This objective, again, was implemented at Atlanta University during Du Bois's first tenure when he called for the institutionalized study of Black Americans in college curriculums. Unfortunately, after his departure and the demise of the first American school of sociology it became less of a priority. There is no question that Karenga is correct when he argues that Black Studies began in earnest after its formal establishment on college campuses as an organized discipline. This fact is beyond dispute. However, I agree with Crouchett who argued that the academic and intellectual foundation for Black Studies was established long before the 1960s and that rich history should not merely serve as a minor footnote in accounts of the discipline's origin and development. Instead, that historical record should be prominently noted within the Black Studies literature.

For those like Crouchett, who argue the Black Studies tradition dates back to pre-emancipation, their understanding of the term is rather broad. For this collective, they agree with Maurice Jackson that "Black Studies, simply put, is the systematic study of black people."[15] Key to Jackson's definition is the idea that Black Studies is a non-deficit-centered scientific examination of Black people:

> Black studies, then, is not the study of black ethnic minority, however valuable that may be. An ethnic minority, by virtue of being a minority, is by definition in a disadvantaged position which facilitates the characterization of black people as problems, as being essentially inferior, and so on. Black studies, in contrast, is the study of black people with a history and a current position with many strong points, with both a rich heritage and a rich complexity, which can be sources of pride. It is the study of people who have done much more than survive under the most difficult and trying circumstances, in and out of slavery, in and out of the ghettoes.[16]

Contrasting with Karenga, Crouchett believed "greater credit must be reserved for the efforts of Dr. W. E. B. Du Bois. Du Bois initiated and taught the first formal 'black curriculum' at Atlanta University in 1897. Here he taught sociology and inaugurated the first scientific study of the conditions of black people covering all important aspects of life."[17] Crouchett's acknowledgement of Du Bois's role in the establishment of Black Studies was powerful yet limited. Moreover, it is consistent with most of the literature and is represented in the writings of Ama Mazama who, in a book co-edited by Molefi Kete Asante and Mualana Karenga, wrote, "although W. E. B. Du Bois . . . may very well be considered one of the forerunners of Africana Studies, he may not be considered one of Africana Studies' founders because Africana Studies was not institutionalized during his lifetime."[18] A more thorough examination and argument that the academic roots of Black Studies started at Atlanta University via Du Bois's Atlanta Sociological Laboratory was published 41 years later.

The idea that Du Bois deserves (some) credit for establishing the academic foundation upon which Black Studies developed was captured by Nagueyalti Warren in her little-cited but important book, *Grandfather of Black Studies: W. E. B. Du Bois*. Warren argued:

> W. E. B. Du Bois' contributions to the development of Black Studies is to be found in his scientific investigation of the Black experience in the United States, and later in the Diaspora and in Africa, and in his thought-provoking essays that constitute a theoretical base for examining issues confronting Black Studies.[19]

Warren's argument centered on a collection of Du Bois's essays, some never published, where he addressed post-secondary curriculum needs for Black students. Specifically, Du Bois argued for the development of courses on the Black experience and the necessity for HBCUs to be the primary distributors of this curriculum, since HWCUs, obviously, had little to no interest in doing so; especially in the South. Weaving together the essays "Conservation of the Races," "The Study of the Negro Problems," "Does the Negro Need Separate Schools," "The Negro College," and "The Field and Function of the American Negro College," Warren made a compelling argument that Du Bois, without using the term Black Studies, was arguing for the establishment of an academic unit dedicated to centering the experiences of Blacks, nationally and internationally, such that objective and non-deficit scientific investigations may be performed. While claims to the discipline's theoretical foundation fluctuated between ancient African cultures, early Black American intellectual societies, and thought emerging from departments of Black Studies, there should be no debate that the scholarly foundation, or forerunner, of Black Studies as an academic enterprise in the United States was established by Du Bois during his tenure at Atlanta University.[20] If it is true that the institutionally housed academic foundation upon which Black Studies now stands was established via the Black sociology efforts of W. E. B. Du Bois at Atlanta University and ended after the *Brown* decision and deaths of Du Bois, Frazier, and Johnson, then the argument that Black sociology reemerged as a reimagined and more defined area called Black Studies and was housed primarily at HWCUs is completely plausible. Moreover, this reimagining of Black sociology serves as a vehicle by which the substantive area, while without an institutional home at HBCUs, continues to exist at various Black Studies departments at HWCUs.

It is important to note that the primary argument offered here is that the institutionally housed academic foundation for Black Studies was developed via the curriculum and research program established at Atlanta University under the direction of W. E. B. Du Bois. Similar to Black Studies, the early efforts of Du Bois's team included centering objective and scientific inquiries into the social, economic, and physical condition of Blacks while employing a Black theoretical lens to understand the data uncovered and develop solutions to the problems identified. As presented in the Introduction, Black sociology differed from mainstream White sociology on the principle of centering Blacks within non-deficit scientific investigations while, simultaneously, developing theories unique to understanding their situation and developing solutions to the problems identified. This is similar to the perspective of many Black Studies scholars who argue that their discipline is separate and distinct from sociology (regardless of distinctions made by this author) and other sciences since it is guided by its own sets of unique disciplinary dogma.[21] Despite the chasm between this belief held by many Black Studies scholars and myself, I remain insistent in my claim that Black sociology, as defined herein, is, at an absolute minimum, a distant cousin to *but* an academic building block for Black Studies and should be recognized accordingly.

While it is noted earlier in this chapter that Jackson offers a generic definition of Black Studies wherein my argument finds refuge, it is also true that he, and scores of other Black Studies scholars, insist that Black sociology cannot be a precursor to Black Studies because of the latter's unique guiding principles. According to Jackson:

> Black studies differs from academic disciplines rooted in European traditions by relating to African history and culture. Although the relationship between Africans and black Americans may not be frequent or strong, the fact that they see themselves, and are seen as alike, as black, makes current African experience as well as African heritage important to black studies.[22]

Contrary to the idea that the sociology practiced at Atlanta University under Du Bois was merely sociology in blackface, I, again, argue that a parallel world of sociology developed at early HBCUs that differed from mainstream sociology, was consistent with the guiding principles of Black Studies, and is manifested through its framing of the research question, research design, and emphasis on policy creation. Thus, and again, while many Black Studies scholars reject the idea that Du Bois's school represented an early Black Studies unit, Chapter 2 of this book provides evidence of my argument to the contrary.

It is sad that HBCUs are no longer the primary domain of Black sociological production. Despite this fact, an argument can be made that the only, or primary, institutional space where the principles of Black sociology continue in the works of individual scholars at HBCUs and HWCUs and is welcomed without suspicion or challenges of being *me-search* is within professional organizations like the Association of Black Sociologists.

The Association of Black Sociologists

When the American Sociological Association was established in 1905 it instantly became the largest and most influential organization of professional sociologists. Despite the relative youth of the discipline and low number of doctorates, very few contributors to the organization's early development were not White and not male.[23] This disparity was problematic for non-White males desiring to secure important placements in the yearly meeting and hold positions of leadership and governance. Michael R. Hill reported that, "Despite the existence of numerous female sociologists during the first years of the twentieth century, the [ASA] was overwhelmingly a male club. When women were invited to participate on the annual programs it was typically as discussants rather than as major presenters."[24] The experiences of Black sociologists mirrored those of female sociologists, especially in governance. Hill again was informative when he noted that "W. E. B. Du Bois, America's most noted and prolific African American sociologist, neither attended ASA meetings nor held any ASA office."[25] The exclusion of women and Black sociologists from significant participation in the organization should not be surprising, since this period was defined by, among other matters, hyper-patriarchal oppression and Jim Crow violence and segregation. Despite these challenges a fortunate few women and Black sociologists, E. Franklin Frazier for example, were granted entree into this space with the approval of specific distinguished gatekeepers.[26] The limited inclusion of both groups continued well into the twentieth century. Dissatisfied with their treatment within ASA and looking to create inclusive spaces that reflected their views, women and Black sociologists established professional organizations separate from the nation's largest. Sociologists for Women in Society was established in 1971 and, more germane to this inquiry, the Association of Black Sociologists was established in 1970.

As the Civil Rights Movement era ended the number of Black sociologists grew exponentially from Greene's count of 30. "James E. Conyers reported that the number of Black doctorates in sociology increased from 132 in 1969 to 185 in 1974. Conyers also found that Black doctorate holders [were] increasingly employed in predominately white academic institutions."[27] During this period there was an increasing critical mass of Black sociologists who, while simultaneously embracing the Black Power era, were intentional in making their presence in the discipline known. Given the integration of Blacks into HWCU departments of sociology, some of whom held important administrative positions, this generation of Black sociologists wanted to, similarly, occupy important positions of governance in professional organizations and have significant participation at yearly sociology meetings, including ASA. The desire for Black sociologists to directly and collectively address ASA specifically concerning these issues came to a head at the 1968 meeting in Boston, Massachusetts.

Led by Tilman Cothran of Atlanta University "the black sociologists in attendance . . . met to map a strategy for enhancing our collective representation and participation in the ASA and the profession."[28] In what can be described as a contentious meeting personifying the differing civil rights philosophies of Martin Luther King Jr. and Malcom X, "Those in attendance were divided between advocates of an ASA Black Caucus and advocates of a separate black sociological association."[29] Members favoring the establishment of a caucus within ASA argued that the separation of sociologists by race was antithetical to the legacy and struggles of persons like E. Franklin Frazier and Charles S. Johnson, who were philosophically aligned with King, who believed the most effective way to gain the advancements desired by Black sociologists was to work within the existing White mainstream sociological structure as represented by ASA. If the objective of Black sociologists was to gain a stronger voice within ASA, then establishing an entirely separate organization would defeat this purpose. Contrarily, members favoring the establishment of a separate professional organization were not convinced ASA would provide the appropriate environment for them to advance a sociological perspective influenced by the unapologetic calls of antiestablishment Blacks to define their own destiny sociologically in ways similar to the philosophy espoused by Malcolm X shortly before his untimely death. These members believed if they became an organ of ASA they would be contributing to their own professional invisibility. Instead, they wanted to create a space where the principles of Black sociology could be developed, supported and nurtured. While the literal establishment of a space to promote Black sociology was not stated, in effect one can draw a parallel. According to Joseph Scott, faculty member at Notre Dame and attendee of this meeting:

> The sentiments at the first meeting ran the gamut between black sep-
> aratism and black integrationism. Black power or black empowerment
> was the call of the day within and without the ASA. The black experience
> had been neglected both inside and outside academia, and the black
> sociologists felt a need for corrective knowledge, courses, programs, and
> departments. Black studies were on nearly everyone's mind.[30]

After a period of deliberation, the Caucus of Black Sociologists (CBS) of the
American Sociological Association was formally established at the 1970
meeting of ASA in Washington D.C.

CBS had an immediate and continuing impact on ASA through the
efforts of persons such as James E. Blackwell, James Conyers, Edgar Epps,
Jacquelyne Johnson Jackson, John Moland, Jr., Charles U. Smith, Preston
Valien, William Julius Wilson, and Ernest Works. Because of the collective
efforts of the Black sociologists of this generation, opportunities for Blacks
specifically, and people of color in general, were created in areas that were
impossible to conceive when ASA was established in 1905.[31] CBS-driven
initiatives that continue within ASA to this day include: 1) creation of the
Minority Fellowship Program, 2) establishment of the Du Bois–Johnson–
Frazier Award (now called the Cox–Johnson–Frazier Award) and 3) establishment of the Committee on Racial and Ethnic Minorities. Despite its
success in making ASA a more democratic and welcoming space for Blacks,
there were some within CBS who continued the push from earlier years to
create a professional organization separate from ASA.

Despite its role in proposing and spearheading the establishment
of the Minority Fellowship Program, Committee on Racial and Ethnic
Minorities, and minority specialist position, some CBS members became
frustrated with the lack of independence in decision making affecting
these and other CBS-sponsored initiatives. This is when CBS reevaluated
its relationship with ASA. "Prior to 1977, CBS enjoyed a special relation
with ASA. In fact, it was called CBS of ASA. However, with the prolifer-
ation of [sociological interest] groups, it became clear from both parties
that ASA could not assume special and permanent responsibility for such
groups."[32] Thus, in 1976 the Caucus of Black Sociologists of the American

Sociological Association formally separated itself from its parent organization and became an incorporated entity now known as the Association of Black Sociologists.[33] Since 1970 the Association of Black Sociologists has been an institutional space of refuge for Black sociologists and adherents of the principles of Black sociology to present their research.

I argue here that ABS is the primary, not only, academic sociological space where the principles of Black sociology are invited, expressed, and given critical and scholarly (not ad hominem) examination and scrutiny. Moreover, it is a space that has embraced the spirit of Black Studies since the organization's establishment. Since 1970 ABS has been a space where sociologists could present research that was not necessarily accepted by their White colleagues as *legitimate* sociological scholarship or belittled by White sociologists for not being as rigorous as that presented at other professional meetings. The idea that one's research is inherently subjective and dismissed out of hand because of their decision to conduct research on one's own community which arrives at conclusions countering existing disciplinary dogma (otherwise stigmatized as *me-search*) is nonsensical. This is why ABS is an important space in the growth and development of Black sociologists for whom other spaces would not provide the necessary rigorous analysis of their work without the dismissal of its reason for being studied. It is for this reason I argue that the primary, not exclusive, remaining institutional space where one can find the principles of Black sociological research actualized is at the annual meetings of the Association of Black Sociologists. Equally important is the fact that ABS continues to be a space where the contributions of early Black sociologists are recognized and canonized accordingly.

Conclusion

When the discipline of sociology emerged in the United States in the mid 1800s its development was influenced by deep-seated racial intolerance of Blacks by Whites. This dogma grew into the creation of the original manifestation of the topical area, sociology of the South. Prior to the end of slavery, sociology of the South proponents busily engaged in pseudo-scientific sociological inquiries designed to validate the continued bondage of kidnapped Africans after emancipation and the need for continued segregation in the land of the free and home of the brave. The desires of sociology of the South proponents were not impeded, even when the topic centered on persons of equal status but of different races. In nearly all matters, public and private, the racialized veil was not pulled back to allow equal-status contact and interactions among colleagues. Du Bois provided an example during a 1960 interview. Speaking directly to the difficulty sociologists experienced attempting to engage in equal status relationships, particularly in the South, Du Bois said:

> We had absolutely no social contact with white Atlanta. Once in a while a white person would call on me—I remember one professor of sociology from Mississippi, who slipped up on the campus at dusk and came to my office. He said, "You're the first person I've visited in Atlanta, and I wouldn't want people to know it." He didn't dare come up to call on me in broad daylight.[34]

When the interviewer probed into the matter and asked Du Bois what his reaction was to his colleague's quandary, his response was:

> I had no simple response. I mean, the way he said it, you knew he was perfectly honest. Here was a situation which I understood as well as he did: a professor from a white Mississippi college couldn't come and visit as a social equal with a Negro professor. He simply couldn't do it. I knew it as well as he did, of course. Of course, on the other hand he knew perfectly well that I wasn't going to call on him no matter where he was; that the next time we meet, on the street or anything of that sort, I was going to fail to see him. I always had difficulties of that sort.[35]

It was in this cultural milieu that the discipline developed. My central argument in this book is that segregation in the United States during the discipline's formative years in this nation led Whites and Blacks to view and employ the tools of the science differently given their social locations on the racial map. White sociologists viewed the discipline as a means to develop theories on the behavior and interactions of the masses in, supposedly, a scientific and objective manner. Black sociologists, I posit, viewed the discipline as a tool to scientifically and objectively investigate, analyze and, if possible, positively impact the condition of a people rendered to second-class citizenship by the leading democratic government in the world. Despite the overbearing weight of individual and institutional racism, the constant threat of domestic terrorism from the Ku Klux Klan, potential loss of funding because of their commitment to objective research, and the virtual impossibility of improving their condition through the electoral process, Black sociologists made canonical contributions to the discipline during the period of American history known as Jim Crow.

It is simultaneously disconcerting and pleasing that sociologists are now beginning to recognize the voluminous contributions of Black sociologists at HBCUs to the discipline. Although the focus of this inquiry centered Atlanta, Tuskegee, Fisk, and Howard, examinations of the contributions of departments of sociology at HBCUs could easily be expanded to include activities at schools like Hampton University, Jackson State University, Johnson C. Smith University, and Texas Southern University. While a broad examination of the contributions of HBCUs to sociology is long overdue, this study is limited to the Big Four of Black sociology.

It is important that the historical record be corrected to note the achievements made by scholars at these schools. The historical record, including introductory textbooks and primary readers in multiple substantive topical areas, should be revised to note that Atlanta University housed the first American school of sociology; established the first program of applied urban sociology; was the first to institutionalize the methodological practices of method triangulation, insider researchers, and limitations and methods sections; and was the first to conduct sociological studies of the substantive areas of religion and family. Had historians not focused so intensely on Booker T. Washington's perceived hostility to the social sciences, in general, and sociology, specifically, they would have noticed that he developed at Tuskegee the first program of applied rural sociology in the nation. The contributions of Fisk sociologists George

Edmund Haynes and Charles S. Johnson were not as substantive as those at Atlanta. However, their applied urban sociology program served as a predecessor to its current manifestation that we call community-based participatory research. Howard, which housed a powerhouse of social science intellectuals rivaled by few, is most notably included here because of its well-developed infrastructure that allowed for the development of a top-notch research-intensive program and what continues to be the nation's only doctoral program at an HBCU. Collectively, this portrait of the contributions and accomplishments of early Black sociologists paints a different picture than existing depictions highlighting the nearly super-human exploits of singular superstar Black sociologists and pointing to them as exceptions to the rule that second-class citizens were not note-worthy figures in the discipline. Instead, the narrative in this inquiry acknowledges the collective efforts of countless and nameless Black men and women who assisted in the molding of this discipline into a tool to be used in the liberation of a subjugated people. The narrative on the contributions of Blacks to the discipline during its formative years in this nation is changing, but more work needs to be done to infuse this body of literature into the canon.

Instead of exclusively lionizing Chicago, North Carolina, and Wisconsin the canon should be more diverse, holistic, and accurate in bestowing proper credit on those who made seminal contributions to the discipline at, relatively speaking, under-resourced HBCUs. Instead of lionizing Max Weber, Karl Marx, and Robert Park, the canon should be more expan-sive and include significant sociological figures including Ida B. Wells-Barnett, George Edmund Haynes, Monroe N. Work, and Lucy Laney and Augustus Granville Dill who, but for their race, gender, and orientation, would already be canonized had they been male, White, heterosexual, and worked at an HWCU. A logical question one might ask in light of the invis-ibility of scores of Black sociologists is, "How did their works become mar-ginalized and ignored?" The answers to this question are addressed in my previous work, "Why Black Folks Tend to Shout!" However, below I offer a brief review of the five answers to this question. While the original paper addresses this topic only as it pertains to the exclusion of Du Bois's Atlanta Sociological Laboratory, the findings remain applicable for explaining the marginalization of the collective of HBCUs. Before I outline the causes of the marginalization of early Black sociologists, I lay out the theoretical lens through which the explanations were derived.

The theoretical lens through which the marginalization of early HBCUs is examined is Karl Mannheim's sociology of knowledge (SoK). SoK is a useful tool because it allows one to place theirself within a specific period of time to understand why and how people arrive at certain conclusions. While it is difficult for us to fully comprehend the veracity of anti-Black thought in both professional and communal settings by American Whites after emancipation and through the modern Civil Rights Movement, viewing their belief system via the SoK lens is one way to *partially understand* American racism. SoK enables one to reach a richer level of interpretation and analysis because "it does not refer only to specific assertions which may be regarded as concealment, falsification, or lies."[36] Moreover, SoK "does not criticize thought on the level of the assertions themselves, which may involve deceptions and disguises, but examines them on the structural, [cultural and/or ideological] level[s], which it views as not being the same for all men, but rather as allowing the same object to take on different forms and aspects in the course of social development."[37] As used in this study, SoK provides space to understand how the contributions of Blacks to sociology could be marginalized and ignored by White sociologists as unimportant at best, and pseudo-science at worst, while Black sociologists simultaneously fully understand and articulate the importance of their research to society and, vicariously, the discipline. Let me be very clear on this matter. I am not making an argument that the historical exclusion of Black sociologists by White sociologists from the canon should be forgiven or minimized. What I attempt to do is, giving most White sociologists a reasonable degree of the benefit of the doubt, make sense of the erasure of the contributions of Blacks at HBCUs by mainstream White sociologists for nearly one hundred years.

The first explanation for the marginalization of early Black sociologists is the idea that their works were mired in *academic obscurity*. Stated more clearly, this notion is rooted in the possibility that the contributions of Blacks at HBCUs were overlooked by White sociologists because their products were simply unknown or not widely disseminated within the academy. Thus, their exclusion from the historical (White) record is more akin to a simple oversight than an overt act with malicious intent. This argument is easily refuted when one considers each case. The Atlanta University publications often included a list of people and institutions from whom requests were received for copies of their research. The list was exhaustive and included a range of entities that received copies of the publications from popular magazines, both Black and White, to high school teachers and professors from Ivy League institutions. Although the printed proceedings of the applied rural sociology program at Tuskegee were not as readily distributed as reports from Atlanta, arguably, this school received more widespread attention than Du Bois's because of Booker T. Washington's status as the leading Black American figure of the era. Washington never shied away from delivering *the good news* concerning Tuskegee's accomplishments in industrial education. Given his nonthreatening posture towards Jim Crow segregation and neutral stance on issues of race and politics, many of his White benefactors eagerly promoted his successful endeavors. Allen Jones supported this position when he wrote:

> The approval and the publicity given the conferences by southern and northern newspapers and magazines was extremely helpful to [Washington] in his crusade to spread the "Tuskegee Idea." The Associated Press sent reports of the annual conferences to its thousands of newspapers detailing the handicaps of the southern Negro farmers and the progress being made by their self-uplifting.[38]

As indicated in Chapters 4 and 5, the applied sociology efforts of George Edmund Haynes, Charles S. Johnson, and their Fisk team were not limited to Nashville. Their research on ways to improve race relations were practiced in multiple cities and distributed around the nation via postal mail.

Also, by the time E. Franklin Frazier led Howard to prominence he had already become a national figure. In addition to his excellent research on the Black family, it would be unusual for Frazier to be an unknown entity within the discipline because of his ascension to the presidency of the Eastern Sociological Society and American Sociological Association (the latter with the assistance of Robert Park) and his establishment of a foundation for the only HBCU doctoral-producing department in the nation.

The second explanation for the marginalization of early Black sociologists is the notion that the *findings of their research were ungeneralizable.* This idea was proposed by Elliott Rudwick and is rooted in the misguided and scientifically racist belief that research on Blacks in America had little to no relevance (i.e., generalizability) to other groups.[39] In order for one to hold this position they must be consciously oblivious to the fact that similarities exist among seemingly dissimilar people such that their lived experience provides space for connections among groups thought previously to be impossible. A counterexample of this is Rudwick's critique of Du Bois's Atlanta Sociological Laboratory. While he lauded Du Bois's effectiveness at improving the *morale* of members of his race, Rudwick ultimately concluded Du Bois's school was an insignificant blip on the sociological radar because its findings were ungeneralizable. If one allows their *veil* to limit perceptions of others, then this posture is understandable. However, if one looks beyond Du Bois's veiled scholarship and *at the work actually performed* they will arrive at a different conclusion. Take, for example, the 1897 Atlanta University study wherein it was discovered Blacks had higher rates of tuberculosis than Whites. Researchers concluded that the high rate of disease was caused by a lack of proper ventilation in apartments where Blacks lived. Now, if one were to believe that only Blacks lived in apartments with little to no ventilation and *all* Whites did not, then Rudwick's position concerning the limitations of research conducted on a singular racial group would be supported. However, it is incontrovertible that not all Whites lived in single-family home units. Many Whites, in fact, also lived in poorly ventilated apartments. Consequently, for Rudwick and other White sociologists desirous of interpreting the works of early

Black sociologists from outside rather than within the veil, their short-sightedness is what cost generations of sociologists and social scientists the opportunity to learn and apply the excellent works produced by these brilliant yet marginalized scholars.

The third explanation for the marginalization of early Black sociologists is the idea that their *methods of research were unsophisticated and of low quality*. Instead of restating the methodologies employed by the schools highlighted earlier, I will simply refer the reader to Chapter 2 and the methodological contributions initiated by Du Bois's Atlanta Sociological Laboratory; Chapter 3 and the methodology employed at Booker T. Washington's farmer's conference that resulted in the first program of applied rural sociology; and Chapter 4, where the methodological foundation laid by George Edmund Haynes and Charles S. Johnson propelled Fisk to becoming one of the earliest applied urban sociology programs in the nation and forerunner to what we now call community-based participatory research.

The fourth explanation for the marginalization of early Black sociologists is the notion that their *findings lacked theoretical analysis*. Yes, in an ideal world every scientific question would include an explanation of its findings via a unit of theoretical analysis. More important than developing theoretical analyses of said research question, at least from the vantage point of Black sociology, was the development of policies and recommendations to address concerns resulting from said research question. In one respect, the prescriptions offered to address said research question by early Black sociologists, those aimed at impacting social policy and the everyday lives of Blacks in America, could be understood as elementary forms of theoretical analysis during the discipline's formative years in this nation. Stated another way, if one defines a theory as a set of interrelated statements that attempt to explain, predict, and/or understand social facts, which are replicable and generalizable, then the products of early Black sociologists qualify for theory status even if they were not presented in the prose deemed acceptable by today's standards. What I ultimately propose is that the shortsightedness of today's conceptions of theoretical constructions should not diminish the products produced by scholars engaged in research during the formative years of the discipline in this nation. Instead, one should analyze the sociological products of early sociologists through a lens that is more accurately attuned to the common practices of that day.

The last, and most significant, explanation for the marginalization of early Black sociologists is *racism*. Again, I will not repeat here that which is found in the Introduction and Chapter 1 on the extent and impact of racism on Blacks during the discipline's formative years in this nation. What is important to note is that, whether consciously or unconsciously, the mainstream White sociological enterprise colluded to render the significant contributions of Black sociologists invisible for more than one hundred years. While nothing can be done to change the past behavior(s) of White mainstream sociologists, at this point I believe it is more important to consider the ways that Black sociologists can be infused into the contemporary curriculum. This book is one effort in that direction.

Crashing Through the Gate

Despite the fact that HBCUs established departments of sociology before many HWCUs, there is a paucity of scholarly research on them. Donald Cunnigen cogently captured this point when he wrote, "It is the rare African-American college that has a published volume on an academic department. . . . With the exception of a brief essay on the Fisk University department by Stanley H. Smith (1974), African-American college sociology departmental histories are almost non-existent in contemporary scholarship."[40] Fortunately, since Cunnigen's proclamation a number of articles and books centering the contributions of sociologists at HBCUs like Atlanta, Fisk, and Howard[41] have been published. *The First American School of Sociology: W. E. B. Du Bois and the Atlanta Sociological Laboratory*, written by this author, was the first book-length singular treatment of a department of sociology at an HBCU. This inquiry is a similarly significant offering on a collective of departments of sociology at HBCUs. It is unfortunate it has taken so long to bring the accomplishments of these men and women to the attention of the mainstream White American sociological community. The historical invisibility of these departments of sociology has made their infusion into the canon extremely difficult, but not impossible. Had there been thorough articulations of the sociological significance of the works conducted by Blacks at HBCUs during or immediately following their terms it is likely their contributions would be canonized today. In lieu of their current relative invisibility, there are several ways one can infuse these works into curriculums.[42]

First, instructors can require research assignments comparing and contrasting the works of early Black sociologists to their contemporaries in courses including, but not limited to, classical theory, crime & deviance, family, historical sociology, and religion. Second, instructors can use selected portions of the works of early Black sociologists as supplemental reading materials. Third, instructors can include as required readings relevant works of early Black sociologists in their classes. Last, instructors may employ a hybrid of the latter two suggestions and customize a book featuring some of the important works of early Black sociologists. The customization of books is becoming increasingly popular and allows instructors more control over the content material. Collectively, when these efforts are combined with citation respect, properly recognizing early Black sociologists for seminal accomplishments made years before White sociologists who are incorrectly cited, the infusion of the works of early Black sociologists at HBCUs into the disciplinary canon will be achieved sooner than later.

I Will Find A Way or Make One

From 1895 to the modern civil rights era, the intellectual center of scientific, objective, and non-deficit centered research on Blacks was HBCUs. More importantly, during this period HBCUs made seminal contributions to the discipline in research methods, applied rural and urban sociology, and substantive topical areas including but not limited to family, race, and religion. It was in these spaces that leading sociologists and social scientists employed the tools of science and principles of Black sociology to counter scientific racism and inequality. In many respects, the accomplishments of these scholars can be summarized by the motto of Atlanta University, "I will find a way or make one." Despite lacking resources comparable to their HWCU peers, the accomplishments made at Atlanta, Fisk, Howard, and Tuskegee are a testament to their commitment and determination to engage in sociological works at a time when White America viewed them as *problems* who were biologically and intellectually inferior. Ironically, it is because of White America's insistence on separating the races in both public and private spaces that the emergence of sociology was an opportunity for Blacks to develop their own brand of scientific inquiry to improve their condition in this nation.

Ultimately, the contributions of Blacks to American sociology extend beyond the exploits of a handful of superstar scholars and include many people we will never know by name but whose works we can still appreciate. It is my sincere desire that more investigations into departments of sociology at HBCUs are conducted such that a more holistic portrait of the scholarly products of these scholars and institutions can be revealed. While the Big Four of Black sociology—Atlanta, Fisk, Howard and Tuskegee—made contributions to the discipline that were on par with any institution in the nation, who can say that in-depth examinations of departments of sociology at schools like Hampton, Tougaloo, and Xavier will not produce equally fascinating findings. Ultimately, this effort is a clarion call for sociologists and social scientists to make the canon more inclusive. This challenge must be accepted and the select scholars on this trip should be guided by the admonition, "I Will Find a Way or Make One."

APPENDIX I

Timeline of Noteworthy Events in *Jim Crow Sociology*

1826 John Brown Russworm (Bowdoin College) becomes the first Black American to graduate from college in the United States.

*   Edward Jones (Amherst College) becomes the second Black American to graduate from college in the United States, two weeks after Russworm.

1854 Lincoln University (Pennsylvania) is the first HBCU established in the United States.

1872 William G. Sumner teaches the first course in sociology in the United States at Yale.

1881 The University of Arkansas becomes the second school in the nation to offer a course in sociology.

1885 Arthur B. Woodford (Indiana University) becomes the first person to have the word *sociology* listed in his instructional title.

1889 The University of Kansas established the first department in the United States with *sociology* in its title (Department of History and Sociology).

1892 The Tuskegee Negro Conference is established by Booker T. Washington.

---- The University of Chicago established the first singularly named department of sociology in the United States.

1893 Fisk University becomes the first HBCU to offer a course on sociology.

1894 Kenyon L. Butterfield (University of Michigan) becomes the first person to have "Instructor of Rural Sociology" in his title.

---- C. R. Henderson (University of Chicago) teaches the first American course on rural sociology.

1895 The Atlanta University Study of the Negro Problem is established by President Horace Bumstead and George Bradford.

1896 First Atlanta University Study of the Negro conference held at Atlanta University under Director George Bradford.

1905 American Sociological Society (later renamed American Sociological Association) founded.

1906   James R. L. Diggs becomes the first Black American to take the PhD with a "specialty" in sociology (Illinois Wesleyan).

1911   Richard R. Wright becomes the first Black American to take the PhD from a department of sociology (University of Pennsylvania).

1937   Anna Johnson Julian becomes the first Black American woman to take the PhD from a department of sociology (University of Pennsylvania).

————   Rural Sociological Society founded.

1954   *Brown vs. Topeka Board of Education* decision desegregates schools.

1970   Association of Black Sociologists founded. (It was initially known as the Caucus of Black Sociologists of the American Sociological Association.)

1972   The first doctoral program in sociology at an HBCU is established at Howard University.

APPENDIX II

Reading list of Early Black Sociologists and Schools of Black Sociology

Atlanta University

Irvine, Russell W. 2001. "Coming South: The Reverend John Howard Hincks, A Five-Year (1889–1994) Window in the Development of Atlanta University and the Social Sciences." *Phylon* 49: 229–265.

Wright II, Earl. 2015. *The First American School of Sociology: W. E. B. Du Bois and the Atlanta Sociological Laboratory.*

Wright II, Earl. 2009. "Beyond W. E. B. Du Bois: A Note on Some of the Lesser Known Members of the Atlanta Sociological Laboratory." *Sociological Spectrum* 29, no. 6: 700–717.

Wright II, Earl. 2002. "The Atlanta Sociological Laboratory, 1896–1924: A Historical Account of the First American School of Sociology." *Western Journal of Black Studies* 26, no. 3:165–174.

Wright II, Earl. 2002. "Why Black People Tend To Shout!: An Earnest Attempt To Explain the Sociological Negation of the Atlanta Sociological Laboratory Despite Its Possible Unpleasantness." *Sociological Spectrum* 22, no. 3: 325–361.

Wright II, Earl. 2002. "Using The Master's Tools: Atlanta University and American Sociology, 1896–1924." *Sociological Spectrum* 22, no. 1: 15–39.

Fisk University

Carlton-LaNey, Iris. 1983. "Notes on a Forgotten Black Social Worker and Sociologist: George Edmund Haynes." *Journal of Sociology and Social Welfare* 10, no. 3:530–539.

Gilpin, Patrick J. 2003. *Charles S. Johnson: Leadership Beyond the Veil in the Age of Jim Crow.*

Hunter, Herbert M. 1988. "The Clinical Sociology of George Edmund Haynes." *Clinical Sociology Review* 6: 42–50.

Richardson, Joe M. 1980. *A History of Fisk University, 1865–1946.*

Sanders-Cassell, Katrina M. 2005. *Intelligent and Effective Direction: The Fisk University Race Relations Institute and the Struggle for Civil Rights, 1944-1969.*

Wright II, Earl. 2010. "The Tradition of Sociology at Fisk University." *Journal of African American Studies* 14, no. 1: 44–60.

Howard University

Dyson, Walter. 1941. *Howard University: The Capstone of Negro Education.*

Holloway, Jonathan S. 2002. *Confronting the Veil: Abram Harris Jr., E. Franklin Frazier, and Ralphe Bunche, 1919-1941.*

Jarmon, Charles. 2003. "Sociology at Howard University: From E. Franklin Frazier and Beyond." *Teaching Sociology* 31: 366–374.

Meier, August. 1960. "The Racial and Educational Philosophy of Kelly Miller, 1895-1915." *The Journal of Negro Education* 29, no. 2: 121–127.

Platt, Anthony M. 1991. *E. Franklin Frazier Reconsidered.*

Williams, Zachery R. 2009. *In Search of the Talented Tenth: Howard University Public Intellectuals and the Dilemmas of Race, 1926-1970.*

Tuskegee Institute

Jefferson, Paul. 1986. "Working Notes on the Prehistory of Black Sociology: The Tuskegee Negro Conference." *Knowledge and Society: Studies in the Sociology of Culture Past and Present* 6: 119–151.

Johnson, John Quincy. 2015. *Report of the Fifth Tuskegee Negro Conference (1896).*

Jones, Allen. 1991. "Improving Rural Life for Blacks: The Tuskegee Negro Farmers' Conference, 1892-1915." *Agricultural History* 65, no. 2: 105–114.

McMurry, Linda O. 1980. "A Black Intellectual in the New South: Monroe Nathan Work, 1866-1945." *Phylon* 41, no. 4: 333–344.

_____. *Recorder of the Black Experience: A Biography of Monroe Nathan Work.*

Washington, Booker T. 1901. *An Autobiography: The Story of My Life and Work.*

APPENDIX III

Reading List for a Course on Black Sociology

Aldridge, Delores P. 2009. *Imagine A World: Pioneering Black Women Sociologists.*

Atlanta University Publication. 1903. *The Negro Church.*

Atlanta University Publication. 1906. *The Health and Physique of the Negro American.*

Atlanta University Publication. 1908. *The Negro American Family.*

Carlton-LaNey, Iris. 1983. "Notes on a Forgotten Black Social Worker and Sociologist: George Edmund Haynes." *Journal of Sociology and Social Welfare* 10, no. 3: 530–539.

Daniels, Kalasia S. and Earl Wright II. 2018. "An Earnest Desire for the Truth Despite Its Possible Unpleasantness: A Comparative Analysis of the Atlanta University Publications and *American Journal of Sociology*, 1895–1917." *Sociology of Race and Ethnicity* 4, no. 1: 35–48.

Duncan, H. G. and Winnie L. Duncan. 1934. "The Development of Sociology in the Old South." *American Journal of Sociology* 39, no. 5: 649–656.

Fitzhugh, George. 1854. *Sociology for the South, or the Failure of a Free Society.*

Green, Dan S. and Edwin Driver. 1976. "W. E. B. Du Bois: A Case in the Sociology of Sociological Negation." *Phylon* 37: 308–333.

Holsey, Albin L. 1923. "The Tuskegee Conference." *Social Forces* 1, no. 3: 285–287.

Hughes, Henry. 1854. *Treatise on Sociology: Theoretical and Practical.*

Hurston, Zora N. 1942. *Dust Tracks on A Road.*

Hurston, Zora N. 1938. *Tell My Horse.*

Hurston, Zora Neale. 1927. "Cudjo's Own Story of the Last African Slaver." *Journal of Negro History* 12, no. 4: 648–663.

Hurston, Zora Neale. 1991. "Folklore and Music." *Frontiers: A Journal of Women Studies* 12, no. 1: 182–198.

Hurston, Zora Neale and John R. Lynch. 1927. "Communications." *Journal of Negro History* 12, no. 4: 664–669.

Jackson, Jacquelyn Johnson. 1974. "Black Female Sociologists." Pp. 267–295 in *Black Sociologists: Historical and Contemporary Perspectives*, edited by J. E. Blackwell and M. Janowitz.

Jefferson, Paul. 1986. "Working Notes on the Prehistory of Black Sociology: The Tuskegee Negro Conference." *Knowledge and Society: Studies in the Sociology of Culture Past and Present* 6: 119–151.

Jones, Allen. 1991. "Improving Rural Life for Blacks: The Tuskegee Negro Farmers' Conference." *Agricultural History* 65, no. 2: 105–114.

Ladner, Joyce. 1973. *The Death of White Sociology* (Part 3, Black Sociology: Toward A Definition of a Theory).

Lemert, Charles. 1994. "A Classic from the Other Side of the Veil: Du Bois's Souls of Black Folk." *The Sociological Quarterly* 35: 383–396.

McMurry, Linda O. 1980. "A Black Intellectual in the New South: Monroe Nathan Work, 1866–1945." *Phylon* 41, no. 4: 333–344.

Richardson, Marilyn (Ed.). 1987. *Maria W. Stewart: America's First Black Woman Political Writer.*

Sanders, Katrina. 2005. *Intelligent and Effective Direction: The Fisk University Race Relations Institute and the Struggle for Civil Rights, 1944–1969.*

Staples, Robert. 1973. "Race and Ideology: An Essay in Black Sociology." *Journal of Black Studies* 3: 395–422.

Stewart, Maria. 1987. *Maria Stewart: America's First Black Woman Political Writer.*

Thompson, E. T. 1945. "Sociology and Sociological Research in the South." *Social Forces* 23, no. 3: 356–365.

Watson, Wilbur. 1976. "The Idea of Black Sociology: Its Cultural and Political Significance." *American Sociologist* 11: 115–123.

Wells-Barnett, Ida B. 1996. *Southern Horrors and Other Writings: The Anti-Lynching Campaign of Ida B. Wells 1892–1900.*

Wright II, Earl. 2014. "W. E. B. Du Bois, Howard Odum and the Sociological Ghetto." *Sociological Spectrum* 34, no. 5: 453–468.

Wright II, Earl. 2012. "Why, Where and How to Infuse the Atlanta Sociological Laboratory into the Sociology Curriculum." *Teaching Sociology* 40: 257–270.

Wright II, Earl. 2010. "The Tradition of Sociology at Fisk University." *Journal of African American Studies* 14, no. 1: 44–60.

Wright II, Earl. 2010. "Beyond W. E. B. Du Bois: A Note on Some of the Lesser Known Members of the Atlanta Sociological Laboratory." *Sociological Spectrum* 29, no. 6: 700–717.

Wright II, Earl. 2002. "Why Black People Tend To Shout!: An Earnest Attempt to Explain the Sociological Negation of the Atlanta Sociological Laboratory Despite Its Possible Unpleasantness." *Sociological Spectrum* 22, no. 3: 325–361.

Wright II, Earl and Thomas C. Calhoun. 2006. "Jim Crow Sociology: Toward An Understanding of the Origin and Principles of Black Sociology via the Atlanta Sociological Laboratory." *Sociological Focus* 39, no. 1: 1–18.

Zuckerman, Phil. 202. "The Sociology of Religion of W. E. B. Du Bois." Sociology of Religion 63, no. 2: 239–253.

NOTES

Preface

1. Elliott Rudwick, "W. E. B. Du Bois and the Atlanta University Studies on the Negro," *Journal of Negro Education* 26 (1957): 466–476.
2. W. E. B. Du Bois, *The College-Bred Negro: Atlanta University Publication No. 5* (Atlanta: Atlanta University Press, 1900), 17.
3. L. L. Bernard, "Sociological Trends in the South," *Social Forces* 27, no. 1 (1948–1949): 14.
4. Ibid.
5. L. L. Bernard, "The Teaching of Sociology in Southern Colleges and Universities," *American Journal of Sociology* 23, no. 4 (1918): 505.

Introduction

1. Earl Wright II and Thomas C. Calhoun, "Jim Crow Sociology: Toward An Understanding of the Origin and Principles of Black Sociology via the Atlanta Sociological Laboratory," *Sociological Focus* 39, no. 1 (2006): 1–18.
2. See Joyce A. Ladner, *The Death of White Sociology* (New York: Random House, 1973); Robert Staples, "Race and Ideology: An Essay in Black Sociology," *Journal of Black Studies* 3 (1973): 395–422; Darryl Le Duff, "Perspectives on the Caucus of Black Sociologists and the 1975 Program," *The Black Sociologist* 5 (1975): 6–7; Robert Staples, *Introduction to Black Sociology*, (New York: McGraw-Hill, 1976); Wilbur Watson, "The Idea of Black Sociology: Its Cultural and Political Significance," *American Sociologist* 11 (1976):115–123; Alford A. Young, Jr. and Donald R. Deskins, Jr., "Early Traditions of African-American Sociological Thought," *Annual Review of Sociology* 27 (2001): 445–477.
3. Wilbur Watson, *Introduction to Black Sociology* (New York: McGraw-Hill, 1976), 3.
4. See Kalasia S. Daniels and Earl Wright II, "An Earnest Desire for the Truth Despite Its Possible Unpleasantness: A Comparative Analysis of the Atlanta

University Publications and *American Journal of Sociology*, 1895–1917," *Sociology of Race and Ethnicity* 4, no. 1 (2018): 35–48.

5. W. E. B. Du Bois, *The Souls of Black Folk* (New York: Dover Publications, [1903]1994), 94.

6. W. E. B. Du Bois, "The Study of the Negro Problems," in *W. E. B. Du Bois: On Sociology and the Black Community*, eds. Dan S. Green and Edwin D. Driver (Chicago, IL: University of Chicago Press, [1898] 1978), 77–78.

7. Ibid., 76.

8. See Aldon Morris, *The Scholar Denied* (Berkeley: University of California Press, 2015).

9. See Elliott Rudwick, "W. E. B. Du Bois and the Atlanta University Studies on the Negro," *Journal of Negro Education* 26 (1957): 466–476.

10. See Earl Wright II, "Using The Master's Tools: Atlanta University and American Sociology, 1896–1924," *Sociological Spectrum* 22, no. 1 (2002a): 15–39; Earl Wright II, "Why Black People Tend To Shout!: An Earnest Attempt To Explain the Sociological Negation of the Atlanta Sociological Laboratory Despite Its Possible Unpleasantness," *Sociological Spectrum* 22, no. 3 (2002b): 325–361; and Kalasia S. Daniels and Earl Wright II, "An Earnest Desire for the Truth Despite Its Possible Unpleasantness," 35–48.

11. Atlanta University, *Mortality Among Negroes in Cities: Atlanta University Publication No. 1* (Atlanta: Atlanta University Press, 1896), 5.

12. Ibid.

13. W. E. B. Du Bois, "The Relations of the Negroes to the Whites in the South," in *W. E. B. Du Bois: On Sociology and the Black Community*, eds. Dan S. Green and Edwin (Chicago: University of Chicago Press, [1904]1978), 58–59.

14. Ibid., 56.

15. Ibid., 56–57.

16. Ibid., 56.

17. Atlanta University, *Mortality Among Negroes in Cities*, 6–7.

18. W. E. B. Du Bois, "The Study of the Negro Problems," 80.

19. W. E. B. Du Bois, *The Autobiography of W. E. B. Du Bois: A Soliloquy on Viewing My Life from the Last Decade of its First Century* (New York: International Publishers, 1968), 46.

Chapter 1

1. L. L. Bernard, "Sociological Trends in the South," 13.

2. Editor's Table, "Sociology and Theology at Yale College," *Popular Science Monthly* 17, (1880): 168.

3. Albion Small, "Fifty Years of Sociology in the United States (1865–1915)," *American Journal of Sociology* 21, no. 6 (1916): 732.

4. L. L. Bernard, "Sociological Trends in the South," 12–19.

5. Floyd N. House, *The Development of Sociology* (New York: McGraw-Hill Book Company, 1936), 245.

6. See Albion Small, "Fifty Years of Sociology in the United States."

7. Ibid., 760.

8. Ibid.

9. Ibid.

10. Ibid.

11. Ibid.

12. Ibid.

13. University of Chicago Committee on Development, *The Quest for Truth* (Chicago: University of Chicago Press, 1925), 9.

14. Ibid., 39.

15. Albion Small, "Fifty Years of Sociology in the United States," 763.

16. Ibid., 764.

17. Ibid., 765.

18. See W. E. B. Du Bois, *The Negro Common School: The Atlanta University Publications, No. 6* (Atlanta, GA: Atlanta University Press, 1901).

19. Ibid., 18.

20. Ibid., 19.

21. Ibid., 18.

22. See W. E. B. Du Bois, *The Negro Common School: The Atlanta University Publications, No. 6* (Atlanta, GA: Atlanta University Press, 1901).

23. Ibid., 21.

24. See W. E. B. Du Bois, *The College-Bred Negro: Atlanta University Publication No. 5* (Atlanta: Atlanta University Press, 1900).

25. See Frank Bowles and Frank DeCosta, *Between Two Worlds: A Profile of Negro Higher Education* (New York: McGraw-Hill, 1971).

26. Ibid., 29.

27. Ibid., 31.

28. Augustus F. Beard, *A Crusade of Brotherhood: A History of the American Missionary Association* (Boston: The Pilgrim Press, 1909), 154–155.

29. Dwight O. W. Holmes, *The Evolution of the Negro College* (New York: Arno Press & The New York Times, 1969), 8.

30. W. E. B. Du Bois, *The College-Bred Negro*, 12.

31. Ibid.

32. Ibid.
33. Ibid., 13.
34. Ibid., 12.
35. L. L. Bernard, "Sociological Trends in the South," 13.
36. Ibid., 14.
37. See Earl Wright II, "W. E. B. Du Bois, Howard Odum and the Sociological Ghetto," *Sociological Spectrum* 34, no. 5 (2014): 453–468
38. H. G. Duncan and Winnie Leach Duncan, "The Development of Sociology in the Old South," *American Journal of Sociology* 39, no. 5 (1934): 649.
39. Ibid., 650.
40. Edgar T. Thompson, "Sociology and Sociological Research in the South," *Social Forces* 23, no. 3 (1945): 357.
41. George Fitzhugh, *Sociology for the South or the Failure of Free Society* (Richmond, VA: A. Morris, 1854), vi.
42. Henry Hughes, *Treatise on Sociology, Theoretical and Practical* (Philadelphia: Lippincott, Grambo and Company, 1854), v.
43. See H. G. Duncan and Winnie Leach Duncan, "The Development of Sociology in the Old South," 649.
44. Francis Galton, "Eugenics: Its Definition, Scope and Aims," *American Journal of Sociology* 10 (1904): 4.
45. George Howard, "Alcohol and Crime: A Study in Social Causation," *American Journal of Sociology* 24, no. 1 (1918): 67–68.
46. Elliott Rudwick, "W. E. B. Du Bois as Sociologist," in *Black Sociologists: Historical and Contemporary Perspectives*, eds. James Blackwell and Morris Janowitz (Chicago, IL: University of Chicago Press, 1974), 48.
47. Ibid., 47.
48. Ibid., 48.
49. Dan S. Green and Edwin D. Driver, "W. E. B. DuBois: A Case in the Sociology of Sociological Negation," *Phylon* 37, no. 4 (1976): 331.
50. Ibid.

Chapter 2

1. Russell W. Irvine, "Coming South: The Reverend John Howard Hincks, A Five-Year (1889–1994) Window in the Development of Atlanta University and the Social Sciences," *Phylon* 49 (2001): 259.
2. Ibid., 251.
3. Atlanta University, *The Negro in Business. Atlanta University Publication No. 4* (Atlanta: Atlanta University Press, 1899), 13.

4. See Clark Atlanta University, "Who's Who Among Atlanta University Graduates and Former Students," *Phylon* 3, no. 2 (1942): 163–169.
5. W. E. B. Du Bois, *The Autobiography of W. E. B. Du Bois: A Soliloquy*, 214.
6. W. E. B. Du Bois, "The Study of the Negro Problems," 80.
7. Ibid.
8. See Aldon Morris, *The Scholar Denied*.
9. W. E. B. Du Bois, "The Study of the Negro Problems," 81.
10. See Earl Wright II, "Using The Master's Tools," 15–39; and Earl Wright II, "Why Black People Tend To Shout!" 325–361.
11. Atlanta University, *Social and Physical Condition of Negroes in Cities. Atlanta University Publication No. 2* (Atlanta: Atlanta University Press, 1897), 5.
12. See Earl Wright II, "Using The Master's Tools"; Earl Wright II, "Why Black People Tend To Shout!!" 325–361; and Earl Wright II, *The First American School of Sociology: W. E. B. Du Bois and the Atlanta Sociological Laboratory* (London: Routledge/Ashgate, 2016).
13. Ibid.
14. Atlanta University, *The Negro American Family: The Atlanta University Publications, No. 13* (Atlanta: Atlanta University Press, 1908), 9–10.
15. See Kalasia S. Daniels and Earl Wright II, "An Earnest Desire for the Truth Despite Its Possible Unpleasantness," 35–48.
16. See Earl Wright II, "Using The Master's Tools," 15–39; and Earl Wright II, *The First American School of Sociology*.
17. W. E. B. Du Bois, *The Negro Common School*, 2.
18. Ibid.
19. See Phil Zuckerman, *Du Bois on Religion* (Oxford: Rowman & Littlefield, 2000).
20. W. E. B. Du Bois, *The Autobiography of W. E. B. Du Bois: A Soliloquy*, 217.
21. See Earl Wright II, "Using The Master's Tools," 15–39; Aldon Morris, *The Scholar Denied*; and Earl Wright II, *The First American School of Sociology*.
22. Phil Zuckerman, *Du Bois on Religion*, 250.
23. W. E. B. Du Bois, *The Autobiography of W. E. B. Du Bois: A Soliloquy*, vi.
24. Earl Wright II, "Why Black People Tend To Shout!" 353.
25. Atlanta University, *The Negro American Family*, 152.
26. Atlanta University, *Mortality Among Negroes in Cities*, 29.
27. Atlanta University, *Social and Physical Condition of Negroes in Cities*, 62.
28. Ibid.
29. Ibid., 56–57.

30. See Phil Zuckerman, *The Social Theory of W. E. B. Du Bois* (Thousand Oaks, CA: Pine Forge Press, 2004).

31. See Earl Wright II, "Using The Master's Tools," 15–39; Earl Wright II, "Why Black People Tend To Shout!" 325–361; and Earl Wright II, *The First American School of Sociology*.

32. See Kalasia S. Daniels and Earl Wright II, "An Earnest Desire for the Truth Despite Its Possible Unpleasantness," 35–48.

Chapter 3

1. Lowrey Nelson, *Rural Sociology: Its Origin and Growth in the United States* (Minneapolis: University of Minnesota, 1969), 28.

2. Ibid.

3. See Lowrey Nelson, *Rural Sociology,* and Dwight Sanderson, "The Teaching of Rural Sociology: Particularly in the Land-Grant Colleges and Universities," *American Journal of Sociology* 22, no. 4 (1917): 433–460.

4. Lowrey Nelson, *Rural Sociology,* 106–107.

5. Ibid., 107.

6. Kenyon Butterfield, "Rural Sociology as a College Discipline," *Annals of the American Academy of Political and Social Science* 40 (1912): 12–18.

7. Lowrey Nelson, *Rural Sociology.*

8. See Dwight Sanderson, "The Teaching of Rural Sociology," 433–460; Carl C. Taylor, "Research in Rural Sociology," *American Journal of Sociology* 33, no. 2 (1927): 211–221; and Emilia E. Martinez-Brawley, "Rural Sociology and Rural Social Work: An Historical Essay," *The Journal of Sociology & Social Welfare* 7, no. 4 (1980): Article 6.

9. W. E. B. Du Bois, "The Talented Tenth," in *The Negro Problem: A Series of Articles by Representative American Negroes of To-day*, ed. unknown (New York: AMS Press, ([1903]1970), 61.

10. Booker T. Washington, *An Autobiography: The Story of My Life and Work* (Atlanta, GA.: J. L. Nichols and Company, 1901), 255.

11. Ibid., 256.

12. Emmett J. Scott, "The Tuskegee Negro Conferences," *Voice of the Negro* (May 1904): 9.

13. Editor, "A Letter from Tuskegee: Reported by Our Special Correspondent," *Southern Workman* (March 1893b): 50.

14. See Kalasia S. Daniels and Earl Wright II, "An Earnest Desire for the Truth Despite Its Possible Unpleasantness," 35–48.

15. Ibid.

16. Carl C. Taylor, "Research in Rural Sociology," 211.

17. Editor. "A Trip Through the South," *Southern Workman* (April 1894b): 57.

18. Paul Jefferson, "Working Notes on the Prehistory of Black Sociology: The Tuskegee Negro Conference," *Knowledge and Society: Studies in the Sociology of Culture Past and Present*, 6 (1986): 135.

19. Editor, "Tuskegee Negro Conference," *Southern Workman* (March 1892): 37.

20. Editor, "A Letter from Tuskegee: Reported by Our Special Correspondent," *Southern Workman* (March 1893a): 41.

21. Editor, "The Tuskegee Negro Conference," *Southern Workman* (March 1894a): 47.

22. Ibid., 48.

23. Editor. "A Trip Through the South," 58.

24. Tuskegee University, *Fifth Tuskegee Negro Conference* (Baltimore: Tuskegee University, 1896), 12.

25. Allen W. Jones. "The Role of Tuskegee Institute in the Education of Black Farmers." *Journal of Negro History* (1975): 261.

26. Ibid.

27. Ibid., 263.

28. Carl C. Taylor, "Research in Rural Sociology," 213.

29. Paul Jefferson, "Working Notes on the Prehistory of Black Sociology," 139.

30. Ibid.

31. Booker T. Washington, *An Autobiography,* 258.

32. Ibid., 259.

33. Allen Jones, "Improving Rural Life for Blacks: The Tuskegee Negro Farmers' Conference, 1892–1915," *Agricultural History* 65, no. 2 (1991): 109.

34. Ibid.

35. W. E. B. Du Bois, *Results of Ten Tuskegee Negro Conferences* (Tuskegee, AL: Tuskegee Institute, 1901), 3.

36. Ibid., 4–5.

37. Paul Jefferson, "Working Notes on the Prehistory of Black Sociology," 127–128.

38. Booker T. Washington, *An Autobiography,* 263.

39. Ibid., 261.

40. Linda O. McMurry, *Recorder of the Black Experience: A Biography of Monroe Nathan Work* (Baton Rouge: Louisiana State University, 1985), 49.

41. Ibid., 49.

42. Ibid., 334.

43. Ibid., 28.

44. Ibid., 334.

45. Earl Wright II, "Beyond W. E. B. Du Bois: A Note on Some of the Lesser Known Members of the Atlanta Sociological Laboratory," *Sociological Spectrum* 29, no. 6 (2009): 704.

46. Stanford M. Lymann, "Robert Park Reconsidered: The Early Writings," *The American Sociologist* 21, no. 4, (1990): 345.

47. Linda O. McMurry, *Recorder of the Black Experience*, 28.

48. Ibid., 74–75.

49. Ibid., 75.

50. Ida B. Wells-Barnett, *Southern Horrors and Other Writings: The Anti-Lynching Campaign of Ida B. Wells, 1892-1900* (Bedford Books: Boston, 1997): 79.

51. Earl Wright II, "Why Black People Tend To Shout!" 350–351.

52. Ida B. Wells-Barnett, *Southern Horrors and Other Writings*, 75.

53. Ibid., 82.

54. Ibid., 157.

55. Ibid., 150.

Chapter 4

1. Frank L. Tolman, "The Study of Sociology in Institutions of Learning in the United States: A Report of an Investigation Undertaken by the Graduate Sociological League of the University of Chicago," *American Journal of Sociology* 7, no. 6 (1902): 797.

2. Joe M. Richardson, *A History of Fisk University, 1865-1946, 1980* (Tuscaloosa: University of Alabama, 1980), 3.

3. A. A. Taylor, "Fisk University and the Nashville Community, 1866-1900," *The Journal of Negro History* 39, no. 2 (1954): 118.

4. See Joseph S. Himes, "The Teacher of Sociology in the Negro College," *Social Forces* 29, no. 3 (1951): 302–305.

5. See Earl Wright II, "The Tradition of Sociology at Fisk University," *Journal of African American Studies* 14, no. 1 (2010): 44–60.

6. Cornelius Wortendyke Morrow, "History of Fisk Sociology" (unpublished manuscript n.d.), 3.

7. "The Talented Tenth: The Re-Examination of a Concept," by W. E. B. Du Bois, 1948, Reel 81, Frame 1090–100 in *The Papers of W. E. B. Du Bois*, ed. Robert W. McDowell. (Sanford, NC: Milcrofilming Corporation of America. [1948]1980), 2.

8. Cornelius Wortendyke Morrow, "History of Fisk Sociology," 4.

9. Joe M. Richardson, *A History of Fisk University*, 64.

10. Preston Valien et al., "History of the Department of Social Sciences, Fisk University, 1911–1948" (unpublished manuscript, 1950), 1.

11. Ibid.

12. Ibid.

13. Iris Carlton-LaNey, "Training African-American Social Workers Through the NUL Fellowship Program," *Journal of Sociology and Social Welfare* 21, no. 1 (1994):44.

14. Ibid., 45.

15. Preston Valien et al., "History of the Department of Social Sciences, Fisk University," 2–3.

16. Ibid., 3.

17. Ibid., 4.

18. Iris Carlton-LaNey, "Fisk Social Work Students' Emergency Relief Work Following the East Nashville Fire of 1916," *Tennessee Historical Quarterly* 44, no. 4 (1985): 373.

19. Ibid., 374.

20. Cynthia Neverdon-Morton, *Afro-American Women of the South and the Advancement of the Race, 1895–1925* (Knoxville: University of Tennessee Press, 1989), 169.

21. Patricia Lengermann and Gillian Niebrugge, "Thrice Told: Narratives of Sociology's Relation to Social Work," in *Sociology in America: A History*, ed. Craig Calhoun (Chicago: University of Chicago Press, 2007), 72.

22. Samuel K. Roberts, "Crucible for a Vision: The Work of George Edmund Haynes and the Commission on Race Relations, 1912–1947" (Ann Arbor: University Microfilm International, 1974), 58.

23. Iris Carlton-LaNey, "Notes on a Forgotten Black Social Worker and Sociologist: George Edmund Haynes," *Journal of Sociology and Social Welfare* 10, no. 3 (1983): 531.

24. Herbert Hunter, "The Clinical Sociology of George Edmund Haynes," *Clinical Sociology Review* 6 (1988): 48.

25. Walter Dyson, *Howard University: The Capstone of Negro Education* (Washington, D.C.: Howard University, 1941), 39.

26. Ibid., 90.

27. Zachery R. Williams, *In Search of the Talented Tenth: Howard University Public Intellectuals and the Dilemmas of Race, 1926–1970* (Columbia: University of Missouri Press, 2009), 41.

28. Ibid., 90.

29. Walter Dyson, *Howard University*, 303.

30. Ibid., 392.
31. Fred J. Kelly, "An Outsider's View of Howard University," *The Journal of Negro Education* 4, no. 4 (1935): 473.
32. Zachery R. Williams, *In Search of the Talented Tenth*, 51.
33. Ibid., 52.
34. Walter Dyson, *Howard University*, 371.
35. Charles Jarmon, "Sociology at Howard University: From E. Franklin Frazier and Beyond," *Teaching Sociology* 31 (2003): 366.
36. W. D. Wright, "The Thought and Leadership of Kelly Miller," *Phylon* 39, no. 2 (1978): 181.
37. See W. D. Wright, "The Thought and Leadership of Kelly Miller," 180–192.
38. Zachery R. Williams, *In Search of the Talented Tenth*, 109.
39. Ibid., 109–110.
40. August Meier, "The Racial and Educational Philosophy of Kelly Miller, 1895–1915," *The Journal of Negro Education* 29, no. 2 (1960): 127.

Chapter 5

1. Letter, "Letter from Charles S. Johnson (National Urban League) to President Thomas Elsa Jones (Fisk University)" by Charles S. Johnson, 1928, Thomas Elsa Jones Collection, Fisk University, Box 34, Folder 21, page 2.
2. Preston Valien et al., "History of the Department of Social Sciences, Fisk University," 1.
3. Letter, "Letter from President Thomas Elsa Jones (Fisk University) to Eugene Kinkle Jones (Executive Secretary of the National Urban League)" by Thomas Elsa Jones, 1927b, Thomas Elsa Jones Collection, Fisk University, Box 34, Folder 21, page 1.
4. Preston Valien et al., "History of the Department of Social Sciences, Fisk University," 7.
5. See Katrina M. Sanders, *Intelligent and Effective Direction: The Fisk University Race Relations Institute and the Struggle for Civil Rights, 1944-1969* (New York: Peter Lang, 2005).
6. Herman Long, "10 Years Perspective on Our Work in Race Relations: Report to the Joint Meeting of the American Missionary Association Divisional Committee and the Policy and Planning Committee of the Board of Home Missions of the Congregational and Christian Churches at Deering, New Hampshire, June 16–17, 1953" (unpublished manuscript, 1953), 4.
7. Ibid., 3
8. Ibid., 7.

9. Ibid., 8.
10. Ibid., 9.
11. Ibid. 12.
12. Ibid., 12.
13. Ibid., 14.
14. Ibid., 15.
15. Ibid., 19.
16. Ibid., 34.
17. Ibid., 33.
18. Ibid., 31.
19. Ibid., 32.
20. Bertram Doyle, "The Introductory Course in Sociology in Negro Colleges and Universities," *Journal of Educational Sociology* 7, no. 1 (1933): 30.
21. Ibid., 36.
22. Frazier, E. Franklin. "Graduate Education in Negro Colleges and Universities," *The Journal of Negro Education* 2, no. 3 (1933): 341.
23. Ibid., 332.
24. Ibid., 330.
25. Ibid., 331.
26. Ibid., 332.
27. Ibid., 341.
28. Ibid., 339.
29. See Jonathan Holloway, *Confronting the Veil: Abram Harris Jr., E. Franklin Frazier, and Ralph Bunche, 1919-1941* (Chapel Hill: University of North Carolina Press, 2002) and Zachery R. Williams, *In Search of the Talented Tenth.*
30. See Zachery R. Williams, *In Search of the Talented Tenth.*
31. Ibid., 4–5.
32. Anthony Platt, *E. Franklin Frazier Reconsidered* (New Brunswick: Rutgers University Press, 1991).
33. Arthur P. Davis, "E. Franklin Frazier (1894–1962): A Profile," *The Journal of Negro Education* 31, no. 4 (1962): 432.
34. Ibid.
35. See Anthony Platt, *E. Franklin Frazier Reconsidered.*
36. E. Franklin Frazier, "Ethnic Family Patterns: The Negro Family in the United States," *American Journal of Sociology* 53, no. 6 (1948): 438.
37. Walter Dyson, *Howard University*, 178.

38. E. Franklin Frazier, "Graduate Education in Negro Colleges and Universities," 339.

39. Zachery R. Williams, *In Search of the Talented Tenth*, 46.

40. E. Franklin Frazier, "Graduate Education in Negro Colleges and Universities," 337.

41. Zachery R. Williams, *In Search of the Talented Tenth*, 3.

42. Walter Dyson, *Howard University*, 168–169.

43. Anthony Platt, *E. Franklin Frazier Reconsidered*, 105.

44. Ibid., 104–105.

45. Ibid., 104.

46. Ibid.

47. W. E. B. Du Bois, *The Autobiography of W. E. B. Du Bois: A Soliloquy*, 223–224.

48. Ibid., 229.

49. W. E. B. Du Bois, "The Atlanta University Studies of Social Conditions among Negroes" (unpublished manuscript, November 10, 1940) 4.

50. Ibid., 5.

51. W. E. B. Du Bois, "The First Phylon Institute and Twenty-Fifth Atlanta University Conference." *Phylon* 2, no. 3 (1941): 275–288.

52. Ibid., 279.

53. Dorothy C. Yancy, "William Edward Burghardt Du Bois' Atlanta Years: The Human Side—A Study Based Upon Oral Sources," *Journal of Negro History* 63 (1978): 64.

54. W. E. B. Du Bois, interviewer unknown. ([1960] 1979). W. E. B. Du Bois Papers 1979, Reel 84, Frame 163.

Chapter 6

1. W. E. B. Du Bois, *The College-Bred Negro,* and *The Negro Common School.*

2. Greene, Harry W., *Holders of Doctorates Among American Negroes* (Boston: Meador Publishing, 1946).

3. Joseph S. Himes, "The Teacher of Sociology in the Negro College," 303.

4. Ibid.

5. Ibid.

6. James E. Conyers, "Negro Doctorates in Sociology: A Social Portrait," *Phylon* 29, no. 3 (1968): 218.

7. See Jerry Watts, "Dilemmas of Black Intellectuals: What Role Should We Play," *Dissent*, Fall (1989): 501–507.

8. See Robert B. Slater, "The First Black Faculty Members at the Nation's Highest-Ranked Universities," *Journal of Blacks in Higher Education* 22 (1998–1999): 97–106.

9. James E. Blackwell, "The Founding of the Minority Fellowship Program: A Commitment to Opportunity and Diversity" (unpublished manuscript, August 2008, presented at the 2008 American Sociological Association Annual Meeting, Boston, Massachusetts), 2.

10. See James L. Conyers, *Africana Studies: A Disciplinary Quest for both Theory and Methods* (Jefferson, NC: McFarland & Company, Inc. Publishers, 1997); Molefi Kete Asante and Maulana Karenga, *Handbook of Black Studies* (Thousand Oaks, CA: Sage Publications, 2006); and Nathaniel Norment, Jr., *The African American Studies Reader* (Durham, NC: Carolina Academic Press, 2007).

11. See Lawrence Crouchett, "Early Black Studies Movements." *Journal of Black Studies* 2, no. 2 (1971): 189–200.

12. Maulana Karenga, *Introduction to Black Studies*, 6.

13. See Earl Wright II, *The First American School of Sociology*.

14. Maulana Karenga, *Introduction to Black Studies*, 19.

15. Maurice Jackson, "Toward a Sociology of Black Studies," *Journal of Black Studies* 1, no. 2 (1970): 132.

16. Ibid., 135.

17. Lawrence Crouchett, "Early Black Studies Movements," 194.

18. Ama Mazama, "Interdisciplinary, Transdisciplinary, or Unidisciplinary?: Africana Studies and the Vexing Question of Definition," in *Handbook of Black Studies*, eds. Molefi Kete Asante and Maulana Karenga (Thousand Oaks, CA: Sage Publications, 2006), 5.

19. Nagueyalti Warren, *Grandfather of Black Studies: W. E. B. Du Bois* (Trenton: Africa World Press, 2011), 62.

20. See Lawrence Crouchett, "Early Black Studies Movements," 189–200.

21. See John W. Blassingame, *New Perspectives on Black Studies* (Urbana: University of Illinois Press, 1971); James P. Shenton, *Black Studies: Threat or Challenge* (Port Washington, NY: Kennikat Press, 1973); T. K. Daniel, "Theory Building in Black Studies," *The Black Scholar* 12, no. 3 (1981): 29–36; James L. Conyers, *Africana Studies: A Disciplinary Quest for Both Theory and Methods* (Jefferson, NC: McFarland & Company, 1997); Molefi Kete Asante and Maulana Karenga, *Handbook of Black Studies*; Nathaniel Norment, Jr., *The African American Studies Reader*; Maulana Karenga, "Names and Notions of Black Studies: Issues of Roots, Range and Relevance," *Journal of Black Studies* 40, no. 1 (2009): 41–64; and Maulana Karenga, *Introduction to Black Studies*.

22. Maurice Jackson, "Toward a Sociology of Black Studies," 133.

23. See William H. Sewell, "Some Observations and Reflections on the Role of Women and Minorities in the Democratization of the American Socio-logical Association, 1905–1990," *The American Sociologist* 23, no. 1 (1992): 57–62.

24. Michael R. Hill, "American Sociological Association," in the *Blackwell Encyclopedia of Sociology, Vol. 1*, ed. George Ritzer (Malden, MA: Blackwell Publishing, 2007), 131.

25. Ibid.

26. Michael R. Hill, "American Sociological Association," 130–134.

27. James B. Blackwell, Maurice Jackson, and Joan W. Moore, "The Status of Racial and Ethnic Minorities in Sociology," *Footnotes* (Special Supplement), August (1977): 3.

28. Joseph W. Scott, "A Brief History of the Association of Black Sociologists" (unpublished manuscript, n.d.), 1.

29. Ibid.

30. Ibid.

31. See James E. Blackwell, "Minorities in the Liberation of ASA?" *The American Sociologist* 23, no. 1 (1992): 11–17; James E. Conyers, "The Association of Black Sociologists: A Descriptive Account from an 'Insider,'" *The American Sociologist* 23, no. 1 (1992): 49–55; and James E. Blackwell, "The Founding of the Minority Fellowship Program," 2.

32. James E. Conyers, "The Association of Black Sociologists," 53.

33. James E. Blackwell, "Minorities in the Liberation of ASA?" 11–17; James E. Conyers, "The Association of Black Sociologists," 49–55; and Joseph W. Scott, "A Brief History of the Association of Black Sociologists" (unpublished manuscript, n.d.), 1.

34. Interview, "Untitled" by W. E. B. Du Bois, 1960, W. E. B. Du Bois Papers, Reel 84, Frame 163.

35. Ibid., 163–164.

36. Karl Mannheim, *Ideology and Utopia: An Introduction to the Sociology of Knowledge* (New York: Harcourt, Brace, & World, Inc., 1968), 238.

37. Ibid.

38. Allen Jones, "Improving Rural Life for Blacks," 112.

39. See Elliott Rudwick, "W. E. B. Du Bois and the Atlanta University Studies on the Negro," 466–476.

40. Donald Cunnigen, "The Legacy of Ernst Borinski: The Production of an African American Sociological Tradition," *Teaching Sociology* 31 (2003): 397.

41. See Earl Wright II, "Using The Master's Tools," 15–39; Earl Wright II, "Why Black People Tend To Shout!" 325–361; Earl Wright II, "The Atlanta Sociological Laboratory, 1896–1924: A Historical Account of the First American School of Sociology," *Western Journal of Black Studies* 26, no. 3 (2002c): 165–174; Charles Jarmon, "Sociology at Howard University," 366–374; Earl Wright II, "Beyond W. E. B. Du Bois," 700–717; Earl Wright II, "The Tradition of Sociology at Fisk University," 44–60; Earl Wright II, "Why, Where and How to Infuse the Atlanta Sociological Laboratory into the Sociology Curriculum," *Teaching Sociology* 40 (2012): 257–270; Aldon Morris, *The Scholar Denied*, and Earl Wright II, *The First American School of Sociology*.

42. See Earl Wright II, "Why, Where and How to Infuse the Atlanta Sociological Laboratory into the Sociology Curriculum," 257–270.

BIBLIOGRAPHY

Asante, Molefi Kete and Maulana Karenga. *Handbook of Black Studies.* Thousand Oaks, CA: Sage Publications, 2006.

Atlanta University. *Mortality Among Negroes in Cities: Atlanta University Publication No. 1.* Atlanta: Atlanta University Press, 1896.

Atlanta University. *Social and Physical Condition of Negroes in Cities. Atlanta University Publication No. 2.* Atlanta: Atlanta University Press, 1897.

Atlanta University. *The Negro in Business. Atlanta University Publication No. 4.* Atlanta: Atlanta University Press, 1899.

Atlanta University. "Who's Who Among Atlanta University Graduates and Former Students." *Phylon* 3, no. 2 (1942): 163–169.

Atlanta University. "Who's Who Among Atlanta University Graduates and Former Students." *Phylon* 3, no. 2 (1942): 163–169.

Beard, Augustus F. *A Crusade of Brotherhood: A History of the American Missionary Association.* Boston: The Pilgrim Press, 1909.

Bernard, L. L. "The Teaching of Sociology in Southern Colleges and Universities." *American Journal of Sociology* 23, no. 4 (1918): 491–515.

———. "Sociological Trends in the South." *Social Forces* 27, no. 1 (1948): 12–19

Blackwell, James E. "Minorities in the Liberation of ASA?" *The American Sociologist* 23, no. 1 (1992): 11–17.

———. "The Founding of the Minority Fellowship Program: A Commitment to Opportunity and Diversity." Unpublished manuscript, August 2008.

Blackwell, James E., Maurice Jackson, and Joan W. Moore. 1977. "The Status of Racial and Ethnic Minorities in Sociology." *Footnotes* (Special Supplement), August, (1977): 1–8.

Blassingame, John W. *New Perspectives on Black Studies.* Urbana: University of Illinois Press, 1971.

Bowles, Frank and Frank DeCosta. *Between Two Worlds: A Profile of Negro Higher Education.* New York: McGraw-Hill, 1971.

Brooks, Marcus and Earl Wright II. 2019. "Augustus Granville Dill: Notes on an Early Black Queer Subjugated Scholar." Department of Sociology, University of Cincinnati, Cincinnati, OH. Unpublished manuscript.

Butterfield. Kenyon L. "Rural Sociology as a College Discipline." *Annals of the American Academy of Political and Social Science* 40(1912): 12–18.

Carlton-LaNey, Iris. 1983. "Notes on a Forgotten Black Social Worker and Sociologist: George Edmund Haynes." *Journal of Sociology and Social Welfare* 10, no. 3 (1983): 530–539.

———. "Fisk Social Work Students' Emergency Relief Work Following the East Nashville Fire of 1916. *Tennessee Historical Quarterly* 44, no. 4 (1985): 371–379.

———. "Training African-American Social Workers Through the NUL Fellowship Program." *Journal of Sociology and Social Welfare* 21, no. 1 (1994): 43–53.

Conyers, James E. 1968. "Negro Doctorates in Sociology: A Social Portrait." *Phylon* 29, no. 3 (1968): 209–223.

———. 1992. "The Association of Black Sociologists: A Descriptive Account from an 'Insider.'" *The American Sociologist* 23, no. 1 (1992): 49–55.

Conyers, James L. *Africana Studies: A Disciplinary Quest for both Theory and Methods.* Jefferson, NC: McFarland & Company, Inc. Publishers, 1997.

Crouchett, Lawrence. 1971. "Early Black Studies Movements." *Journal of Black Studies* 2, no. 2 (1971): 189–200.

Cunnigen, Donald. "The Legacy of Ernst Borinski: The Production of an African American Sociological Tradition." *Teaching Sociology* 31 (2003): 397–411.

Daniel, T. K. "Theory Building in Black Studies." *The Black Scholar* 12, no. 3 (1981): 29–36.

Daniels, Kalasia S. and Earl Wright II. "An Earnest Desire for the Truth Despite Its Possible Unpleasantness: A Comparative Analysis of the Atlanta University Publications and *American Journal of Sociology*, 1895–1917." *Sociology of Race and Ethnicity* 4, no. 1 (2018): 35–48.

Davis, Arthur P. "E. Franklin Frazier (1894–1962): A Profile." *The Journal of Negro Education* 31, no. 4 (1962): 429–435.

Doyle, Bertram W. "The Introductory Course in Sociology in Negro Colleges and Universities." *Journal of Educational Sociology* 7, no. 1 (1933): 30–36.

Du Bois, W. E. B. "The Study of the Negro Problems." In *W. E. B. Du Bois: On Sociology and the Black Community*, edited by Dan S. Green and Edwin D. Driver, 70–84. Chicago, IL: University of Chicago Press, [1898]1978.

———. *The Negro in Business: The Atlanta University Publications, No. 4.* Atlanta, GA: Atlanta University Press, 1899.

———. *The College-Bred Negro: Atlanta University Publication No. 5.* Atlanta: Atlanta University Press, 1900.

———. *The Negro Common School: The Atlanta University Publications, No. 6.* Atlanta, GA: Atlanta University Press, 1901.

———. *Results of Ten Tuskegee Negro Conferences.* Tuskegee, AL: Tuskegee Institute, 1901.

———. "The Talented Tenth." In *The Negro Problem: A Series of Articles by Representative American Negroes of To-day,* edited by unknown editor, 31–76. New York: AMS Press [1903]1970.

———. *The Souls of Black Folk.* New York: Dover Publications, [1903] 1994.

———. "The Relations of the Negroes to the Whites in the South." Pp. 253–270 in *W. E. B. Du Bois: On Sociology and the Black Community,* edited by Dan S. Green and Edwin, 253–270. *W. E. B. Du Bois: A Soliloquy on Viewing My Life from the Last Decade of its First Century.* New York: International Publishers, [1904] 1978.

———. *The Negro American Family: The Atlanta University Publications, No. 13.* Atlanta: Atlanta University Press, 1908.

———. "The Atlanta University Studies of Social Conditions among Negroes." Unpublished manuscript, November 10, 1940. *The Papers of W. E. B. Du Bois,* edited by Robert W. McDowell, Reel 80, Frames 796–801, [1948] 1980.

———. "The Talented Tenth: The Re-Examination of a Concept." Unpublished manuscript, [1948]1980, *The Papers of W. E. B. Du Bois,* edited by Robert W. McDowell, Reel 81, Frame 1090–100, [1948]1980.

———. "Interview." Unpublished manuscript, ([1960]1979), *The Papers of W. E. B. Du Bois,* edited by Robert W. McDowell, Reel 84, Frame 163, ([1960] 1979).

———. *The Autobiography of W. E. B. Du Bois: A Soliloquy on Viewing My Life from the Last Decade of its First Century.* New York: International Publishers, 1968.

———. 1979. W. E. B. Du Bois Papers. Special Collections and University Archives, W. E. B. Du Bois Library, University of Massachusetts Amherst, 1979.

Duncan, H. G. and Winnie Leach Duncan. "The Development of Sociology in the Old South." *American Journal of Sociology* 39, no. 5 (1934): 649–656.

Dyson, Walter. *Howard University: The Capstone of Negro Education.* Washington, D.C.: Howard University, 1941.

Editor's Table. "Sociology and Theology at Yale College." *Popular Science Monthly* 17: 265–269, 1880.

Frazier, E. Franklin. "Graduate education in Negro Colleges and Universities." *The Journal of Negro Education* 2, no. 3, (1933): 329–341.

Frazier, E. Franklin. "Ethnic Family Patterns: The Negro Family in the United States." *American Journal of Sociology* 53, no. 6, (1948):435–438.

Fitzhugh, George. *Sociology for the South or the Failure of Free Society*. Richmond, VA: A. Morris Publisher, 1854.

Galton, Francis. "Eugenics: Its Definition, Scope and Aims." *American Journal of Sociology* 10, (1904): 1–25.

Green, Dan S. and Edwin D. Driver. "W. E. B. DuBois: A Case in the Sociology of Sociological Negation." *Phylon* 37(4), (1976): 308–333.

Greene, Harry W. *Holders of Doctorates Among American Negroes*. Boston: Meador Publishing, 1946.

Hill, Michael R. "American Sociological Association." In *Blackwell Encyclopedia of Sociology, Vol. 1*, edited by George Ritzer, 130–134. Malden, MA: Blackwell Publishing, 2007.

Himes, Joseph. S. 1951. "The Teacher of Sociology in the Negro College." *Social Forces* 29, no. 3 (1951): 302–305.

Holloway, Jonathan S. *Confronting the Veil: Abram Harris Jr., E. Franklin Frazier, and Ralph Bunche, 1919-1941*. Chapel Hill: University of North Carolina Press, 2002.

Holmes, Dwight O. W. *The Evolution of the Negro College*. New York: Arno Press & The New York Times, 1969.

House, Floyd N. *The Development of Sociology*. New York: McGraw-Hill Book Company, 1936.

Howard, George E. 1918. "Alcohol and Crime: A Study in Social Causation." *American Journal of Sociology* 24, no. 1 (1918): 61–80.

Hughes, Henry. *Treatise on Sociology, Theoretical and Practical*. Philadelphia: Lippincott, Grambo and Company, 1854.

Hunter, Herbert M. "The Clinical Sociology of George Edmund Haynes." *Clinical Sociology Review* 6 (1988): 42–50.

Irvine, Russell W. "Coming South: The Reverend John Howard Hincks, A Five-Year (1889–1994) Window in the Development of Atlanta University and the Social Sciences." *Phylon* 49 (2001): 229–265.

Jackson, Maurice. "Toward a Sociology of Black Studies." *Journal of Black Studies* 1, no. 2 (1970): 131–140.

Jarmon, Charles. "Sociology at Howard University: From E. Franklin Frazier and Beyond." *Teaching Sociology* 31 (2003): 366–374.

Jefferson, Paul. "Working Notes on the Prehistory of Black Sociology: The Tuskegee Negro Conference." *Knowledge and Society: Studies in the Sociology of Culture Past and Present* 6 (1986): 119–151.

Jones, Allen. "The Role of Tuskegee Institute in the Education of Black Farmers." *Journal of Negro History* (1975): 252–267.

———. "Improving Rural Life for Blacks: The Tuskegee Negro Farmers' Conference, 1892–1915." *Agricultural History* 65, no. 2 (1991): 105–114.

Karenga, Maulana. "Black Studies and the Problematic of Paradigm: The Philosophical Dimension." *Journal of Black Studies* 18, no. 4 (1988): 395–414.

———. "Names and Notions of Black Studies: Issues of Roots, Range and Relevance." *Journal of Black Studies* 40, no.1 (2009): 41–64.

———. *Introduction to Black Studies.* Los Angeles: University of Sankore Press, 2010.

Kelly, Fred J. "An Outsider's View of Howard University." *The Journal of Negro Education* 4, no. 4 (1935): 468–475.

Ladner, Joyce A. *The Death of White Sociology.* New York: Random House, 1973.

Le Duff, Darryl. "Perspectives on the Caucus of Black Sociologists and the 1975 Program." *The Black Sociologist* 5 (1975): 6–7.

Lengermann, Patricia and Gillian Niebrugge. "Thrice Told: Narratives of Sociology's Relation to Social Work." In *Sociology in America: A History*, edited by Craig Calhoun, 63–114. Chicago: University of Chicago Press, 2007.

Logan, Rayford W. *Howard University: The First Hundred Years, 1867–1967.* New York, NY: New York University Press, 1968.

Long, Herman. "10 Years Perspective on Our Work in Race Relations: Report to the Joint Meeting of the American Missionary Association Divisional Committee and the Policy and Planning Committee of the Board of Home Missions of the Congregational and Christian Churches at Deering, New Hampshire." Unpublished manuscript, 1953.

———. "Racial Desegregation in Railroad and Bus Transportation." *The Journal of Negro Education* 23, no. 3 (1954): 214–221.

Lymann, Stanford M. "Robert Park Reconsidered: The Early Writings." *The American Sociologist* 21, no. 4 (1990): 342–351.

Mannheim, Karl. *Ideology and Utopia: An Introduction to the Sociology of Knowledge.* New York: Harcourt, Brace, & World, Inc, 1968.

Mazama, Ama. "Interdisciplinary, Transdisciplinary, or Unidisciplinary?: Africana Studies and the Vexing Question of Definition." In *Handbook of Black Studies*, edited by Molefi Kete Asante and Maulana Karenga, 3–15. Thousand Oaks, CA: Sage Publications, 2006.

Martinez-Brawley, Emilia E. "Rural Sociology and Rural Social Work: An Historical Essay." *The Journal of Sociology & Social Welfare* 7, no. 4, (1980): Article 6

Meier, August. "The Racial and Educational Philosophy of Kelly Miller, 1895–1915. *The Journal of Negro Education* 29, no. 2 (1960): 121–127.

McMurry, Linda O. "A Black Intellectual in the New South: Monroe Nathan Work, 1866–1945." *Phylon* 41, no. 4 (1980): 333–344.

———. *Recorder of the Black Experience: A Biography of Monroe Nathan Work.* Baton Rouge: Louisiana State University, 1985.

Morris, Aldon. *The Scholar Denied.* Berkeley: University of California Press, 2015.

Morrow, Cornelius Wortendyke. "History of Fisk Sociology." Unpublished manuscript, n.d.

Nelson, Lowrey. *Rural Sociology: Its Origin and Growth in the United States.* Minneapolis: University of Minnesota Press, 1969.

Neverdon-Morton, Cynthia. *Afro-American Women of the South and the Advancement of the Race, 1895–1925.* Knoxville: University of Tennessee Press, 1989.

Norment, Jr., Nathaniel. *The African American Studies Reader.* Durham, NC: Carolina Academic Press, 2007.

Platt, Anthony M. *E. Franklin Frazier Reconsidered.* New Brunswick: Rutgers University Press, 1991.

Richardson, Joe M. *A History of Fisk University, 1865–1946.* Tuscaloosa: University of Alabama Press, 1980.

Roberts, Samuel K. "Crucible for a Vision: The Work of George Edmund Haynes and the Commission on Race Relations, 1912–1947." Ann Arbor: University Microfilm International, 1974.

Rudwick, Elliott. "W. E. B. Du Bois and the Atlanta University Studies on the Negro." *Journal of Negro Education* 26 (1957): 466–476.

———. "W. E. B. Du Bois as Sociologist." In *Black Sociologists: Historical and Contemporary Perspectives,* edited by James Blackwell and Morris Janowitz, 25–55. Chicago, IL: University of Chicago Press, 1974.

Sanders, Katrina M. *Intelligent and Effective Direction: The Fisk University Race Relations Institute and the Struggle for Civil Rights, 1944–1969.* New York: Peter Lang, 2005.

Sanderson, Dwight. "The Teaching of Rural Sociology: Particularly in the Land-Grant Colleges and Universities." *American Journal of Sociology* 22, no. 4 (1917): 433–460

Scott, Emmett J. "The Tuskegee Negro Conferences." *Voice of the Negro* (May 1904), 5.

Scott, Joseph W. "A Brief History of the Association of Black Sociologists." Unpublished manuscript, n.d.

Scott Jr., Nolvert P. "On the Advantages Arising from the Incorporation of the Caucus of Black Sociologists." *The Black Sociologist* 5, no. 2 (1976): 6–7.

Sewell, William H. "Some Observations and Reflections on the Role of Women and Minorities in the Democratization of the American Sociological Association, 1905–1990." *The American Sociologist* 23, no. 1 (1992): 57–62.

Shenton, James P. *Black Studies: Threat or Challenge*. Port Washington, NY: Kennikat Press, 1973.

Slater, Robert B. "The First Black Faculty Members at the Nation's Highest-Ranked Universities." *Journal of Blacks in Higher Education* 22 (1998–1999): 97–106.

Small, Albion. "Fifty Years of Sociology in the United States (1865–1915)." *American Journal of Sociology*, 21, no. 6 (1916), 721–864.

Southern Workman. 1892. "Tuskegee Negro Conference." *Southern Workman*, (March 1892), 36–37.

———. "A Letter from Tuskegee: Reported by Our Special Correspondent," (March 1893a), 40–42.

———. "A Letter from Tuskegee: Reported by Our Special Correspondent," (March 1893b), 50–51.

———. "The Tuskegee Negro Conference," (March 1894a), 47–48.

———. "A Trip Through the South," (April 1894b), 55–58.

Staples, Robert. "Race and Ideology: An Essay in Black Sociology." *Journal of Black Studies* 3 (1973): 395–422.

———. *Introduction to Black Sociology*. New York: McGraw-Hill, 1976.

Taylor. A. A. "Fisk University and the Nashville Community, 1866–1900." *The Journal of Negro History* 39, no. 2 (1954): 111–126.

Taylor, Carl C. "Research in Rural Sociology." *American Journal of Sociology* 33, no. 2 (1927): 211–221.

Thomas Elsa Jones Collection, Fisk University, Box 34, Folder 20, page 1. (1927a). Letter from Eugene Kinkle Jones (Executive Secretary of the National Urban League) to President Thomas Elsa Jones (Fisk University).

Thomas Elsa Jones Collection, Fisk University, Box 34, Folder 21, page 1. (1927b). Letter from President Thomas Elsa Jones (Fisk University) to Eugene Kinkle Jones (Executive Secretary of the National Urban League).

Thomas Elsa Jones Collection, Fisk University, Box 34, Folder 21, page 2. (1928). Letter from Charles S. Johnson (National Urban League) to President Thomas Elsa Jones (Fisk University).

Thompson, E. T. "Sociology and Sociological Research in the South." *Social Forces* 23, no. 3 (1945): 356–365.

Tolman, Frank L. "The Study of Sociology in Institutions of Learning in the United States: A Report of an Investigation Undertaken by the Graduate Sociological League of the University of Chicago." *American Journal of Sociology* 7, no. 6 (1902): 797–838.

Tuskegee University. *Fifth Tuskegee Negro Conference*. Baltimore: Tuskegee University, 1896.

University of Chicago Committee on Development. *The Quest for Truth*. Chicago: University of Chicago Press, 1925.

Valien, Preston with Johnnie R. Clarke and Ruth E. Vaughn. "History of the Department of Social Sciences, Fisk University, 1911–1948." Unpublished manuscript, 1950.

Warren, Nagueyalti. *Grandfather of Black Studies: W. E. B. Du Bois*. Trenton: Africa World Press, 2011.

Washington, Booker T. *An Autobiography: The Story of My Life and Work*. J. L. Nichols and Company: Atlanta, GA, 1901.

Watson, Wilbur. "The Idea of Black Sociology: Its Cultural and Political Significance." *American Sociologist* 11 (1976): 115–123.

Watts, Jerry. "Dilemmas of Black Intellectuals: What Role Should We Play." *Dissent* (Fall 1989): 501–507.

Wells-Barnett, Ida B. *Southern Horrors and Other Writings: The Anti-Lynching Campaign of Ida B. Wells, 1892-1900*. Boston: Bedford Books, 1997.

Williams, Zachery R. *In Search of the Talented Tenth: Howard University Public Intellectuals and the Dilemmas of Race, 1926-1970*. Columbia: University of Missouri Press, 2009.

Wright II, Earl. "Atlanta University and American Sociology, 1896–1917: An Earnest Desire for the Truth Despite Its Possible Unpleasantness." PhD dissertation, Department of Sociology, University of Nebraska–Lincoln (2000).

———. "Using The Master's Tools: Atlanta University and American Sociology, 1896–1924." *Sociological Spectrum* 22, no. 1 (2002a): 15–39.

———. "Why Black People Tend To Shout!: An Earnest Attempt To Explain the Sociological Negation of the Atlanta Sociological Laboratory Despite Its Possible Unpleasantness." *Sociological Spectrum* 22, no. 3 (2002b): 325–361.

———. "The Atlanta Sociological Laboratory, 1896–1924: A Historical Account of the First American School of Sociology." *Western Journal of Black Studies* 26, no. 3 (2002c): 165–174.

———. "Beyond W. E. B. Du Bois: A Note on Some of the Lesser Known Members of the Atlanta Sociological Laboratory." *Sociological Spectrum* 29, no. 6 (2009): 700–717.

———. "The Tradition of Sociology at Fisk University." *Journal of African American Studies* 14, no. 1 (2010): 44–60.

———. "Why, Where and How to Infuse the Atlanta Sociological Laboratory into the Sociology Curriculum." *Teaching Sociology* 40 (2012): 257–270.

———. "W. E. B. Du Bois, Howard Odum and the Sociological Ghetto." *Sociological Spectrum* 34, no. 5 (2014): 453–468.

Wright II, Earl and Thomas C. Calhoun. "Jim Crow Sociology: Toward an Understanding of the Origin and Principles of Black Sociology via the Atlanta Sociological Laboratory." *Sociological Focus* 39, no. 1 (2006): 1–18.

Wright, W. D. "The Thought and Leadership of Kelly Miller." *Phylon* 39, no. 2 (1978): 180–192.

Yancy, Dorothy C. "William Edward Burghardt Du Bois' Atlanta Years: The Human Side—A Study Based Upon Oral Sources." *Journal of Negro History* 63 (1978): 59–67.

Young, Jr., Alford A. and Donald R. Deskins, Jr. "Early Traditions of African-American Sociological Thought." *Annual Review of Sociology* 27 (2001): 445–477.

Zuckerman, Phil. *Du Bois on Religion*. Oxford: Rowman & Littlefield, 2000.

———. *The Social Theory of W. E. B. Du Bois*. Thousand Oaks, CA: Pine Forge Press, 2004.

INDEX

A

Addams, Jane, 14, 21, 69–70

agriculture and agricultural colleges, 38

  see also rural sociology

alcohol consumption

  by Blacks and Native Americans, 44–45

  "Intemperance as a Cause for Immorality" (King), 71

Allen University, 38

American Baptist Home Mission Society, 114

American Journal of Sociology (AJS)

  data collection and analysis, 59, 76, 87, 91

  racism in, 44, 45

  Tolman's articles in, 113–15

  use by HBCUs, 159

American Missionary Association, 49, 118, 150

American Sociological Association (American Sociological Society), xiv, 44, 46

  establishes Caucus of Black Sociologists (CBS), 190, 197

  founding and influence of, 130, 187

  Frazier becomes first Black president of, 18, 19, 166

  includes *Methods* section, 59, 76

position of blacks and women within, 188

and study of sociology at HBCUs, 158, 197

Amherst College, 35

Ante-Bellum schools, 37–38

applied sociology

  at Fisk University, xix, 17, 121–31, 148–50, 193–94, 196

  at HBCUs and HWCUs, 116–18

  in rural settings, 80–81, 86

  and Washington, 86

Arkansas Baptist College, 38

Asante, Molefi Kete, 185

Association of Black Sociologists, xiv, 181, 187–91

Atlanta Sociological Laboratory

  accomplishments of, xiv, 56–60

  as first American school of sociology, xviii–xix, 49–52, 61, 76, 199

  Health and Physique of the Negro American (1906), 67

  influence upon Work, 102

  methodological contributions of, 198

  publications, xv–xvi, 66

  Rudwick's critique of, xiii–xiv, 197

  use of citizen researchers, 62–63, 108–9

Atlanta Sociological Laboratory *(cont.)*
  women's contribution to, 68–73
  see also Du Bois, W. E. B.
Atlanta University (now Clark Atlanta
    University)
  beginnings of research programs,
    52–56
  Bumstead as president of, 5, 6,
    11, 53
  on centering of Blacks as research
    subjects, 7, 10
  curriculum of, xviii–xix, 26, 49–52,
    62
  Du Bois on faculty of, xi, 19, 23,
    184–85, 193
  and engagement with local
    community, 116–17, 183–84
  establishment of Black sociology
    at, 11, 14
  founding of, 38, 49
  Georgia withdraws taxpayer-
    based funding for, 65, 66
  "I will find a way or make one"
    motto, 201
  publications distributed to
    outsiders, 196
  racial tensions effect upon
    teaching, 165
  as second-tier HBCU, xvi
  study of tuberculosis (1897), 9, 197
  as template for other HBCUs, 77
  Tolman recognizes as nation's
    highest performing HBCU, 114
  see also Atlanta Sociological
    Laboratory; Atlanta
    University Study of the Negro
    Problems; Phylon Institute

"Atlanta University and American
    Sociology: An Ernest Desire
    for Truth Despite Its Possible
    Unpleasantness (Wright, xiv)
Atlanta University Study of the Negro
    Problems
  (1896–1898), xii
  (1896–1917), 8
  Bradford and Bumstead co-found
    program, 61
  Bumstead on principles of Black
    sociology, 5–6, 9, 11
  Du Bois assume leadership of,
    53–54
  Du Bois's original plans for, 63–64
  first conference held (1896), 5
  publications, 64–65
  upperclassmen assist with data
    collection, 62
  Work writes essays for, 102
Auburn University, 93

B
Baltimore Afro-American (newspaper),
    143
Beard, Augustus F., 37
Benedict College, 38
Bennett College, xviii
Berea College, 65
Berlin, H. E. ("The Civil War as Seen
    through Southern Glasses"), 45
Bernard, L. L., xvii–xviii, 39, 115–18
Bethlehem House, 126–27
birth rates of Black women, 71
Blackmar, Frank, 28–29
Black sociology
  at Atlanta Sociological Laboratory,
    xviii–xix, 49–52, 61, 76, 199

Smith, Stanley H., 199
Social Forces (journal), 159
social gospel movement
  at Dartmouth College, 121–22
  at Fisk University, 120–21
  principles of, 120
  at Up South, 133–35
social policy/ reform, 10–11, 150, 198
social work, 125, 128, 129–31, 167
Sociologists for Women in Society, 188
sociology
  at Atlanta University, 49–52
  development and spread of in
    U. S. colleges and universities,
    25–30
  emergence as legitimate academic
    field, 38–39
  first time term used for professor
    title, 26–27
sociology of knowledge (Sok), 195
Sociology of the South, 13, 15, 41–43
South Carolina, 33
Southern Sociological Association, xiv
Spelman College, 65
Spencer, Herbert (*Study of Sociology*),
  25, 26, 27
Stanford University (formerly Leland
  Stanford Junior University), 30
  funding and philanthropic
    support for, 30, 65
  study of sociology at, 182
state colleges, 38
Straight University, xviii
Sumner, William Graham
  Folkways, 159
  teaches sociology at Yale, 25, 79,
    130
syphilis, 9–10

T
Taylor, Carl C. ("Research in Rural
  Sociology,"), 87–88
Tennessee State University (formerly
  State Normal School), 128
Terrerll, Mary Church, 14, 21, 68–69
Texas Southern University, 193
Thirkield, Wilbur P., 136
Thirteenth Amendment to the
  Constitution, 47, 82, 119, 131
Thomas, William I., 29, 45, 59, 102
Thompson, Edgar T., 42
"Thrice Told: Narratives on Sociology's
  Relation to Social Work" (
  Lengermann and Niebrugge), 129
Tolman, Frank L., 113–16
triangulation, xiv, 58
tuberculosis (consumption), 9, 197
Tufts College, 37
Tuskegee Institute
  develops first program of applied
    rural sociology, xix, 15, 21, 23,
    95, 193, 198
  on local community engagement,
    183
  principles of Black Sociology at, 11
  publishes *The Negro Year Book,*
    104–8
  receives more attention that
    Atlanta University, 196
  Work at, 103–4
Tuskegee Negro Conference. (later
  Tuskegee Farmer's Conference),
  15, 85–99
Tuskegee Study of Untreated Syphilis
  in the Negro Male, 9–10

Earl Wright II is a professor of sociology at Rhodes College in Memphis, TN. He earned his Bachelor of Arts in History and his Masters in Sociology from the University of Memphis. In 2000, Earl earned a doctorate in Sociology at the University of Nebraska, where he founded a chapter of the Black Graduate Student Association. Over his career, Dr. Wright has served as faculty at the University of Central Florida, Fisk University, Texas Southern University (as chairperson of the Department of Sociology), the University of Cincinnati, and now, Rhodes College. His groundbreaking research has altered our understanding of the discipline's formative years in this nation. He is the author of *The First American School of Sociology: W. E. B. Du Bois and the Atlanta Sociological Laboratory* and *What to Expect and How to Respond: Distress and Success in Academia.*